GRO

Edited by
Jenny J. F

First published in Great Britain in 2007 by

The Policy Press
University of Bristol
Fourth Floor
Beacon House
Queen's Road
Bristol BS8 1QU
UK

Tel +44 (0)117 331 4054
Fax +44 (0)117 331 4093
e-mail tpp-info@bristol.ac.uk
www.policypress.org.uk

British Library Cataloguing in Publication Data
A catalogue record for this book is available from the British Library.

Library of Congress Cataloging-in-Publication Data
A catalog record for this book has been requested.

ISBN 978 1 86134 731 2 paperback
ISBN 978 1 86134 732 9 hardcover

The right of Betsy Thom, Rosemary Sales and Jenny J. Pearce to be
identified as editors of this work has been asserted by them in accordance
with the 1988 Copyright, Designs and Patents Act.

The statements and opinions contained within this publication are solely
those of the editors and contributors, and not of The University of Bristol or
The Policy Press. The University of Bristol and The Policy Press disclaim
responsibility for any injury to persons or property resulting from any
material published in this publication.

The Policy Press works to counter discrimination on grounds of gender, race,
disability, age and sexuality.

Cover design by Qube Design Associates, Bristol.
Front cover photograph kindly supplied by Getty Images.
Printed and bound in Great Britain by MPG Books, Bodmin.

Contents

List of tables, figures and boxes

Tables

Figures

Boxes

Acknowledgements

This book arose out of a seminar organised by the Social Policy Research Centre at Middlesex University. We are grateful to all those colleagues who attended and whose ideas contributed to the development of some of the central themes of the book. We would like to thank in particular those colleagues, at Middlesex and elsewhere, who read and gave valuable comments on earlier drafts of the chapters: Virginia Berridge, Bernard Burgoyne, Anne Daguerre, Panos Hatziprokopiou, Rachel Herring, Eleonore Kofman, Susanne MacGregor, Louise Ryan, David Shemmings, Sue Tapsell and Jenni Ward. We would also like to thank Emily Watt at The Policy Press for responding so quickly and efficiently to all our queries and for her flexibility in accommodating to the changes in timetable and the shape of the book.

Notes on contributors

David Ball has a PhD in science and is Director of the Centre for Decision Analysis and Risk Management and Professor of Risk Management at Middlesex University. His area of interest covers how decisions are made in relation to safety, health, environment, technology and business. He is the author of *Environmental Health Policy* (Open University Press, 2006).

Marina Barnard is a Professorial Research Fellow at the Centre for Drug Misuse Research, Glasgow University. Her research and publications have most recently concerned the impact of drug problems on families, but also gender and drug problems, HIV and AIDS, and prostitution. She is author of *Drug Addiction and Families* (Jessica Kingsley Publications, 2006). Professor Barnard was a member of the Prevention Working Group of the Advisory Council on the Misuse of Drugs (ACMD), which produced *Hidden Harm: Responding to the Needs of Children of Problem Drug Users* (2003).

Mariana Bayley, MSc, works as a Research Fellow in the Social Policy Research Unit at Middlesex University. Her research interests include child and pedestrian road safety and car marketing/advertising to young people. She has recently published Bayley, M., Curtis, B., Lupton, K. and Wright, C.C. (2005) 'Are cars visually threatening to pedestrians?', *Municipal Engineer*, vol 158, ME3, pp 201-6.

Julia Borossa is a Senior Lecturer in Psychoanalysis in the School of Health and Social Sciences, Middlesex University. Her research is concerned with the history and politics of psychoanalysis, and with the question of trauma, memory and resilience. Her publications include *Hysteria* (Icon, 2001) and articles in publications including the *Journal of European Studies* and the *Oxford Literary Review*.

Rachel Hek works at the University of Birmingham as a Lecturer and Placement Manager on the MA and BA in social work. Her main research interests are the experiences and aspirations of young refugees, the impact of horticultural therapy on children and substance use and parenting. Recent publications include *The Experiences and Needs of Refugee and Asylum Seeking Children: A Literature Review* (DfES, 2005).

Lesley Hoggart is a Senior Research Fellow at the Policy Studies Institute, London. Her research interests include sexual health policy and practice; young people's sexual behaviour; feminist political action; and the politics of reproductive choice. Her book *Feminist Campaigns for Birth Control and Abortion Rights in Britain* was published in 2003 (Edwin Mellen Press).

Lesley Jordan is a Visiting Senior Research Fellow in the Social Policy Research Centre at Middlesex University. Her research relates to the impact of policy, provision and practice on disabled people. A recent paper with Lock, S., Bryan, K. and Maxim, J. (2005) is 'Work after stroke: focusing on barriers and enablers', *Disability & Society*, vol 20, no 1, pp 33-47. Other publications include articles in a range of academic and professional journals in the fields of communication impairment, rehabilitation and care.

Kenneth Lupton is a Lecturer in Geographical Information Systems at Middlesex University. He is also the group coordinator of the Transport Management Research Group and has been actively involved with the group's research since 1990. Much of his research has been in the area of road safety, in particular, the spatial characteristics of road accidents and, more recently, road accidents involving children.

Neil McKeganey is the Founding Director of the Centre for Drug Misuse Research, which opened at the University of Glasgow in 1994. His research covers a wide range of topics including the impact of parental drug use on children, pre-teen drug use, the link between drugs, crime and prostitution and research on establishing the prevalence of problem drug use in Scotland. Professor McKeganey has acted in an advisory capacity to the World Health Organization and the US Department of Justice. He is the author of over 150 academic papers on aspects of illegal drug use and is the author along with Jim McIntosh of *Beating the Dragon: The Recovery from Dependent Drug Use* (Prentice Hall, 2001).

Veena Meetoo is a Research Assistant at the Social Policy Research Centre, Middlesex University. Her areas of interest include racism and gender. She is co-author with Reena Bhavnani and Heidi Safia Mirza of *Tackling the Roots of Racism: Lessons for Success* (The Policy Press, 2005).

Heidi Safia Mirza is Professor of Equalities Studies in Education and Director of the Centre for Equalities and Human Rights in Education at the Institute of Education, University of London. She is known internationally for her work on ethnicity, gender and identity in education with best-selling books such as *Young, Female, and Black* (Routledge, 1992) and *Black British Feminism* (Routledge, 1997). Her most recent co-authored book is *Tackling the Roots of Racism: Lessons for Success* (The Policy Press, 2005).

Jenny J. Pearce is Professor of Young People and Public Policy at the University of Bedfordshire. She is Chair of the National Working Group on Young People and Sexual Exploitation and is a board member of the UK Network of Sex Work Projects. She has published on young women, community safety and sexual exploitation, and conducted multidisciplinary training in this field. Her publications include *It's Someone Taking a Part of You: A Study of Young Women and Sexual Exploitation* (Joseph Rowntree Foundation, 2002).

David Porteous is a Senior Lecturer in Criminology at Middlesex University. His research in recent years has been geared towards understanding the impact of changes in youth justice in England and Wales and developing critical perspectives on the criminal victimisation of children and young people. He is the co-editor of *Working with Young People in Europe* (Russell House Publishing, 2002).

Alan S. Reid is a Lecturer in Law at The Robert Gordon University in Aberdeen, Scotland. His research interests include European Union (EU) law and information technology law. A recent publication is: 'Is Society Smart Enough to Deal with Smart Cards?', (2007) *Computer Law and Security Report*, vol 23(1), pp 53–61. He is currently completing an EU law textbook for W. Green publishers, and the Communications Law Re-issue of the *Stair Memorial Encyclopaedia of the Laws of Scotland*, published by Lexis-Nexis.

Rosemary Sales is Professor in Social Policy at Middlesex University. Her research interests are in refugee and migration policy in Britain and Europe. She is currently involved in several studies of new migrants in London, including Polish and Chinese migrants. Her book *Understanding Immigration and Refugee Policy: Contradictions and Continuities* will be published by The Policy Press in 2007.

Betsy Thom is a Reader in Drug and Alcohol Studies and Head of the Social Policy Research Centre at Middlesex University. Her main research interests are in alcohol policy and she is author of the book *Dealing with Drink* (Free Association Books, 1998). She is Coordinating Editor of the journal *Drugs: Education, Prevention and Policy*.

Jenni Ward is a Senior Research Fellow in the Social Policy Research Centre, Middlesex University. Her research interests include young people's drug-using lifestyles, youth transitions, 'looked-after' young people, care leavers and illicit drug markets. A recent publication is Ward, J., with Patel, N. (2006) 'Broadening the discussion on "sexual exploitation": Ethnicity, sexual exploitation and young people', *Child Abuse Review*, vol 15, pp 341-50.

ONE

Introduction

Betsy Thom, Rosemary Sales and Jenny J. Pearce

Nowhere is the tension between the need to prevent risk and the necessity of learning to manage and take calculated risks more apparent than in the process of growing up from childhood to adulthood. Survival of the individual and of the social group has always relied on ensuring a balance between protecting the very young from danger and allowing the child to experiment and learn to navigate the risks and dangers encountered in daily life. In some circumstances, risk taking is socially approved and rewarded – in business life, in record-breaking sports activities or in action in military service, for instance. Increasingly, however, the concept of 'risk' has become associated with harmful or negative events and behaviours, which can be predicted, measured and avoided or minimised through timely, responsible action (Douglas, 1992; Lupton and Tulloch, 2002; McWhirter and South, 2004).

The move towards a 'culture of caution', where, for most people most of the time, risks must be prevented, has come to dominate social and health policy. This, it could be argued, is to the detriment of understanding and responding to risk as an essential, unavoidable and sometimes positive element of the human condition (Green et al, 2000). It also undermines the important relationship between risk taking and building resilience. An individual's resilience – the capacity to draw on their own resources to withstand unpredictable events that are a part of everyday life – is developed through taking risks and learning to cope with the unexpected (Gilligan, 1997). However, much of the discourse on risk views risk-taking actions and behaviour as bound up with 'ignorance' and 'irrationality' and often fails to take into account the voluntary nature of risk taking and the pleasures and benefits that can be derived from 'risky' activities. How risk is defined and understood has important implications for the development of policy and intervention to address the dangers that children and young people face as they grow up.

Over time, in health and social welfare (as in other policy domains), we have seen shifts in the perception of risk. The pre-modern notion of risk as an unpredictable 'act of God' was replaced with the modern 'scientific' view that it was an inevitable aspect of life, which could nevertheless be managed and contained. The welfare state was based on collectivising individual risks of, for example, unemployment and sickness, through collective responsibility and 'no fault' protection of the individual (Kemshall and Pritchard, 1997). More recently, crises in welfare states in western countries have led to policy changes promoting individual and family responsibility, shared to a decreasing extent with state provision.

The apparent consensus on risk avoidance, risk assessment and measurement and responses to risk begs a number of questions. Who decides what the important 'risks' are and how they should be tackled? Who is seen to be 'at risk' and who is responsible for 'risky behaviour'? Whose task is it to ensure that risks are prevented or minimised? Who benefits from the identification and management of risk? To what extent is 'risk' a social construct that reflects social and political anxieties within a particular historical context? Examination of policy, practice and research reveals a diversity of views on these questions and on the conflicting perspectives that emerge in attempting to balance the interests of different stakeholders – the state, industry and business, professionals, parents and the young, themselves, to name just a few.

This book addresses these questions in relation to 'growing up' and, in doing so, highlights the contested nature of policy and practice concerned with the identification and management of risk in the lives of the young. We illustrate the varying ways in which society constructs and reconstructs the definitions and parameters of risk from birth to early adulthood. We address a number of themes, which illustrate the ambiguities and tensions inherent in current policy and practice regarding children and young people. For instance, the potential benefits of risk and risk taking need to be balanced by the need for protection and by recognising specific vulnerabilities; care has to be seen alongside control; concern to foster the autonomy of the young needs to be placed in relation to the realities of dependence; the desire to protect young people from risk needs to be balanced against their need to make mistakes and build resilience to cope with unknown adversity; and young people's rights need to be recognised as well as their responsibilities. The policy and practice dilemmas that arise in responding to differing needs, value systems and professional and lay perspectives run throughout the chapters. The topics have been selected to provide a critical analysis of 'risk', 'risk management' and related concepts and each chapter provides a specific policy case study to illustrate these cross-cutting themes and issues. The focus is on UK policy although some chapters refer to European and international policy contexts and the themes are relevant to policy debate more generally.

Growing up with risk

Much has been written around the transition from childhood to adulthood in contemporary societies where adulthood is no longer marked by well-defined, traditional ceremonies and 'rites of passage'. Consent to sexual intercourse and to marriage, permission to leave school, to drive a car, to purchase certain goods such as alcohol, and to vote, are all achieved at different ages, which not only vary within and between countries but change over time. The definition of a 'child' is flexible. For the purposes of the UN Convention on the Rights of the Child, which came into force in 1990, 'a child means every human being below the age of eighteen years unless under the law applicable to the child, majority is attained earlier'. The Convention was needed 'because people under 18 years old often need special care and protection that adults do not' (UN, 1989, Part 1, Article 1). Young people in some contexts are deemed not to need such protection, for example in the area of criminal responsibility, which at 10 years of age in Britain is lower than in most European states; or in the armed forces where 17-year-olds have been among British casualties in Iraq. Much research, however, understands 'young people' as those up to the age of 25, reflecting the complexity of the process of growing up and the extended nature of dependence in modern states. The chapters in this book cover the whole age range from birth up to young adulthood, with chapters dealing with different age groups in relation to their specific themes.

Growing up and the perception and experience of risks throughout that time is not the same for all children and young people. For a child in a London family, playing in the streets may be regarded by parents as risky whereas a child in a rural area may be allowed much more freedom of movement outdoors and out of sight of parents. Gender is a major determinant of expectations of risk taking, with boys generally enjoying greater leeway and legitimation of risk-taking behaviour than is granted to girls. Despite this apparent freedom for risk taking, it is young men who are more likely to be 'at risk' of committing offences or of being involved in violent crime (Newburn and Stanko, 1994). Other factors such as class, religion and ethnicity enter the picture and militate against the tendency to discuss 'the young' as if they were all alike. As subsequent chapters illustrate, exposure to risks, experiences of risk and toleration of 'risky' behaviour differs for different behaviours, different individuals and groups and in different social settings. Most importantly, as other work on young people's lives has demonstrated, experiences and opportunities throughout the growing-up years are structured by wider socioeconomic and political factors and, within those structures, all is not equal (Aggleton et al, 2006).

Categorising risk

There are numerous ways of categorising 'risk'. Adams (1999), for instance, proposes three broad categories: *directly perceptible risks* such as crossing the road or riding a bicycle; *risks perceptible with the help of science*, which includes risks of disease from microbes or contamination made visible through technologies such as the microscope; and *manufactured virtual risks* produced by human activity, food additives, Creutzfeld-Jakob disease (CJD) and global warming. Lupton (1999) suggests a more extended categorisation, comprising environmental (pollution, chemical, floods, dangerous road conditions and so on), lifestyle (drug use, 'unsafe sex', some leisure pursuits and so on), medical (surgery, drug therapy, reproductive technologies and so on), interpersonal (social interactions, gender roles, sexuality, parenting and so on), economic (unemployment, investment, bankruptcy and so on) and criminal (being a participant in or potential victim of crime) risks.

The variety of different risks discussed by these authors suggests the enormous range of phenomena covered by the term 'risk' and the different ways in which it can be understood. As Gabe (1995, pp 1–14) has noted, the 'risk industry' has spread in recent decades and incorporates research and literature from many disciplines. These include engineering, toxicology, biostatistics and actuarial science, which are concerned predominantly with risk assessment and the technicalities of measurement, monitoring and surveillance. Psychological analyses focus on perceptions of risk and the different ways that individuals understand and assess risk. Both of these approaches tend to adopt a positivist model, which treats risks as objective phenomena to be measured and explained by clearly defined causes. Cultural and social theories, by contrast, consider risk to be 'socially constructed or framed and collectively perceived' (Gabe, 1995, p 8). As the chapter by Porteous in this volume shows (Chapter Fifteen), even a validated assessment instrument to measure risk can be seen as a 'social product', which reflects the concerns and definitions of 'risk' current within a particular group at a particular time, rather than a technical, objective measure of a potential danger. Moreover, the high public profile of some risks suggests that the construction of risk, and the policy response to it, often bear little relation to 'rational' calculation of the actual costs and benefits. The level of media coverage of 'bird flu', for example, far outweighs the concern devoted to other continuing risks such as car accidents, which regularly kill hundreds annually (see Chapter Five by Lupton and Bayley).

The categories of risk listed above suggest the complexity of risk and the interconnections between the physical environment and human activity in producing risk situations. Flooding, for example, may be a result of the natural event of heavy rainfall, but its impact is heavily dependent on the built environment in which it falls, as the recent flooding in New Orleans illustrated. Furthermore, the shape of the built environment reflects relations of power based on class, gender and race, and the policy response to risky events is deeply implicated in these divisions. Thus, the degree of risk for individuals is mediated by class, gender and other forms of social disadvantage. Notions of risk associated with human relationships are also embedded in particular social and historical situations, as changing attitudes to sexuality, and the debate about the 'risk' of homosexuality and the identification of a so-called 'gay gene', demonstrate.

The focus of this book is on risk related to human activity and lifestyle, a focus reflecting dominant policy concerns in contemporary Britain. Global environmental risks, such as nuclear war or radiation from nuclear industry or chemical pollution – issues at the forefront of much risk theory – are beyond the scope of this volume, although the chapter on the spread of new technologies and their relevance to child protection (Reid, Chapter Six) serves as a reminder of the importance of such global threats for national perceptions and policies. Other chapters that discuss the risks associated with the physical environment (Ball on children's playgrounds, Chapter Four; Lupton and Bayley on road safety, Chapter Five) focus on the social and policy contexts in which these risks are defined and experienced.

The chapters in this book draw on research and policy debate that emerge from different traditions; but it is within the social-cultural perspective that the discussions presented here are located. They are illustrative of the complex, contested nature of policy and of the power relationships embedded in them. They fit within an approach that seeks to examine how the meaning and significance of risk and responses to it are constructed in different social and material contexts and how definitions and responses to risk vary between actors. The analyses of risk discourses across different policy and practice domains illustrate how even policies aimed at the protection of children and young people – where we might expect a high level of consensus – warrant Taylor-Gooby's (2001, p 205) conclusion that a risk society is 'complex and is not experienced in the same way by all its members'. (For a fuller discussion on risk theories, see Lupton, 1999; Lupton and Tulloch, 2002.)

The adoption of a 'constructionist' approach does not mean a denial of the reality of risk and danger in the lives of children and young people. Nor does it mean rejecting the reality of risks arising, for instance, from genetic predisposition to disease or disability. Rather, it suggests that the meaning and importance ascribed to different forms of risks and dangers and the responses to it are based in the specific contexts of people's lives, in their relationships with one another and with the social groups to which they belong. This opens the door to examining the interaction between individuals and social institutions, to analysing the importance of collective as well as individual responses, and to including consideration of the changing material and structural bases of life within which identification and management of risk takes place. For example, chapters in this book examine differences in risk perception and responses to risk between professionals, parents and young people (Hek, Chapter Seven; Pearce, Chapter Twelve); and differences between strategies to address perceived risks for 'mainstream' children (Ball, Chapter Four; Lupton and Bayley, Chapter Five) compared to those who may be marginalised because of physical disability (Jordan and Sales, Chapter Ten), living with drug-using parents (McKeganey and Barnard, Chapter Eight), or belonging to an asylum-seeking family (Sales, Chapter Thirteen). The inclusion in this volume of a chapter from a psychoanalytic point of view (Borossa, Chapter Two) adds a perspective so far lacking in the literature. Borossa's analysis presents 'risk' as part of the psyche, an inescapable fact of human existence, central to the development of a sense of self and identity.

The 'risk society'?

There is already a considerable body of literature that addresses the questions we raise in the broader context of the 'risk society' and 'reflexive modernisation'. According to these theorists, 'reflexive modernisation' is characterised by greater awareness of risk and by both public and private concern to identify and manage it. Risk is seen as a product of human action and interaction rather than a result of fate or accident (for example, Beck, 1992; Adam et al, 2000). In this view, individualism is considered to have replaced traditional, collective life as the defining feature of societies. In contemporary, developed societies, individuals act as autonomous, self-regulating social actors, reflecting on themselves and on the social structures, institutions and networks that both constrain and enable them to carve out their own identities and biographies. However, as Taylor-Gooby (2001) points out, this view of risk, which has impacted importantly on New Labour policy in Britain, especially in relation to social welfare, implicitly assumes value consensus, ignoring differences in perceptions between groups and individuals, and in outcomes for different social groups, especially the less powerful.

New Labour has shifted the emphasis of welfare policy away from the protection of individuals towards empowering individuals and communities to engage with and manage risk – an approach that redefines the relationship between the state and the individual in particular circumstances. As well as bestowing greater individual autonomy, it imposes greater responsibility for risk management onto individuals, families and communities (Giddens, 1998). Risk, as Lupton and Tulloch (2002, p 318) comment, 'is closely linked to reflexivity, accountability and responsibility'. The focus on tackling social exclusion, which has replaced the traditional Labour goal of eliminating poverty through some level of income redistribution, relies primarily on individual efforts to develop the skills to ensure integration within the labour market, and thus avoid the risk of unemployment. These developments are linked to changes in welfare state provision so that:

> [S]ocial policy is no longer about the alleviation of the needs of the individual or the pursuit of the collective good. Instead it is about the prevention of risk and the displacement of risk management responsibilities on to the 'entrepreneurial self' who must exercise informed choice and self-care to avoid risks. (Kemshall, 2002, p 22)

The factors underlying this shift are complex and contested. Global economic restructuring has undermined the political and economic structures that underpinned the post-war welfare states. This has also led to questioning of some of the certainties associated with the welfare state, in particular, of professional expertise and the social control aspects of welfare provision, as well as to broader critiques of the notion of progress. Service providers have become preoccupied with risk management as a result both of their increased role as gatekeepers to the effective use of resources and of increased accountability for service delivery (Kemshall and Pritchard,1997). Thus, '(r)isk has become the key criterion for targeting scarce resources, protecting the most vulnerable, and making professionals and agencies accountable' (Parton, 1996, p 104). Services are increasingly driven by the aim of identifying and targeting 'at-risk' groups through risk assessment. Some key events have been pivotal in shifting these attitudes, such as child abuse scandals (see Chapter Seven by Hek) and more recently the outcry over released foreign prisoners who have not been deported.

The assumptions of individual and local empowerment underpinning such policy shifts are contentious. The residualisation of the welfare state and the focus on social exclusion has revived the relevance of the 'deserving' and 'undeserving' poor and precipitated punitive intervention in families and young people who do not conform (see Chapter Twelve by Pearce and Chapter Seven by Hek) including the use of Anti-Social Behaviour Orders (ASBOs) to punish behaviour that has not hitherto been understood as criminal. As Hoggart's chapter suggests, teenage pregnancy, a key target of social exclusion policy, is often the result of poverty and the lack of opportunities to exercise individual choice (Chapter Eleven). The emphasis on risk avoidance and management, and the growing litigation arising from mistakes by professionals, can lead to caution and defensiveness on the part of service providers, which may have serious consequences for those whom the services are designed to support. This is illustrated in the chapters discussing disability (Jordan and Sales, Chapter Ten) and 'honour killings' (Meetoo and Mirza, Chapter Nine). As Porteous's chapter demonstrates (Chapter Fifteen), risk assessment tools are themselves flawed instruments, a fact illustrated by the current panic over reoffending by released prisoners, deemed by professionals to be low risk.

Young people and risk

The position of children and young people within risk discourse is complex and contradictory. A central concern is the extent to which they are able and permitted to be independent, self-defining agents at different ages. The literature on 'risk' is replete with research studies that examine the influence of 'risk factors' on the opportunities of children and young people growing up as integrated members of society or as marginalised, excluded and 'deviant' youth (for example, Lloyd, 1998; Hayes, 2002; Rhodes et al, 2003). Youth policy and government initiatives to combat 'social exclusion' rely, to a great extent, on the predictive value of 'risk factors' in devising strategies to counter individual behaviour and social circumstances which threaten the well-being and integration of the young, or – seen from another perspective – to curb the threat of rebellious youth (Barry, 2005).

On the other hand, it is apparent, as Daniel and Ivatts (1998, pp 1-2) argue, that children as autonomous agents have been largely absent from the social policy literature although their life conditions and experiences are affected by the impact of health, social and economic policies on their families and on the environments in which they grow up. The voices of children and young people are generally filtered through an adult screen and in policy discourse children typically assume one of three roles – as threat, victim or investment (Hendrick, 1994). For instance, recent media coverage of 'binge' drinking and city-centre disturbance portrays young people as a 'threat' to community safety; public alarm concerning reports of drug dealers at the school gates or child pornography on the internet see children as victims; throughout history, children have been valued as 'investments' for ageing parents or, as workers and members of the armed forces, for the economic and military power of the state. As a result, children and young people may become the emotive drivers of policy action that 'is developed according to a set of implicit assumptions and values, often embedded in wider concerns such as the relationship between the state and the family, or the future of the nation' (Daniel and Ivatts, 1998, p 5). As Chapter Three by Ward and Bayley shows, children's perceptions of which risks are important may be very different from that assumed by adults, including their parents, and policy makers. They also find ways of negotiating risk for themselves, thus acting as autonomous agents rather than fitting the categories of threat and victim.

All three roles of threat, victim and investment are visible in the policy and practice discourses discussed in this book. Indeed, several chapters show how policy and professional discourses around specific social problems, such as drug and alcohol problems, abortion or sexual exploitation, often reveal all three of these stereotypical roles functioning at the same time. Without denying the intention to protect and ensure children's well-being, it is also apparent that concern is frequently used to build consensus or public alarm to secure support for particular policies (for example on alcohol, see Chapter Fourteen by Thom). In the frequent clash of 'traditional' values and ideologies with the reality of changing lifestyles and family structures, fear of 'risk' and 'moral panics' over issues such as unsafe sex or drug and alcohol misuse or 'honour killings' become part of a battle between competing moral and religious frames for understanding current social issues. These may be used politically as a means of sustaining the status quo and maintaining a precarious balance between care and control responses, especially in the private sphere of the family.

Much of the focus in recent policy debate has been on parents. They occupy a central place in both the protection and control of the young and as the 'bearer of core social values' (Hek, Chapter Seven). The family (in particular the mother) has traditionally been seen as the main vehicle responsible for rearing the citizens of the future. As intermediaries between the state and the child, parents represent the divide between the public and private spheres of life. However, the reality of the state–family divide and the ideal of family privacy have been challenged as a self-perpetuating ideology easily dismissed if we look at social policies aimed at children. Here 'the state plays a significant part through its legislative and social policy framework in shaping family relationships and obligations' (Daniel and Ivatts, 1998, p 8). Policy, as Daniel and Ivatts argue, frequently subsumes the interests and welfare of the child under 'the family' and can result in children being worse off. The family becomes at once a source of protection and risk, a theme that is taken up centrally by Hek (Chapter Seven), McKeganey and Barnard (Chapter Eight) and by Meetoo and Mirza (Chapter Nine).

The structure of the book

The chapters are arranged in three broad sections. Chapters Two to Six explore the concept of 'risk' and its uses in policy and practice in the everyday lives of children and young people. The second group of chapters (Seven to Nine) considers circumstances where parents and the family are seen to constitute a risk or potential risk to the welfare of the young. Finally, six chapters (Ten to Fifteen) examine different aspects of risk among young people who may be seen as 'marginalised' or at risk of 'marginalisation' because of the ways in which society, policy and professional activity label particular individuals, families or types of behaviour.

Chapter Two by Julia Borossa presents the argument that the human condition is one of fundamental and unavoidable risk within which risk taking and risk management are necessary for negotiating a place in the world, for the development of a sense of 'self' and for establishing a relationship between the individual psyche (identity) and the social-structural contexts within which identity evolves and changes as the child grows up.

In the third chapter, Jenni Ward and Mariana Bayley remind us that there is frequently a mismatch between adult views and young people's views of the world. Drawing on discussions with samples of young people at two transition points in school life, the authors highlight how young people focus on the immediate risks and dangers that they experience or expect within their families and environments. A key theme is gendered risk and, as Borossa's analysis notes in Chapter Two, the importance of risk activity in the constructions of young people's self-identity. The role of risk in the child's developing maturity is examined within the context of parental and other external influences on young people's views and experiences.

Chapters Four and Five present case studies of how environmental risks that affect most children are perceived and contested by professionals, parents and young people. David Ball (Chapter Four) tells the story of how issues around playground safety and fears of litigation have, in large part, undermined the value of playgrounds as a space where children can explore risk and experience 'adventure'. The chapter illustrates changes over time in attitudes towards the balance between fostering children's development of independence and autonomy and protecting them from harm; it raises questions regarding the meaning of 'risk' and 'safety' for different groups of stakeholders, and documents growing concern regarding excessive or unnecessary restrictions on children's play activities.

In Chapter Five, Kenneth Lupton and Mariana Bayley review the literature and national data on road accidents for children and examine children's own perceptions of risk in the road environment and their strategies for dealing with risk. The children's comments highlight the complex understandings of risk taking – for example, as part of a 'dare' – and raise issues regarding responsibility for achieving a reduction in risk as much through environmental change and change in adult and driver behaviour as through education and the control of children's behaviour.

Questions of responsibility for responding to risk also run through Chapter Six by Alan Reid. The development of new communication technologies – the internet and mobile phones – brings dangers as well as benefits for children and young people. Reid discusses legal issues surrounding the availability and use of new technology and examines the technical and regulatory controls and educational initiatives that aim to reduce risk. He argues that there is a need to work towards an information technology-aware society where an appropriate balance is struck between overcautiousness, which would compromise the benefits of technology, and foolhardiness, which would fail to deal with dangers such as paedophile activity, cyberbullying or gambling. Reid's chapter also emphasises the importance of different stakeholder interests and perceptions, notably the cyber-industry and children and their parents.

As noted above, the literature on risk contains a vast number of studies that explore 'risk factors'. In an attempt to predict and prevent risk, identification of individuals and groups that may be at risk of incurring harm becomes a key feature of current policy and practice. The family occupies a central position in the list of risk factors, both as a protection against harm, when it operates well, and as a threat to the well-being of the young and to society as a whole, when it operates badly. The next section of the book examines circumstances in which risk is seen to originate within the family but where understanding of the issues requires a broader perspective of community, cultural, social and economic contexts.

Rachel Hek (Chapter Seven) discusses how risk assessment has become central to social work with families and is a key element in determining priorities for professional involvement. Her chapter focuses on the ways risk is defined and applied, highlights how risk is viewed and identified by government policy makers and social care service providers, and describes how it is experienced by families who have been pulled into a system that brands them as 'risky'. Parents may be seen as a risk to their children, either through 'omission' (for example, neglect or lack of control) or 'commission' (for example, physical cruelty or sexual abuse). Children can also be seen as presenting a risk to society if parents do not control them, when they become labelled as antisocial. The analysis demonstrates how different groups of parents and children are treated in different ways and considers the implications for risk responses in labelling families as 'deserving' or 'undeserving'.

Similar issues arise in Chapter Eight, by Neil McKeganey and Marina Barnard. Drawing on qualitative research that gives a 'voice' to drug-using parents and their children, they examine the experiences of young people living with drug-using parents and the complex issues that face professionals involved with these families. The authors contend that the needs of children and families have attracted too little attention because the policy focus has been elsewhere – on reducing the risk of acquiring and spreading HIV infection and on reducing drug-related crime. The chapter highlights one of the 'thorniest' questions facing professionals: 'how much adversity is it tolerable for children to experience at the hands of their addict parents?'.

Chapter Nine by Veena Meetoo and Heidi Safia Mirza tackles the uneasy relationship between policies designed to recognise diversity and the need to protect people from abuse carried out in the name of 'traditional values'. The authors use the issue of so-called 'honour killings' of young women to examine policy responses to risk and gender-related violence in minority ethnic communities in Britain. They suggest that the risks that some young women face are heightened by multicultural policies, which can engender non-intervention when dealing with domestic violence that is seen as rooted in cultural and religious practices. The chapter provides a critique of structural and institutional racism and sexism, which can lead on the one hand to sensationalising particular cases of violence, thus entrenching stereotypes of some cultures, particularly Muslim, as backward and oppressive, while on the other hand ignoring risk situations in the private sphere of the family.

The final group of six chapters deals with a range of 'risks' and risk situations that may set individual young people apart from their contemporaries and result in 'marginalisation' and social exclusion. These chapters discuss how the risks are defined, experienced and dealt with by different social groups.

Lesley Jordan and Rosemary Sales (Chapter Ten) explore notions of risk associated with different models of disability and consider contemporary policy and practice in relation to childhood disability. They argue that disabled young people are at greater risk than their peers of poverty, family breakdown and isolation, and of being unable to make the transition to adulthood and a full and independent human life. From one viewpoint, these risks are seen as coming from the nature of the impairment itself. From another viewpoint, the 'social model' sees the risks as arising mainly from society's attitudes and behaviour towards those with disabilities. The way in which disability is defined and understood, therefore, has serious implications for human rights and social integration. The chapter offers a critique of government policy based on evidence of the impact of particular policies and services on disabled children and their families.

The concept of risk has become central to policy debate on young people and sexual behaviour. Chapters Eleven and Twelve consider different aspects of this debate. Lesley Hoggart (Chapter Eleven) provides an insight into contested meanings attached to risk in the area of sexual health and young people. In particular, she draws on the views and experiences of a group of teenage mothers and places their understandings of unprotected sex, abortion and motherhood in the context of current sexual health policy and practice and New Labour's teenage pregnancy strategy. In Chapter Twelve, Jenny Pearce looks at the relationship between risk and resilience by considering how we understand and respond to young people in sexually exploitative relationships. Young women's accounts of sexual exploitation form the basis for examining risk and resilience factors and for arguing that greater support for specialist therapeutic outreach services is needed to help build resilience in this group of young people.

Chapter Thirteen by Rosemary Sales focuses on young people in the process of claiming asylum, either on their own behalf or as members of asylum-seeking families. Public discourse and policy in Britain towards young refugees has been deeply ambivalent. On the one hand they are seen as 'at risk' both as children and as refugees who have endured difficult and sometimes traumatic circumstances; but on the other hand they are asylum seekers, who are presented as a risk to society. These groups face uncertainty in relation to their status and future residence in Britain in addition to the risks related to their refugee experience. The chapter examines developments in immigration policy and the implications for the rights of young refugees and suggests that the target of reducing the number of asylum seekers is increasingly taking precedence over the protection of the rights of the child in national policy.

The final two chapters take up the notion of young people as a risk to society in relation to current concerns and increasing policy attention to alcohol and drug use and crime and antisocial behaviour by the young. Betsy Thom (Chapter Fourteen) looks at two historical periods; the turn of the 19th century, when the emphasis in the debates lay on the protection of children from alcohol misuse; and the late 20th century until the present time, when the balance shifted considerably towards state control of youth behaviour, including alcohol use, and the perceived threat to public health and social order. She argues that both the protection of children from risks and the protection of communities from the threat of 'antisocial' youth behaviour are often a good platform on which to build consensus for policy action. Finally, in Chapter Fifteen, David Porteous provides an analysis of the language and policies and practices associated with risk in the new youth justice. All young people referred to Youth Offending Teams in England and Wales are now assessed using a common, structured risk assessment profile known as *Asset*. This is intended to guide practitioners' judgements as to the 'riskiness' of a young person and to enable them to identify the precise 'risk factors' contributing to their offending behaviour so that interventions can be tailored to individual needs. As with issues considered in previous chapters, this analysis demonstrates that current policy constitutes a blend of particular academic, administrative and political discourses, each of which define and mobilise the concept of risk in different ways.

References

Adam, B., Beck, U. and Van Loon, J. (eds) (2000) *The Risk Society and Beyond: Critical Issues for Social Theory*, London: Sage Publications.

Adams, J. (1999) 'Review of Franklin J. (ed) 1998 *The Politics of Risk Society*, Polity: London', *Journal of Forensic Psychiatry*, vol 10, no 1, p 226.

Aggleton, P., Ball, A. and Mane, P. (eds) (2006) *Sex, Drugs and Young People*, London: Routledge.

Barry, M. (ed) (2005) *Youth Policy and Social Inclusion*, London: Routledge.

Beck, U. (1992) *Risk Society: Towards a New Modernity*, London: Sage Publications.

Daniel, P. and Ivatts, J. (1998) *Children and Social Policy*, Basingstoke: Palgrave.

Douglas, M. (1992) *Risk and Blame: Essays in Cultural Theory*, London: Routledge.

Gabe, J. (ed) (1995) *Medicine, Health and Risk*, Oxford: Blackwell.

Giddens, A. (1998) *The Third Way: The Renewal of Social Democracy*, Cambridge: Polity Press.

Gilligan, R. (1997) 'Beyond permanence? The importance of resilience in child placement practice and planning', *Adoption and Fostering*, vol 21, no 1, pp 12-20.

Green, E., Mitchell, W. and Bunton, R. (2000) 'Contextualising risk and danger: an analysis of young people's perceptions of risk', *Journal of Youth Studies*, vol 3, no 2, pp 109-26.

Hayes, M. (2002) *Taking Chances: The Lifestyles and Leisure Risk of Young People*, London: Child Accident Prevention Trust.

Hendrick, H. (1994) *Child Welfare 1870-1989*, London: Routledge.

Kemshall, H. (2002) *Risk, Social Policy and Welfare*, Buckingham: Open University Press.

Kemshall, H. and Pritchard, J. (eds) (1997) *Good Practice in Risk Assessment and Risk Management, Volume 2: Risks, Rights and Responsibilities*, London: Jessica Kingsley Publishers.

Lloyd, C. (1998) 'Risk factors for problem drug use: identifying vulnerable groups', *Drugs: Education, Prevention and Policy*, vol 5, no 3, pp 217-32.

Lupton, D. (1999) *Risk*, London: Routledge.

Lupton, D. and Tulloch, J. (2002) '"Risk is part of your life": risk epistemologies among a group of Australians', *Sociology*, vol 36, no 2, pp 317-34.

McWhirter, J. and South, N. (2004) *Young People and Risk: Towards a Shared Understanding*, Final Report to Government Office East, University of Essex: Community Safety Fund.

Newburn, T. and Stanko, B. (eds) (1994) *Just Boys Doing Business?*, London: Routledge.

Parton, N. (1996) *Social Theory, Social Change and Social Work*, London: Routedge.

Rhodes, T., Lilly, R., Lalam, N., Giorgino, E., Kemmesis, U. E., Ossebaard, H. C., Faasen, I., Spannow, K. E. and Fernández, C. (2003) 'Risk factors associated with drug use: the importance of 'risk environment'', *Drugs: Education, Prevention and Policy*, vol 10, no 4, pp 303-29.

Taylor-Gooby, P. (2001) 'Risk, contingency and the Third Way: evidence from the BHPS and qualitative studies', *Social Policy and Administration*, vol 35, no 2, pp 195-211.

UN (United Nations) (1989) 'Convention on the Rights of the Child', adopted and opened for signature, ratification and accession by General Assembly resolution 44/25 of 20 November 1989, entry into force 2 September 1990, in accordance with Article 49 of the Convention on the Rights of the Child, www.un.org

TWO

Mothering, deprivation and the formation of child psychoanalysis in Britain

Julia Borossa

Introduction

In the classic account of psychoanalysis, it is childhood that provides the key to the ailments of the suffering adult patient. The experiences and fantasies of the first few years of life, visceral, uncanny and mostly unresolved, continue to inhabit us in ways that we are not conscious of, and throw more or less serious obstacles in our path as we attempt to progress through life. Thus, the psychoanalyst's main task is seen as providing an access to this childhood world that survives in the psyche, hidden, distorted but intact, and, in so doing, to defuse its hold over the patient. It is significant yet paradoxical that, in this account, 'the child' means above all the child that lives on in the adult, fleshed out in retrospect through the therapeutic encounter, the dialogue between patient and analyst. Even though some of the earliest published psychoanalytic cases, such as Freud's (1909) 'Analysis of a phobia in a five year old boy' and Ferenczi's (1913) 'The little rooster man', were each essentially based on the observation of a troubled little boy as he interacted with his family, it would be decades before the so-called 'talking cure' came to be seriously deemed applicable to the dependent, sometimes pre-verbal, young, and child psychoanalysis considered as something more than a quirky, lesser offshoot of the main profession, the psychoanalysis of adults (Geissmann and Geissmann, 1998). However, it will be argued that it is precisely the idea of the child as part of a network of social relationships that provides psychoanalysis with the impetus to question itself as a profession and a discipline.

The tasks that this chapter sets itself are multi-fold. On the one hand, it will recount how, in Britain, the analysis of children emerged from the years of the Second World War as an acceptable, even high-profile, professional activity, marking and defining British psychoanalysis generally. This development was partly due to the particular nature of internal theoretical and institutional conflicts, known as the Controversial Discussions, which divided psychoanalytic practitioners during those years and the specific interest that the two leaders in the conflict, Anna Freud and Melanie Klein, had in treating children. It will be necessary to address the background and the theoretical underpinnings of the disputes in order to understand what was at stake in the idea of analysing a child and how this influenced the general development of psychoanalysis in Britain.

However, of great significance is the way in which psychoanalytic discourse from the years around the Second World War highlighted the mothering relationship providing a point of contact with other contemporary discourses on childhood. It will be argued that a key factor at play in this respect was the temporary crossover and eventual divergence between psychoanalysis and the emerging field of social work during those same years, as professionals from different fields were brought together in their attempt to deal with the logistics of the wartime evacuation scheme, as well as its disturbing human fallout. It was during those years that deprivation, theorised mainly in terms of a disruption or a disturbance of mothering, came to take a central place in British psychoanalysis' understanding of what poses a risk to the child's and consequently the adult's emotional and psychological well-being.

However, as the debates and divergences on technique, in other words the differing views on the therapeutic relationship and the professional role of the psychoanalyst, discussed in the chapter show, the view of childhood as a condition demanding special consideration constitutes something problematic for psychoanalysis and the term risk itself does not figure easily, if at all, in the discourse of the profession. Indeed, our contemporary notions of child protection and the 'care and protection' of the young and vulnerable are at odds with a psychoanalytic conception of childhood. But through a consideration of the work of the paediatrician and psychoanalyst Donald Winnicott, a key figure in post-war British psychoanalysis, especially in its intersection with that of Clare Britton, an eminent social worker who was to train eventually as a psychoanalyst and become Winnicott's wife, a context is found for an understanding of what a childhood at risk might mean in psychoanalytic terms. This involves a rethinking of the relationship between the concepts of 'inner' and 'outer' or, in other words, the 'psychic' and the 'social'.

Psychoanalysis and child psychoanalysis: controversies and remits

Britain was one of the first countries to institutionalise psychoanalysis, early in the 20th century. During the interwar years, many talented people from fields ranging from medicine to pedagogy, some closely allied with the Bloomsbury group of writers and intellectuals, were drawn to the new profession. A training institute, with an adjacent clinic, offering low-cost psychoanalytic treatment was established in the mid-1920s. It was not the only place in London where psychoanalysis was practised: it also featured prominently among the more eclectic offerings of the Tavistock Centre, an institution founded by the army psychiatrist Hugh Crichton-Miller in 1920 in order to pursue a double agenda of psychotherapeutic treatment and social research (Dicks, 1970). As Nazism gained ground in central Europe, colleagues fleeing from Austria, Germany and Hungary joined this thriving movement. Two such immigrants were Melanie Klein, arriving in 1926, and Anna Freud, who sought refuge in England with her father in 1938.

In addition to general cultural clashes between the emigré psychoanalysts and their hosts (Steiner, 2004), there were two specific areas of controversy that had a bearing on the integration of the newcomers. The first of these was an ongoing discussion among all existing national psychoanalytic societies about the relation of their profession to medicine and the legitimacy of the work of 'lay analysts', meaning non-medically trained practitioners. Practical issues were involved, as well as epistemological ones pertaining to the nature of psychoanalytic knowledge, and to the conditions of its transmission. Should psychoanalysis seek its legitimation in an overt allegiance with medical training bodies, possessing their own, already well-defined remits and systems of accreditation? To what extent would or should psychoanalytic training institutes newly established in Berlin, London and Vienna be dependent on, modelled on, or subservient to older, established models of education?

The question of psychoanalysis' relationship to medicine was intensely debated, as the British Psychoanalytic Society was divided on whether that relationship should be one of independence or subservience. While in North America the decision was made to restrict psychoanalytic practice to qualified doctors, European societies, where a number of leading analysts came from non-medical backgrounds, generally did not follow suit. Freud himself explicitly defended the idea of an independent psychoanalysis, expressing his doubts as to whether psychoanalysis was best served by people possessing the kinds of skills that a medical education has been known to develop. Perhaps, he argued, the cause of psychoanalysis was better served by those who are merely cultured. If the latter was the case, how was one to define, quantify and transmit the cultural capital necessary to become a good analyst? (Freud, 1926). The British Medical Association, distrustful of the fledgling profession, appointed a committee to look into the matter and its final conclusions implicitly recognised that medicine had no solid means at its disposal to assess psychoanalytic treatment (Kohon, 1986, p 28).

Alongside the issue of the remit and alliances of psychoanalysis – in other words, the question of its professional identity (something that in the British context was left patently wide open by this non-engagement with medicine) – another debate was coming to the fore: the question of how and whether one should analyse a child. It was this question that finally contributed in a decisive manner to the formation of a British psychoanalytic culture that fruitfully intersected for a time with post-war government policies about childhood.

With no qualifications other than an apprenticeship with two of Freud's most respected colleagues, Sándor Ferenczi and Carl Abraham, Melanie Klein emigrated to England in 1926, at the height of the debates about the professional nature of psychoanalysis and its relationship to medicine. London proved a welcoming base for her to pursue and develop her work, which was moving the discipline in a new direction both clinically and theoretically. She was starting to publish papers that addressed the psychological conflicts experienced during the earliest years of life. In articles such as 'The psychological principles of infant analysis' (Klein, 1926) and 'Infantile anxiety situations'(Klein, 1929) she presented her understanding of the psyche, as derived from her work with children. Not only did her vision involve the young child's terrifyingly vivid inner world, whereby its relations with its mother were delineated by dependence, frustration, aggression, guilt and anxiety, but she also argued that this world was fully accessible to psychoanalytic treatment. Among those colleagues who were attracted by her work early on, two stand out as also having been influential in their work with children in a different professional context from psychoanalysis. One was Susan Isaacs, an eminent teacher and sociologist who was the head of an experimental school in Cambridge and then taught pioneering university courses on child development (Isaacs, 1930; Sayers, 2000). The other was Donald Winnicott, a paediatrician at Paddington Green Hospital, who was destined to be a central figure in post-war psychoanalysis.

However, from the outset, the overall reception of Melanie Klein's ideas was fraught with difficulties. Within the psychoanalytic movement, the principal challenge came from Anna Freud, who trained in Vienna as a teacher before following in her father's footsteps. A series of debates in the psychoanalytic journals of the late 1920s polarised the views of the two women and their followers. Melanie Klein, as we have seen, wished to apply the same fundamental principles to the analysis of children as the ones that underpinned the analysis of adults, and in so doing was implicitly arguing for the independence and specificity of psychoanalysis as a practice. The only difference was that instead of words, the free associations of adult patients on the couch, it was the way children played that served as communications from the unconscious, and it was the interpretation of that play that would eventually relieve psychic distress. Anna Freud, on the other hand, proposed a much more pedagogical method for the treatment of children in a handbook on child analysis, based on lectures she had been giving in Vienna. Her stated position was that the child is not a miniature adult but was brought to analysis, and the analyst has to ally herself with the child's parents, and the child's ego. In other words, the child psychoanalyst in *loco parentis*, was to be squarely modelled on the figure of the teacher. This was a position that differed radically, both in terms of theoretical understanding and in terms of practice, from the one taken by Klein and her colleagues, who, as we have seen, refused to turn children into a distinct category of patient and to overtly model psychoanalysis on any profession other than itself. Anna Freud's work was hotly debated in 1927 in the pages of the *International Journal of Psychoanalysis* (Klein et al, 1927).

Once Anna Freud settled in London, and became by that token a colleague of Klein's within the same institution, the British Psychoanalytic Society, it was no longer possible to ignore the professional differences between the two principal theorists and practitioners of child psychoanalysis. From 1940 onwards, they and their followers officially debated their positions in a series of formal meetings of the Society, which came to be known as the Controversial Discussions. It was apparent from the outset that what was at stake was much more than theoretical and clinical issues: it was also a political matter, a leadership crisis within British psychoanalysis and the renegotiation of its training system. In other words, what was at the bottom of the disputes was nothing less than the quest to control the future education of British psychoanalysts, and therefore the way psychoanalysis in general, and not only child psychoanalysis, would come to be practised in Britain.

Psychoanalytic truths and institutional power

Clearly in this context, the issue of organised institutional power was inextricable from that of 'scientific' truth. What all parties aspired to was a recognition of the validity of their beliefs and the efficacy of their technique, as well as the means of transmitting a knowledge and a technique that they believed to be the correct one, that is to say, a dedicated institutional platform. But instead of examining the topics of theory, technique and transmission together, the discussion followed two separate tracks. On the one hand, key papers by Kleinian analysts were opened to lengthy public debate through a series of Scientific Discussions (King and Steiner, 1992). In 1942, the Training Committee of the British Psychoanalytic Society itself met to address the issue of proper practice. Its task was to address the charge of indoctrination (versus a more neutral kind of teaching), to ensure the fair representation of all theoretical tendencies and to discuss possible reforms (King and Steiner, 1992, pp 617-52).

James Strachey, Freud's English translator and editor, was the secretary of the committee and produced the main memorandum. With good strategic sense, he started off by admitting that their task as a committee was to address themselves **to** something that was 'ultimately a *political* and *administrative* problem and not a scientific one' (King and Steiner, 1992, p 602, emphasis in original). However, his text went on to pick up on the slipperiness of what might constitute scientific truth. The way out of this impasse was to propose that psychoanalytic legitimacy lay not in the veracity of theory but in the validity of technique. 'If [a person's] technique is valid, then any gaps in his knowledge [...] will only have what I may call a *local* effect, they will not lead to any *generalized* distortion of the analytic picture, and it will moreover always be possible for the gaps to be filled in and the mistakes corrected' (King and Steiner, 1992, p 607, emphasis in original).

Be that as it may, the separation of theory and technique was clearly untenable and Strachey still referred to an ideal against which mistakes in technique were to be judged, but that psychoanalytic truth needed to be propped up in technical matters by theory, and vice versa. Therefore, the stumbling block of his proposition was exactly the point where practice and elaboration, institution and transmission, might meet: the realm of the clinical, the therapeutic interaction – or, in other words, something, by its very nature, specific and notoriously difficult to control and regulate (Borossa, 1997).[1]

The conflict was ultimately resolved in a compromise, which averted an outright split, focusing on methods of training and leaving in abeyance the entire argument about the possibility of laying down a definite psychoanalytic law, dependent on the legitimacy of either Anna Freud's or Klein's versions of childhood and of psychoanalytic truth. Such a solution was rendered inevitable by the growing number of unaligned analysts, whose work cut across the two positions and thus presented a challenge to their implacable polarisation.[2] In effect, the unaligned were choosing a psychoanalytic identity that lay in a structure other than that of an explicit discipleship, and an overt allegiance to a specific theoretical line. Unlike Kleinians or Anna Freudians who bear the mark of discipleship in their names, the other group were initially known, descriptively and literally, as the Middle group, or alternatively as the Independents, and later on as the British School of Object Relations.

Institutionally, the existence of a tripartite British Psychoanalytic Society was supported by an actual rehaul of the training system, specifically building in a space for the non-aligned, whereby trainees could choose their analysts according to their theoretical preference, but the stipulation being that at least one of their supervisors had to be free of any group affiliations. Anna Freud stayed on in England but distanced herself from British Psychoanalytic Society affairs. With her American-based colleagues, she became engaged in a new publishing venture, *The Psychoanalytic Study of the Child*, realising that this might lend support to the clinical work she had started doing with separated children during the Second World War in her clinic, the Hampstead War Nursery, later known as the Hampstead Clinic. Increasingly, she disengaged herself from ongoing developments in Britain and made America and Ego psychology, a psychoanalytic orientation widely adhered to in America, the context of her work. As for Melanie Klein, she continued practising and writing theoretical papers that were influential within the field of psychoanalysis. However, it is within the Independent group that Donald Winnicott, also deeply interested in the treatment of children, in his role as a paediatrician as well as a psychoanalyst, emerged as an increasingly dominant figure in British psychoanalysis, and one of its key representatives in the public sphere. The final section of this chapter will go on to examine his contribution.

The therapeutic relationship, mothering and deprivation

As we have seen, the issue of the professional remit of psychoanalysis lies at the heart of the Controversial Discussions. The debates were necessary to the establishment of the parameters of the field, and functioned as a forum for the negotiation of training and the acquisition of institutional power. But what emerged clearly from the meetings was that these two spheres in turn were intrinsically dependent on the private therapeutic encounter between patient and analyst. The centrality of the question of the appropriate manner in which children, dependent on others in practical terms and in the face of the law, should be treated, highlights the difficulties inherent in any attempt to isolate that encounter from environmental and historical factors.

It is useful here to pause and reflect on the timing of these meetings: taking place between 1941 and 1945, they largely coincided with the years of the Second World War. One is compelled to wonder just what it is that a story centred on discussions internal to psychoanalysis leaves out, and it is to this crucial remainder that we now must turn in order to fully understand the development of psychoanalysis in Britain. As we have already seen, the positions affirmed during the Controversial Discussions opposed differing understandings of the role of the psychoanalyst, and differing perspectives on the appropriate model for the therapeutic relationship with child (and by implication adult) patients. On the one hand, Melanie Klein's purist way seemed to bracket off the child's actual parents and external reality in general[3] and, on the other hand, Anna Freud's more socially grounded alternative appeared to compromise psychoanalysis' hard-earned distinct identity by allying it overtly with something else (pedagogy) and might as a consequence appear as a treatment that was overly adaptive to social situations and expectations, rather than engaged with unconscious processes. It was unsurprising that she turned more and more to American colleagues whose own practice was historically linked to medicine, and equally encouraging of social adaptation.

Nevertheless, common concerns united the practitioners across the factions of the British Psychoanalytic Society, even as they quarrelled over their professional identity and institutional position, concerns that were also part of the general British discourse on childcare during the inter- and post-war years (Riley, 1983). The first of these concerned the relationship between the inner and outer spheres, or, in other words, the individual psyche and the specific social structures in which it develops. It was during the years following the First World War that thinking through the implications of this relationship became an increasingly urgent question for psychoanalysis. Freud's great texts on society, such as 'Group psychology and the analysis of the ego' (Freud, 1921) and 'Civilisation and its discontents' (Freud, 1930), date from those years and show more clearly than earlier texts the extent to which psychoanalysis conceives of the individual in social terms, their psyche constructed through and through by their relationships with others. To be sure, these relationships are from the outset a source of anxiety, conflict and pain, but it is precisely in this that they are significant; indeed, for psychoanalysis, it is these relationships that shape the individual in a very fundamental way. As Robert Young (1991, p 141) among others puts it, 'psychoanalysis is already a theory of the articulation of the subject with the social: if desire, for instance, is the desire of the Other, this means that desire is a social phenomenon'.

In *The Development of Psychoanalysis*, Sándor Ferenczi and Otto Rank (1925) argued for changes in therapeutic practice, whereby the focus of the clinical encounter would be primarily the relationship between patient and analyst, and the ways in which that relationship repeats, in the here and now, significant relationships from the patient's past, rather than the elucidation of the patients' dreams and fantasies. In the technical language of psychoanalysis this repetition was known as transference (Ferenczi and Rank, 1925). In both the realms of theory and technique, the emphasis was shifting towards a more systemic view of the interaction, a move from a one-person to a two-person psychology, or even multi-person psychology, as patients were understood to bring to the consulting room a complex inner landscape made up of the significant others that shaped them and continued to inhabit them. 'Object' and 'object relationship' were short cuts to describing this crowded psychic scene. These terms became increasingly important for psychoanalysis, particularly as practised in Britain. As we saw earlier, the British School of Object Relations was another name by which the non-aligned faction of the splintered British Psychoanalytic Society became known. This may seem a little puzzling. But as Laplanche and Pontalis (1988 (1973), p 273) state in their classic reference book, *The Language of Psychoanalysis*, 'object is understood here in a sense comparable to the one it has in the literary or archaic 'the object of my passion, of my hatred, etc'. It does not imply, as it does ordinarily, the idea of a thing, of an inanimate and manipulable object as opposed to an animate being or person'.

And it was the mothering bond that was considered as the first and most significant object relationship of all, ensuring the marginalisation of the father's role, particularly in British psychoanalytic work. This development contrasted with earlier views, embodied in the Oedipus Complex that depended on the family as a patriarchal unit, and on the importance of the father as that family's legislator and the child's rival for the mother's affection. This new-found concentration on the role of the mother stood as the second area of concern, cutting across all the warring factions of the British Psychoanalytic Society in the

1930s and 1940s. For Melanie Klein and her followers, its relationship with a maternal figure was the most powerful part of the very young child's fantasy life and the work of Kleinian analysts developed that insight further. Conversely, for their other colleagues, the emphasis lay in the concrete relationship that was observed to be sustaining and frustrating to the child in specific psychically significant ways. Indeed, increasingly, for British psychoanalysts generally, and particularly so for those of the 'Object Relations' school, the mother–child relationship came to serve as a model for the psychoanalytic relationship itself (Phillips, 1988, p 10).

Beyond the terminology specific to psychoanalysis, discussions about the centrality of the mother–child bond formed a significant part of the social discourse of the interwar years. Following on from the 1918 Education Act that increased the age of compulsory school attendance to 14, movements for education reform and child guidance in the 1920s and 1930s were partly predicated on nurture being increasingly perceived as playing a more and more important role in the development of a child. Conventional social arrangements placed mothers in the key nurturing role; but what happened if mothers were unable or unwilling to fulfil that task? Emerging disciplines such as social work, as well as more established ones such as criminology and education, were loci where an expert discourse on the management of childhood circulated. And the experts were in overall agreement that the essential element of a well-adjusted childhood was the mothering bond (Riley, 1983; Rose, 1988). Furthermore, if this bond were broken or somehow faulty the potential consequences would be devastating, not only for the child, but for society. Work with children who were deprived of a family, abandoned or orphaned, and therefore were being brought up in institutional contexts, was providing the empirical basis for this discourse. A deprived child and deprivation were understood as much in psychological as material terms, a deprived child running a serious risk of becoming socially and psychologically maladjusted.

At the beginning of the Second World War, it became government policy to evacuate children from British cities threatened with bombardment. Most left their homes unaccompanied, and the enforced separation of a large number of children from their mothers provided a context for the consolidation of that kind of expert discourse on child development. The evacuation policy was widely criticised as having exaggerated the risks of bombing and underestimated the turmoil that the breaking up of families would cause. Whereas some children gave the appearance of settling well in loving foster homes that offered them a fair approximation of the mothering bond, others could not adjust. They exhibited difficult, sometimes delinquent, behaviour, such as persistent bedwetting, truancy and theft, could not be placed with private individuals and were forced into institutional living (Winnicott and Britton, 1947; Younghusband, 1981; Holman, 1995). John Bowlby, a psychiatrist who was the head of the children's section at the Tavistock Clinic, wrote an influential post-war report to the World Health Organization, partly based on work with such children. It synthesised research conducted across different fields in order to state clearly that 'the prolonged deprivation of the young child of maternal care may have grave and far-reaching effects on his [sic] character and so on the whole of his [sic] future life' (Bowlby, 1951, p 46). Going on to review the work of his psychoanalyst colleagues who treated disturbed children, he concluded that maintaining intact family relationships was critical for producing a healthy child and therefore necessary for society itself. As Denise Riley (1983) and others have shown, the adverse consequences of such a discourse for women, such as the closure of day nurseries and other post-war pro-natalist policies, aimed at encouraging women away from the workplace and back into the home.

Deprived of ordinary maternal devotion: views from social work and psychoanalysis

As we have already seen, psychoanalysis had a specific contribution to this debate in its conceptualisation of the object relationship, and in the way this related to technical aspects of therapeutic relationships with both children and adults. In order to reach a better understanding of what this implied, we will now turn to its points of contact and eventual divergence with the preoccupations of social work, as illustrated by the work of Donald Winnicott and Clare Britton.[4]

Clare Britton gained her training in psychiatric social work by completing two courses at the London School of Economics and Political Science (LSE): a one-year theoretical social science course in 1937, followed two years later by the renowned 13-month course in mental health. Like many others, she found work with the evacuation scheme, first in Reading, then full time in Oxfordshire, where she cared for some 80 children in five different hostels. Following the Second World War, she and Winnicott both contributed to the wide-ranging government enquiry into public provisions for childcare that culminated in the influential 1948 Curtis Report. She taught for several years at the LSE, training a generation of leading social workers. She was appointed Director of Child Care Studies at the Home Office in 1964 and was awarded an OBE in 1971 for her work with children (Holman, 2001; Kanter, 2004).

Britton had met Winnicott during the course of her work in Oxfordshire. Travelling up from London once a week, he was the consultant for the region, but his practice was already permeated by his deep involvement with psychoanalysis. Their collaboration resulted in only one co-written paper, and remained largely unacknowledged, but their individual writings show how two very different disciplinary perspectives on childhood came together at a given historical moment.

In her 1963 paper 'Face to face with children', Britton described her understanding of the major differences at play, but in so doing also deconstructed them:

> The psychotherapist starts from the inside and is concerned with inner conflicts which hamper social development. He or she remains, usually until the very end of treatment, a subjective figure in the child's world. The effectiveness of treatment depends on the degree of subjectivity that can be maintained. The social worker, on the other hand, starts off as a real person concerned with the external events and people in the child's life. In the course of her work with him she will attempt to bridge the gap between the external world and his feelings about it, and in so doing she will enter his inner world too. (Winnicott, 1963, p 171)

Rather than confining the contribution of the social worker to the outer world, Britton goes on to elaborate on the bridging function that she fulfils, one where an attentiveness to the child's inner world allows her to translate the child's needs. In an earlier paper, she put it this way: 'we *become*, so to speak, a reliable environment' (Winnicott, 1955, pp 145-65, emphasis in original), illustrating that statement with various clinical vignettes of work with children that show the social worker engaging effectively with their charges in ways that are often inter-psychic. 'Of course we shall not always understand what is going on or what they are trying to convey to us, and often this does not matter. What matters most is that we respond in a way that conveys our *willingness to try to understand*.... This in itself can provide a therapeutic experience' (Winnicott, 1963, p 173, emphasis in original). Those sentences describe a world that might seem quite lost to the contemporary social worker, whose practice is often constrained by the demands of bureaucracy and accountability and allows little opportunity for the kind of casework that Britton refers to (Kanter, 2004), but resonate quite strikingly with a British 'Object Relations' perspective on the therapeutic experience.

Masud Khan, a key member of the 'Object Relations' group and editor of Winnicott's work, put it in the following terms:

> It is my clinical experience that we offer (that is promise) one thing to our patients, namely the space, time and opportunity to say their hurt and deprivation in the idiom they are capable of and yet make simultaneously a contrary demand, namely of compliance with the rigidly organised regime of our techniques to speak to us in a way vastly beyond their means and capacity. (Khan, 1974, p xxxiii)

Discussing Winnicott's practice, Kahn states that:

> for Winnicott, the human individual was an unknowable isolate, who could personalise and know himself only through the other.... It is to the explication of this crucial human paradox that he applied the extreme diligence of his clinical effort and acumen. (Khan, 1974, pp xiii–xiv)

Addressing this 'crucial human paradox' in his work with both child and adult patients meant for Winnicott a sustained reflection on the mothering bond. In his many writings, he elaborated in different ways the deceptively simple idea that psychological and consequently social adjustment depended on the individual's need for a basic contact in the earliest months of their life, a contact that was sustaining, and would mediate the outside world. But by its very nature this contact could never be perfect and would always cause a measure of suffering and frustration. Such was the function of weaning, for example:

> In extremely subtle ways the mother is introducing the world to the baby, in limited ways, by warding off chance impingements, and by supplying what is needed *more or less* in the right way and at the right time.... Nevertheless there are two whole human beings, intimately interrelated and independent. (Winnicott, 1954, p 6, emphasis in original)

Winnicott's ideas reached a wide public during the Second World War and afterwards through radio broadcasts addressed to 'the ordinary devoted mother', a crucial figure in his theoretical elaboration of psychic health, expert in giving what was 'more or less' needed. The popularisation of Winnicott's thought, as well as that of the more prescriptive Bowlby, weighed on a generation of women who felt immense pressure in their mothering relationship (Riley, 1983). This powerful discursive regime has remained with us to this day, to a greater or lesser extent, and is currently flourishing again in our risk-adverse culture, extending beyond the family into schools and playgrounds, offering up its models for being a mother and for being a child.

But what if, as Winnicott and his colleagues were asking, the child's basic need for contact was fundamentally disrupted, as was understood to be the case with many children living in an institutional setting? In a remarkable essay called 'The antisocial tendency' Winnicott (1956) discusses several cases of children who were deprived of ordinary maternal devotion. The prognostic appears to be bleak: deprivation leading to 'antisocial tendency', leading to a label of 'maladjustment', leading to either treatment in a 'hostel for maladjusted children' or an appearance before the courts and the label of delinquency (Winnicott, 1956, p 307). However, he points out, strikingly, that, in fact:

> lack of hope is the basic feature of the deprived child who, of course, is not all the time being antisocial. In the period of hope the child manifests an antisocial tendency.... This understanding that the antisocial act is an expression of hope is vital in the treatment of children who show the antisocial tendency. Over and over again one sees the moment of hope wasted, or withered, because of mismanagement or intolerance. This is another way of saying that the treatment of the antisocial tendency is not psycho-analysis but management, a going to meet and match the moment of hope. (Winnicott, 1956, p 308)

The term 'management', borrowed from social work, is in fact one that has become associated with Winnicott's practice, his technical stance within his analytic therapeutic relationships often challenging an impassivity and non-interference, which were the established norms in psychoanalysis (Khar, 1996) and the distinction is somewhat disingenuous. In one particular case of a young evacuee, who showed many signs of problem behaviour, including persistent truancy, Winnicott describes how he specifically provided care that made allowance for the boy's antisocial tendency, his hope, which Winnicott interpreted as an unconscious attempt to preserve his lost home and mother (Winnicott, 1947, pp 194-203). The exact disciplinary positioning of Winnicott's treatment of that boy is unclear: it was an informal fostering relationship, since he took him into his home for three months, 'three months of hell' (Winnicott, 1947, p 199). But the essay, as with many of Winnicott's writings, draws a strong explicit parallel with the mothering bond as well as with the work that the psychoanalyst does with his/her patients as a matter of course. Significantly, it ends on a note of cautious optimism.

Conclusion

While children such as that boy could be described as having been, and continuing to be, 'at risk', as well as constituting a potential risk to society, risk is not a term that is classically associated with psychoanalytic conceptions of psychic development. In fact it sits uneasily with the general remit of psychoanalytic work with both adults and children, as unfolded in the preceding pages. Indeed, it scarcely came up in explicit form in the course of this chapter. However, what can be said is that psychoanalysis is dependent on a particular, deeply ambivalent, view of the human condition, one that posits a fundamental and unavoidable risk, whereby a certain amount of deprivation or loss is necessary to the acquisition of subjectivity, as the growing infant negotiates its own place in the world, separate from its primary carer. At the same time, early neglect and lack of a loving bond came to be understood, increasingly, by child psychoanalysis (in step with the general social discourse on childhood of the immediate pre- and post-war years) to be at the root of psychic distress, as the child negotiates levels of anxiety felt to be unbearable. In turn, this was discussed as leading to major emotional and psychological damage causing behaviour patterns that were damaging and potentially dangerous to society. These conceptualisations function necessarily as commentaries and judgements on the nature of the parent–child bond, and wider considerations pertaining to what a given society considers as being its duties and responsibilities towards its young, and the manner in which they might be fulfilled.

In attempting to formulate what a 'childhood at risk' might mean in psychoanalytic terms, we have been brought back to the very issues concerning the profession's auto-conceptualisation, and its relationship with other disciplines, with which we started. Central to Freud's, Klein's and Winnicott's theories of psychic distress is an understanding of childhood itself as a potential danger zone. None of these authors would ever have put it within the terms of our contemporary discourse about children at risk, and requiring care and protection – indeed, if anything, it is the condition of childhood *itself* that constitutes the risk. However, Donald Winnicott's work has been evoked as being conceptually and historically closest to that discourse, especially in the responsibility placed on the carer, in the weight of its vision of the relationship of mothering.

But within the terms of psychoanalytic theory, there is no prospect for any of us to escape unscathed from our childhood. Indeed, for Freud and his heirs, growing into adults capable of engaging in the business of living means accepting the state of childhood in general as an intensely difficult, painful state. The best that can be done in such circumstances is to allow for a respectful space (both psychic and literal), if not a safe one, in which the young can come to terms with that state and work through the anxieties that make us human. The burdens placed on the mothering bond are social and discursive ones as well as the psychic ones that psychoanalysis focuses on, and they came to a particular prominence in the period that we have been discussing, the decades of the consolidation of child psychoanalysis in Britain. As for safety, it is a concept that remains even more elusive at the psychic than at the physical level.

Notes

[1] Psychoanalytic societies within the European Union are currently struggling with government pressures to make their practice more accountable, and are coming up against issues that are not dissimilar to the ones that psychoanalysts were facing more than 50 years earlier. For a conceptual background of the situation in France see Roudinesco (2004) and in Britain see Casement (2004).

[2] As Adam Phillips (1988, p 46) discusses, Winnicott, in attempting to resolve the contradiction between Klein's and Anna Freud's positions regarding the practice of child psychoanalysis, specifically evoked the adaptability of technique to every individual patient.

[3] This is particularly striking in her wartime psychoanalytic treatment of a young boy evacuated to Cambridgeshire. Klein's interpretations seem to consistently ignore the reality of war and refer back to his fantasy life (Klein, 1961).

⁴ In order to avoid confusion between Donald and Clare Winnicott's names, Clare Winnicott's maiden name of Britton has been retained throughout this chapter (excluding references).

References

Borossa, J. (1997) 'Freud's case studies and the institutionalisation of psychoanalysis', in I. Ward (ed) *Case Material and Clinical Discourse*, London: Freud Museum, pp 45-63.

Bowlby, J. (1951) *Maternal Care and Mental Health*, Geneva: World Health Organization.

Casement, A. (ed) (2004) *Who Owns Psychoanalysis?*, London: Karnac.

Dicks, H.V. (1970) *Fifty Years of the Tavistock Clinic*, London: Routledge.

Ferenczi, S. (1913) 'The little rooster man', in J. Borossa (ed) (1999) *Sándor Ferenczi: Selected Writings*, Harmondsworth: Penguin, pp 84-91.

Ferenczi, S. and Rank, O. (1925) *The Development of Psychoanalysis*, New York and Washington, DC: Nervous and Mental Diseases Publishing Co.

Freud, S. (1909) 'Analysis of a phobia in a five year old boy', in J. Strachey (ed) (1953-74) *The Standard Edition of the Complete Psychological Works of Sigmund Freud*, London: Hogarth, vol 10.

Freud, S. (1921) 'Group psychology and the analysis of the ego', in J. Strachey (ed) (1953-74) *The Standard Edition of the Complete Psychological Works of Sigmund Freud*, London: Hogarth, vol 18.

Freud, S. (1926) 'The question of lay analysis', in J. Strachey (ed) (1953-74) *The Standard Edition of the Complete Psychological Works of Sigmund Freud*, London: Hogarth, vol 20.

Freud, S. (1930) 'Civilisation and its discontents', in J. Strachey (ed) (1953-74) *The Standard Edition of the Complete Psychological Works of Sigmund Freud*, London: Hogarth, vol 21.

Geissmann, C. and Geissmann, P. (1998) *A History of Child Psychoanalysis*, London: Routledge.

Holman, B. (1995) *The Evacuation: A Very British Revolution*, Oxford: Lion Publishing.

Holman, B. (2001) *Champions for Children*, Bristol: The Policy Press.

Isaacs, S. (1930) *Intellectual Growth in Young Children*, London: Routledge and Kegan Paul.

Kanter, J. (2004) 'Clare Winnicott: her life and legacy', in J. Kanter (ed) (2004) *Face to Face with Children: The Life and Work of Clare Winnicott*, London: Karnac, pp 1-98.

Khan, M. (1974) 'Introduction', in D. W. Winnicott (1992) *Through Paediatrics to Psychoanalysis*, London: Karnac, pp xi-1.

Khar, B. (1996) *D. W. Winnicott: A Biographical Portrait*, London: Karnac.

King, P. and Steiner, R. (eds) (1992) *The Freud–Klein Controversies 1941–1945*, London: Routledge.

Klein, M. (1926) 'The psychological principles of infant analysis', in J. Mitchell (ed) (1986) *The Selected Melanie Klein*, Harmondsworth: Penguin, pp 57–68.

Klein, M. (1929) 'Infantile anxiety situations reflected in a work of art and in the creative impulse', in J. Mitchell (ed) *The Selected Melanie Klein*, Harmondsworth: Penguin, pp 84–94

Klein, M. (1961) *Narrative of a Child Analysis: The Conduct of the Psycho-Analysis of Children as Seen in the Treatment of a Ten-Year-Old Boy*, London: Hogarth.

Klein, M., Riviere, J., Searl, N., Sharpe, E., Glover, E. and Jones, E. (1927) 'Symposium on child analysis', *International Journal of Psychoanalysis*, no 8, pp 339–91.

Kohon, G. (ed) (1986) *The British School of Psychoanalysis: The Independent Tradition*, London: Free Association.

Laplanche, J. and Pontalis, J. B. (1988 (1973)) *The Language of Psychoanalysis*, London: Karnac.

Phillips, A. (1988) *Winnicott*, London: Fontana.

Sayers, J. (2000) *Kleinians: Inside Out*, Cambridge: Polity.

Steiner, R. (2004) 'Analysts in transition, analysis in translation', in J. Szekacs-Weisz and I. Ward (eds) *Lost Childhood and the Language of Exile*, London: Freud Museum, pp 133–49.

Riley, D. (1983) *War in the Nursery: Theories of the Child and Mother*, London: Virago.

Rose, N. (1988) *The Psychological Complex*, London: Routledge.

Roudinesco, E. (2004) *Le Patient, le Thérapeute et l'État*, Paris: Fayard.

Winnicott, C. (1955) 'Casework techniques in the child care services', in J. Kanter (ed) (2004) *Face to Face with Children: The Life and Work of Clare Winnicott*, London: Karnac, pp 145–65.

Winnicott, C. (1963) 'Face to face with children', in J. Kanter (ed) (2004) *Face to Face with Children: The Life and Work of Clare Winnicott*, London: Karnac, pp 166–83.

Winnicott, D.W. (1947) 'Hate in the countertransference', in D.W. Winnicott (1992) *Through Paediatrics to Psychoanalysis*, London: Karnac, pp 194–203.

Winnicott, D.W. (1954) 'Needs of the under-fives in a changing society', in D.W. Winnicott (1957) *The Child and the Outside World*, London: Tavistock, pp 3–13.

Winnicott, D.W. (1956) 'The antisocial tendency', in D.W. Winnicott (1992) *Through Paediatrics to Psychoanalysis*, London: Karnac., pp 306–15.

Winnicott, D.W. and Britton, C. (1947) 'Residential management as treatment for difficult children', in D.W. Winnicott (1957) *The Child and the Outside World*, London: Tavistock, pp 98–116.

Young, R. (1991) 'Psychoanalysis and political literary theories', in J. Donald (ed) *Psychoanalysis and Cultural Theory: Thresholds*, London: Macmillan, pp 139–57.

Younghusband, E. (1981) *The Newest Profession: A Short History of Social Work*, London: IPS Business Press.

THREE

Young people's perceptions of 'risk'

Jenni Ward with Mariana Bayley

Introduction

Young people's lives are construed as almost synonymous with 'risk' and risk taking (Mitchell et al, 2001). It is well accepted that the transition from childhood to adolescence is marked by the forging of greater levels of independence (Jessor and Jessor, 1977; Lyng, 1990; Smith and Rosenthal, 1995; Shucksmith and Hendry, 1998; Coleman and Hendry, 1999; Farthing, 2005). The lifestyle changes that accompany this independence may result in exposure to a broader range of risks, including both behavioural and environmental risks (Millstein and Halpern-Felsher, 2002a). Adolescence is a period of enhanced risk taking and boundary testing and is typically coupled with feelings of invulnerability. Rarely, however, are understandings of youth activities located in young people's everyday lives and the wider arenas in which young people live their lives.

Academic and policy concerns with risk and young people typically centre on negative health behaviours such as smoking, drinking, drug use and sexual activity (Shucksmith and Hendry, 1998; Shucksmith, 2004). As young people move towards adulthood there can indeed be engagement in risk behaviours such as experimentation with illegal substances and exploring sexual relationships (Plant and Plant, 1992). Thus, much health information and policy intervention work concentrates on ways of diverting and halting these behaviours. There are, however, limits to which social policy health agendas embrace the broader social, cultural and economic milieux of young people's lives. Mitchell et al (2001) conclude from their research on risk and young men and young mothers: 'It is important to recognise the difficulty and one-dimensionality of trying to isolate particular risks, such as health risks within young people's multi-dimensional lives' (Mitchell et al, 2001, p 218). They stress that they are 'often interwoven and experienced collectively' (p 218). Hence they highlight the importance of exploring young people's everyday accounts of risk and risk taking, within the broader social and economic contexts in which they live.

Another important point is that we rarely hear young people's versions of how they comprehend their own risk worlds and risk-taking behaviour (McWhirter and South, 2004). Shucksmith and Hendry (1998, p 2) have argued that most of our views on risk and health behaviour are shaped by adult views of what is 'risky' for young people and not enough attention has been paid to the views and agendas of young people themselves. They conclude that 'qualitative data drawn from young people's own understandings of health issues might help health educators to formulate interventions or programmes for young people, which were salient, realistic and better targeted' (p 2). Since the early 1990s the practice of consulting with young people has been used to help shape more relevant prevention, education and policy initiatives. There would be benefits in broadening this to incorporate understandings of young people's risk worlds.

Leigh (1999) makes an important distinction between individual and population-based perspectives on health-risk behaviours. She cites Jeffrey (1989) to emphasise that public health initiatives build on population-based definitions of risk, but these differ from individuals' own perspectives. While some health risks have enormous significance at the population level, 'they carry only a small absolute personal risk of harm' (Leigh, 1999, p 373). This idea can be applied to the world of young people. On a population-wide basis, the risks of drinking, drug use and sex may appear to be a key feature of youthful lives, but to many young people these can be minor issues compared to other risks they face in their everyday school, family and social lives.

This chapter examines the way young people conceive of risk and what they view as the most relevant factors in their lives in terms of risk. We draw on evidence from a series of focus group interviews with young people to enhance the limited evidence base on this subject. The chapter provides insights into how young people define risk, what they consider to be risk in their worlds and how they manage and judge risk. We wanted to test whether the dominant perceptions of youth and risk such as drugs, alcohol and sex were key issues, or whether there were other concerns and realities that do not receive the same levels of attention. A key theme of the chapter is gendered risk and the importance of risk activity in the constructions of young people's self-identity. Risk is a gendered experience (Mitchell et al, 2001; Thom, 2003), and young men are more likely to engage in certain types of risky activity than young women (Erol and Sahin,

1995; Smith and Rosenthal, 1995), a difference that has been connected to early socialisation. Others have found risk to be closely correlated with identity construction, particularly among young men (Green, 1997; Mitchell et al, 2001). The notion of risk and developing maturity is also examined, as is parental influences on young people's views of risk. This raised the issue of sociocultural difference, which was found to influence risk perceptions, experience and engagement in risky activities (Smith and Rosenthal, 1995).

The study methods

The study collected information from young people who were at two different 'transitional stages'. These were young people making the transition from primary school to secondary school, thus typically aged 11 and 12 years old. The second group were moving into the final stage of secondary education. They were mainly aged 17. We assumed these to be two significant life stages, which were likely to be accompanied by greater levels of independence and therefore changing notions of risk and risk experience. The older age groups were differentiated by those who had remained in secondary school to complete their education, and those who had moved on to a sixth form college. We expected the sixth form group to seek greater levels of independence compared to their secondary school peers and therefore to display different perspectives on risk and risk taking. In fact there was not a significant difference between the responses of these two groups. A total of eight focus groups were held in three different educational establishments: a primary school, a secondary school and a sixth form college (see Table 3.1). The schools were located in two neighbouring North London boroughs.

A convenience sampling strategy was used. We included schools in the local area where access was facilitated through previous research links with the University of Middlesex. Each focus group consisted of

Table 3.1: Focus groups by school type

Primary school	One, year 6 girls
	One, year 6 boys
Secondary school	One, year 7 girls
	One, year 7 boys
	One, year 12 girls
	One, year 12 boys
Sixth form college	One, year 12 girls
	One, year 12 boys

between five and six young people. All were mixed-sex schools, although the focus groups were single sex. We considered this would allow greater freedom to discuss sensitive issues.

The boroughs were marked by social, economic and cultural diversity and a broad representation of young people was included. The majority of participants were from minority ethnic backgrounds. This had an impact on the research, as the young people were growing up amidst a variety of cultural traditions that sanctioned adherence to particular cultural codes. This highlighted the relevance of sociocultural difference in respect to risk perception at both the individual and community level, an area in which there are gaps in the knowledge base.

Three of the focus groups were made up of close friends. These were natural groupings, which came forward in response to the teachers' request for students to participate in a focus group discussion. The others were invited to participate from within timetabled subjects, thus not knowing each other so well. This may have led to some young people feeling inhibited and not raising certain topics relevant to them, such as engagement in sexual activity. This applies particularly to the older groups and was observed in one group of young women. In selecting school attenders, our study did not involve the most excluded young people. It would be interesting to contrast the views of non-school attenders to assess similarities or differences in risk perception.

Conceptualising 'risk'

The focus of our study was the way young people conceived of risk and we aimed not to pre-empt responses. We began by asking the two different age groups (10- to 12-year-olds and 16- to 17-year-olds) what they associated with the word 'risk'. The groups gave quite sophisticated understandings of the concept, although not unexpectedly responses differed by age. The notion of 'harm' linked to an action was pervasive. The younger age group gave responses such as 'something you shouldn't be doing', 'a 50/50 chance of dying', 'a challenge'. For the older age group, responses were more often connected to engaging in an action that carried consequences:

> behind every risk there is a consequence and normally when you take a risk you don't really think about the consequences so much, 'cos it's normally spur of the moment. (Female, aged 17)

Risk was also typically linked with uncertainty with responses such as 'something not predictable', 'something you had not expected to happen', 'not knowing what's going to happen next'. Indeed, it was the unpredictability that lay behind some young people distancing themselves from risk engagement:

> I associate risk with uncertainty, 'cos I'm someone who if I don't know exactly what is going to happen I don't tend to go for it, if it's a risk and it's with uncertainty I normally don't go for it, just in case. (Female, aged 17)

One young man conceived of a risk as 'something you *don't* have to do', thereby linking it to individual choice and responsibility:

> it was not really a risk 'cos I had to come here [speaking about his transfer to a new secondary school], it's not a risk, a risk is something you *don't* have to do. (Male, aged 17)

To him, risk was more related to choosing to engage in particular activities that may carry harm, such as riding with a dangerous driver. Thus, he conceived of risk, or more precisely risk engagement, as something he was in control of. It was something where the odds and potential outcomes were weighed up and engagement was based on that knowledge.

The majority of young people from both age groups viewed risk as associated with 'danger' or harm, or participating in a certain action that might result in a harmful outcome such as injury, or at worst death. A few, however, embraced the notion that risk and risk taking could also be positive, with benefits attached. This was rationalised from the perspective that, even if the outcome turned out to be negative, one could learn from the experience and that such lessons would be useful in judging risk in the future:

> I think risks are always good because, even if the consequence is bad you still learn from it, so it turns out positive. (Female, aged 17)

The comment below also illustrates the perceived benefits of risk, and highlights the highly personalised and intersubjective nature of risk (Simpson, 1996):

> I've spent five years with the same people so going to uni scares me 'cos it's different people. So I think that going to uni would be a good risk because I would get to find out more about myself and have confidence to mix with other people. (Female, aged 17)

Some risk activity was considered straightforward 'fun', such as drinking alcohol and 'getting drunk'. A few young men associated risk with 'doing something that gave you an adrenaline buzz', thereby linking it to something physical and to 'heroic' type activity.

In many ways, the responses recorded in our study mirrored those of Lupton and Tulloch's study (2002a, 2002b), which examined lay understandings of risk. They sought to understand what risk as a concept meant to people and found that, for many, risk involved the weighing up of whether or not an action should be undertaken (2002a, p 323). While they found that risk was often associated with uncertainty and emotions of 'fear and dread', in certain contexts risk was seen as positive and was explained using notions of 'self-actualisation' and 'self-improvement'.

Voluntary and involuntary risk

In addition to conceptualising risk, we asked the young people what were the most prominent risks they faced in their everyday lives. The responses were varied and introduced notions of voluntary and involuntary risk taking. Voluntary risks could be defined as those one chose to engage in and therefore had control over, such as being out at night with friends, or choosing to take an unfamiliar route home. Descriptions of such incidents were framed within the potential to meet trouble. Conversely, involuntary risk could be defined as unexpected risks that a person has no control over. These included life-stage transitions and the risks presented in this process. For instance, moving on to secondary school where peer pressure and 'bullying' from older teenagers was anticipated, or moving to university where new friendships needed to be negotiated.

Not unexpectedly, responses differed by age. Few young people perceived themselves as active risk takers in the stereotypical way we think of youth risk – such as through drugs, alcohol and sexual participation. One young man acknowledged that he was an 'automotive' risk taker and described multifaceted risk taking. This included his enjoyment of dangerous driving and illegal risks such as driving without a licence or insurance:

> When I get my licence I will have a lot greater risks, I will be driving a lot more and with a licence I will be more confident, which is not a good thing because I will just go too fast, I always push it to see how fast I can go. (Male, aged 18)

Responses were more typically placed within the context of leisure- and pleasure-oriented spheres and within the context of urban living. By virtue of growing up in a large urban landscape, various risks were present such as road safety, crime and being out and about in local areas where the sometimes aggressive and acquisitive desires of other youths threatened safety (Lupton and Bayley, 2002; Bunting, 2005). Young people's perceptions of risk are influenced by their social ecology (Smith and Rosenthal, 1995; Shucksmith and Hendry, 1998) and the young people we interviewed identified specific crime 'hotspot' areas that were perceived as 'risky' should they be out in such places.

Obviously age and increasing maturity has an impact on how, and what, young people conceptualise as risk – 'a result of their experience with these activities' (Smith and Rosenthal, 1995). This was evident in our research. The younger participants expressed high levels of fear and anxiety in respect to everyday situations such as travelling on a bus, 'stranger danger' and the 'imagined' potential for harm from other young people, such as having their mobile phone stolen or being 'mugged' (see also Lupton and Bayley, 2002). Older participants spoke more from direct experience and engagement with risk situations and 'risk environments' (Smith and Rosenthal, 1995; Millstein and Halpern-Felsher, 2002b).

Involuntary risks were more a part of the younger groups' narratives. For instance, going to secondary school was perceived as a significant risk in which they feared encountering 'bullies', 'drugs' and 'being a teenager':

> risks are drugs, bullies and making the right friends at secondary school, 'cos it is hard to choose your friends. At first you have to go around with nobody at the start.... I think bullies are a risk because if you get on the wrong side of them, then you can get really hurt and if you tell somebody, they will come and stab you or something like that. And drugs because lots of people in secondary school will tempt you to take it. (Male, aged 10)

These risks were viewed as part and parcel of a world they were soon to inhabit. The extent of anxiety this caused seemed to be connected to the amount of preparatory work undertaken by the school system and by their parents to assist them to make this leap.

It was apparent, then, that young people had a range of concerns both in their daily lives and in connection with their longer-term plans. Thus, when we think about young people and risk there are issues that are not receiving the same attention as those that appear to be at the forefront of professionals' priorities, such as alcohol, drugs and sex.

Risk and gender

There were similarities in male and female risk narratives, yet there were also distinct differences. Risk is a gendered experience, mirroring the gender-role stereotypes that exist in society (Erol and Sahin, 1995; Smith and Rosenthal, 1995; Green et al, 2000; Harris and Miller, 2000; Thom, 2003). For instance, McWhirter and South (2004), in their work on young people's risk perceptions, found that girls were more likely than boys to associate risk with accidents at home and personal safety. Boys more often described outdoor and electrical-related incidents and sport and skill mastery. This is related to understandings of male risk linked to physical and heroic behaviour (Farthing, 2005). To some extent, these differences were revealed in our study. Males typically constructed their risk worlds around physicality while girls' accounts were constructed in more emotive terms. These were around romance relationships, body image and appearance, and empathised with parental concerns such as financial issues and family arguments.

Risk, peer groups and male identity construction

A key theme permeating our discussions was 'identity construction', particularly in regard to 'masculine identity'. This was often discussed in connection with notions of peer group acceptance and belonging. If they did not join in certain group-focused risk behaviours, the young person risked being ostracised, or at least risked compromising their group membership.

It was apparent from our research that masculine identity was frequently tested out by other males. This was both within their own friendship groups, and through anonymous encounters while out on the streets with other groups of young men (compare Bunting, 2005).

For young males, friendship groups were viewed as key sites for engaging in risk activity:

> A: I think you do tend to take more risks when you are with your friends, not that they are so much an influence, but maybe sometimes you want to prove something to them.

> D: That's true, if you are on your own there is no point in taking a risk 'cos you don't have a consequence, 'oh yeah I did this', but does anyone really know you did that ...?

> A: When you take risks, your friends rate you for it, so the next day – 'remember that time when you did so and so?' It makes you feel good in yourself. (Males, aged 17)

Male risk activity was also associated with achieving 'status', which appeared to be an important attribute for some young men:

> It's also for status, it's like trying to show how manly you are; it is not how you think about it at the time, but that is what it really comes down to. (Male, aged 18)

Contrasting views on engaging in risk activity to attain status were made clear in the following debate between two young men. One acknowledged an understanding of how status can benefit a person, yet the other questioned its relevance when attained through risk activity, namely drug involvement:

> T: You do get into some social groups.

> A: But is it good to get into social groups that are with drugs? It's not worth it.

> T: But I'm saying you do get access to some things.

> A: So you get well known?

> T: Yeah, you get a different status. (Males, aged 17)

Shucksmith and Hendry (1998, p 101) noted the importance of 'socially oriented risk' in young people's lives, arguing: 'It is obvious, in that very few risky behaviours are carried out alone. They need an audience to be elicited'. Mitchell et al (2001) also highlighted the links between risk and identity. In their study exploring risk in young people's lives, they found that both male and female accounts suggested that young men who did not engage in risk-taking activities 'might find themselves socially isolated, even disempowered in terms of hegemonic masculinity' (Mitchell et al, 2001, p 224).

The notion of friendship groups being key sites for risk engagement raises the issue of 'peer pressure'. Peer pressure has commonly been understood as lying at the root of young people's decisions to engage in risky behaviours. Coggans and McKellar (1994) challenge this view, arguing that 'peer preference' rather than peer pressure is the key organising feature of young people's lives. They argue that youths actively seek out, and connect with, like-minded people, be they those who endorse 'antisocial behaviours', or those whose group norms coalesce around compliance and general law-abiding behaviours.

The older male groups in our study tended to downplay the dynamic of peer pressure, apparently because they had mastered ways of managing it. Yet, concerns about how they were viewed by peers if they did not participate in certain behaviours created situations where they had to weigh up whether to succumb or not. Real-life examples of peer group pressure to earn acceptance included 'being dared to steal something'. For the younger boys this was at a level of stealing from a local newsagent. For older males it was stealing from a person, that is, stealing a mobile. The dilemmas that faced one young man in connection to this were made clear:

> Say, for example, your friends hang around with gangs, dealing drugs, like going around jacking people [stealing from people], and one time we might be with them and then, for example, they might say, 'oh it's your turn now, and you have to go and do this and that' and you don't want to do it, and you don't want to look stupid in front of them so you might go along with it, but then at the end of the day, you don't want to risk getting yourself in for trouble, so that is like the risk you get with some friendships. (Male, aged 18)

It was evident, that a process of 'peer preference' and 'selection' was at work in young people's management of their risk worlds. This appeared to be an ongoing undertaking as they moved through the child, adolescent and young adult years. Young people described making continual judgements on what they considered to be 'good or bad groups' and the outcome of association with, or belonging to, a particular group. This, however, was most pertinent at key transition points, such as moving into arenas that would open them up to a broader range of friendship groups and thereby varied pressures. The younger group envisaged encountering situations on entry to secondary school where they would be pressurised unwillingly into activities:

> You have to really consider who you want to be your friends and who you don't. Even if they are the coolest people in school, you've got to ask, are they really going to be my friends, or are they just wanting me to do things? (Male, aged 10)

Risk and female identity

The peer group as a site for identity construction, and risk taking, specifically involving group-sanctioned behaviours, appeared to be less of an issue for young women, whose narratives were markedly different from the young men's. Young women gave the impression that physical appearance and clothing, or not looking the right way, or indeed 'making sure you looked the right way', was more of a risk. This was connected to being scrutinised by other young people and the award of friendship based on this factor. One young woman viewed teenage 'girl' magazines as a form of risk, as the typical endorsement of a particular body image could lead to female insecurities:

> I think magazines are very major ... because it has got to do with appearances and if you are an insecure person ... (Female, aged 17)

Although not categorically stated, it was implicit in young women's discussions that group cohesiveness and belonging may have been linked to sexual activity. It seemed group membership, specifically among the older young women, naturally formed around whether they were 'engagers' or 'non-engagers' in sexual activity, as alluded to in the following comment:

> The majority of the people in my close friendship group are virgins, and it is not, we don't have boyfriends it's just we're not interested, we've got guy friends, but not

> boyfriends ... there doesn't seem to be much in between.
> Half the people I know just aren't interested and the other
> half are kind of far too interested. I guess those guys are the
> people that get the name for us, that all young people are
> having lots of unprotected sex or whatever. (Female, aged
> 18)

Rather than sexual engagement being an openly pressurised activity, as male street-based risk behaviour seemed to be, female friendship group formation and identity seemed to be underpinned by shared sexual attitudes. As girls moved towards exploring their sexual identities at different rates, particular group cohesions followed. This was guided by the different moral values they held in regard to sexual engagement. A few young women declared they intended to stay virgins until they were married. In this case they shared few concerns with the other young women they knew, who were sexually active.

In discussing sexual activity and risk, abstaining from sex was regarded as the ultimate risk avoidance strategy in regard to sexual health, early pregnancy and indeed boyfriend troubles. In contrast, other young women discussed the positive aspects of sexual relationships, suggesting that they introduced a different level of understanding and responsibility. They were viewed as a normal part of the maturing process. Thus, female group formation could in many ways be linked to the notion of peer preference/selection. Young women socialised with those who shared the same issues and concerns as they did.

Although not an immediate feature of their lives, both younger and older females perceived of 'marriage' as a form of risk. It was considered to have uncertain outcomes in that the true character of the person was not known. It was noted it was meant to be for life, but 'how were you to be sure?'

> Marriage, moving out of home 'cos you marry someone
> for the rest of your life, but you can never be sure about
> that. (Female, aged 17)

The risk of 'arranged marriage' was mentioned, reflecting the different sociocultural backgrounds of the participants. One young woman discussed a problem she faced in that her parents wanted an arranged marriage for her, but she already had a boyfriend of two years whom she loved and wanted to marry. Two other young girls expressed anxiety about arranged marriage as they had parents in arranged marriages:

> If you've got an arranged marriage and you don't really
> like the person who's been arranged for you, you might
> run away and your family might not talk to you for ages.
> (Female, aged 10)

Coleman and Hendry (1999) suggest that the nature of female relationships is deeper, more emotional and personal than male action-centred, instrumental and competitive relationships, a difference that can be observed for the 'rest of our lives' (Coleman and Hendry, 1999, p 142). This was to some degree confirmed in our study in the way young men and women discussed risk and the pervasiveness of risk activity in the construction of masculine identity.

Risk, developing maturity and parental influences

Young people's risk narratives were bound up within conceptions of developing maturity and forging independent lives. In this context, some situations that could be construed as risky were presented as positive challenges that were part of learning how to negotiate the way through life, and sifting out right from wrong. This reflects the comments made earlier whereby risk was seen as having functions of 'self-actualisation'. Young people rationalised the outcomes of their decisions to engage in something risky as helping to shape them into the person they were becoming and to develop confidence to confront the unfamiliar arenas into which they were moving. The view that risk taking may be potentially adaptive rather than deviant has also emerged in work by Chassin et al (1989) who argued that 'risk-taking can serve a positive constructive role in adolescent development' (cited in Smith and Rosenthal, 1995, p 230).

Views on parents' risk perceptions highlighted the issues – and at times conflicts – around positive and negative aspects of risk taking. Some young people considered that their parents' 'imagined' fears of potentially dangerous situations affected the amount of freedom they were given:

> Just going out at night and staying out late, my parents are
> like, 'ooh it's a risk' ... they think about it as a huge risk ...
> parents think of it differently. (Male, aged 17)

Parental fear had led some young people to develop a sense of fear themselves, which they did not find helpful. While it was accepted that their parents were only trying to protect them, one young woman described how the continual 'drumming' into her that the streets were not safe and the consequent restrictions on her movements had stifled her confidence:

> All of my life my mum has been drumming it into my head that if I ever go out alone something will happen to me. So even if I am going down the road I fear that someone is going to come and grab me or something, I have just got it into my head, I fear going out alone so I prefer to go with someone ... and now that she is allowing me to go out I fear it, it's like great! (Female, aged 17)

Adult and parental fear was viewed as pervasive in the area of sexual advice and communication. This was in part interpreted as problematic in that the young people felt they were ill-informed as a consequence. One young woman construed the lack of communication by her parents to be indicative of a fear that if young people knew about sex, then they would be more inclined to engage in it:

> Parents believe that if you talk about sex, it is going to encourage your child to go and do it, but really you are just educating them, you are not telling them to go do it. But I think they are afraid of speaking about it, because they are afraid if your child knows too much about it they are going to go and do it, but really you are not, you are just educating them, telling them, guiding them on what's right and what's not right. (Female, aged 17)

The same young woman commented on the way the school system had dealt with sex education. This had been provided at an age that was not synchronised with actual sexual activity and interest. Now that they were at the age when they needed information and advice on how to negotiate sexual relationships there was no school-based provision.

On this theme of a disjunction between parental attitudes and risk, defying family was construed as a risk. One group of mainly South Asian young men described their parents' marital/cultural expectations for them as a form of risk, in that if they did not comply with the rules of the culture within which they were being raised, they risked being excluded from the family. This was becoming an important matter in their lives as they began to establish romantic attachments to young women who were from different cultural backgrounds. In some respects this can be linked to identity construction and emphasises issues of 'dual identity' (Singh Ghuman, 2003). Singh Ghuman has contended that young people born to immigrant parents face significant challenges and difficulties as they try to balance parental traditions and values alongside their experiences of being born and raised in the UK. This was verified in the following comment:

> 'cos if you marry someone out of your religion they don't really want to keep in contact with you, because they don't think it is right and then you think it's going to disappoint them but you will disappoint yourself in a way because it is something you want to do, so it's kind of restricting your options in a way. (Male, aged 17)

These young men's explanations were embedded within a discourse of growing up in a multicultural city. Their lives were entrenched within friendships and relationships formed in school, college and leisure environments where they were friends with young men and women from a range of different cultures. They were constructing identities that fitted with 21st-century inner-city life, which to some extent conflicted with parental traditions and values. This was set alongside immense family loyalty and a feeling that they 'owed' their parents for all they had done in bringing them up. They also pointed out that their parents' expectations were not a major burden as they had devised ways of managing it. This, however, involved a level of dishonesty, which they viewed as common to young person–parent relationships. They suggested that if the romance were to flourish, negotiations with parents would be entered into; this might be when they faced conflict.

Although it has been suggested that social and cultural differences are a distinct feature of risk perception (Lupton and Tulloch, 2002a), there appears to be very little work that has examined this issue. Over the last few years in the UK there has been increasing attention on the conflict between young people and their parents' cultural expectations. The serious harm that can be caused to young people who do not follow their parents' traditions has been highlighted with, at its most extreme, 'honour killing' (see Meetoo and Mirza, this volume, Chapter Nine). A more in-depth understanding of how young people negotiate their dual identities and manage the risks involved would provide a significant addition to our conceptualisation of risk. This raises sensitivities, but it is no longer acceptable that such issues are viewed within a multiculturalist discourse in which they are considered to be the business only of the 'community', especially when young people's mental health and safety are at stake.

Conclusion

Our study revealed that risk behaviours are complex and bound up within peer relationships, status and identity. Unless these are confronted within a much broader framework incorporating sociocultural, socioeconomic and social ecology perspectives, we will miss the contextual factors that shape risk-behaviour development. The study confirms that risk was broadly conceptualised by young people, although it was generally associated with an unexpected outcome, or something that carried a harmful consequence. Notions of voluntary and involuntary risk were distinguished, for instance risk that carried a personal choice hence there being an element of control, compared to the more unexpected and unavoidable nature of involuntary risk. It was apparent that both younger and older groups had relatively sophisticated rationalisations and systems in place for managing and judging the voluntary risk they faced in their lives.

Much health intervention work with young people relates to behaviours such as sexual activity, and drug and alcohol consumption, with some work around accidents and road traffic awareness and safety. Little attention seems to have been paid to some of the broader fears and concerns of young people. Our study revealed that there was a range of less obvious risks young people faced in their growing-up years. These differed for the two age groups, but typically involved friendship selection and management and the particular pressures that come through friend and peer attachments. This was often bound up with teenage identity construction, status and anxiety about how they were viewed by others.

Our research suggested that young people of both age groups were well versed in how to be 'safe' in terms of road safety, sexual protection issues and drug and alcohol use. It was in the context of their social relationships that the biggest challenges were presented. They appeared to be less confident in managing and negotiating social relationships that involved general teenage pressures to engage in risk activity such as theft, drug use and casual sexual encounters.

Although school-based Personal, Social and Health Education (PSHE) should not be considered the only arena in which young people learn about life issues, it is an important educational forum that can incorporate dynamic styles of information provision and learning. It would appear, however, that PSHE focuses on the physical aspects of harm prevention, such as condom use and drug facts, at the expense of relationship and peer group management. We acknowledge, however, that school-based sex education is moving towards incorporating relationship education (DfEE, 2000). Yet what is needed is an active engagement with young people in deciding and developing what goes on the agenda. An Office for Standards in Education report on school-based PSHE has recommended that pupils should be consulted more systematically to ensure that it was more relevant to their needs (Ofsted, 2005). Our research suggests that young people are keen to discuss these issues and that they would be well received if tackled within health education by specialists who were independent, knowledgeable and trustworthy.

There is a need to address sociocultural differences and relationships within our understanding of risk. These were important issues for some of the young people in our study, and were related to deep-rooted cultural traditions. This would require boundary-pushing approaches compared to the so-far restrained practice in this area, and could usefully involve parents, and other people who hold community status and influence.

It thus appears that there would be benefits to broadening consultations on young people's health and social lives to encompass their risk worlds. This would enable young people to foreground their own concerns of risk and how risk interacts with their daily lives. As Shucksmith and Hendry (1998) have argued, such information would provide a better-informed policy agenda. While our findings do not point directly to ways in which interventions might be shaped differently, the views of the young people presented in this chapter contribute to the limited evidence on young people's perceptions of risk. This exploratory study can perhaps feed into informing and shaping approaches to interventions within health education policy and expands our understandings of risk lifestyles and risk groups as they pertain to young people.

References

Bunting, M. (2005) 'Threats, fear and control', *The Guardian*, 23 May, p 17.

Chassin, L., Presson, C.C. and Sherman, S. J. (1989) 'Constructive versus destructive deviance in health related behaviours', *Journal of Youth and Adolescence*, vol 18, no 3, pp 246-62.

Coggans, N. and McKellar, S. (1994) 'Drug-use amongst peers: peer pressure or peer preference', *Drugs: Education, Prevention and Policy*, vol 1, no 1, pp 15-26.

Coleman, J. and Hendry, L.B. (1999) *The Nature of Adolescence* (third edition), London: Routledge.

DfEE (Department for Education and Employment) (2000) *Sex and Relationship Education Guidance*, London: DfEE, available at: www.dfes.gov.uk/sreguidance/sexeducation.pdf

Erol, N. and Sahin, N. (1995) 'Fears of children and the cultural context: the Turkish norms', *European Child and Adolescent Psychiatry*, vol 4, no 2, pp 85-93.

Farthing, G.W. (2005) 'Attitudes toward heroic and non-heroic physical risk-takers as mates and as friends', *Evolution and Human Behaviour*, vol 26, no 2, pp 171-85.

Green, E., Mitchell, W. and Bunton, R. (2000) 'Contextualising risk and danger: an analysis of young people's perceptions of risk', *Journal of Youth Studies*, vol 3, no 2, pp 109-26.

Green, J. (1997) 'Risk and the construction of social identity: children's talk about accidents', *Sociology of Health and Illness*, vol 19, no 4, pp 457-79.

Harris, M. B. and Miller, K. C. (2000) 'Gender and perceptions of danger', *Sex Roles*, vol 43, no 11-12, pp 843-63.

Jeffery, R.W. (1989) 'Risk behaviours and health: contrasting individual and population perspectives', *American Psychologist*, vol 44, pp 1194-202.

Jessor, R. and Jessor, S. L. (1977) *Problem Behaviour and Psychosocial Development: A Longitudinal Study of Youth*, New York: Academic Press.

Leigh, B. (1999) 'Peril, chance, adventure: concepts of risk, alcohol use and risky behaviour in young adults', *Addiction*, vol 94, no 3, pp 371-83.

Lupton, D. and Tulloch, J. (2002a) 'Risk is part of your life: risk epistemologies among a group of Australians', *Sociology*, vol 36, no 2, pp 317-34.

Lupton, D. and Tulloch, J. (2002b) "Life would be pretty dull without risk': voluntary risk-taking and its pleasures', *Health, Risk and Society*, vol 4, no 2, pp 113-24.

Lupton, K. and Bayley, M. (2002) 'Children – how they interact with the street environment', *Traffic Engineering and Control*, vol 43, no 6, pp 224-8.

Lyng, S. (1990) 'Edgework: a social psychological analysis of voluntary risk-taking', *Amercian Journal of Sociology*, vol 95, no 4, pp 851-86.

McWhirter, J. and South, N. (2004) *Young People and Risk: Towards a Shared Understanding*, Final Report to Government Office East, University of Essex: Community Safety Fund.

Millstein, S. G. and Halpern–Felsher, B. L. (2002a) 'Perceptions of risk and vulnerability', *Journal of Adolescent Health*, vol 31, no 1, pp 10-27.

Millstein, S. G. and Halpern–Felsher, B. L. (2002b) 'Judgements about risk and perceived invulnerability in adolescents and young adults', *Journal of Research on Adolescence*, vol 12, no 4, pp 399-422.

Mitchell, W. A., Crawshaw, P., Bunton, R. and Green, E. E. (2001) 'Situating young people's experiences of risk and identity', *Health, Risk and Society*, vol 3, no 2, pp 217-33.

Ofsted (Office for Standards in Education) (2005) *Personal, Social and Health Education in Secondary Schools*, London: Ofsted, available at: www.ofsted.gov.uk

Plant, M. and Plant, M. (1992) *Risk Taker: Alcohol, Drugs, Sex and Youth*, London: Tavistock/Routledge.

Shucksmith, J. (2004) 'A risk worth the taking: self and selfhood in adolescence', in E. Burtney and M. Duffy (eds) *Young People and Sexual Health: Individual, Social and Policy Contexts*, New York: Palgrave Macmillan, pp 5-14.

Shucksmith, J. and Hendry, L.B. (1998) *Health Issues and Adolescents: Growing Up, Speaking Out*, London: Routledge.

Simpson, R. (1996) 'Neither clear nor present: the social construction of safety and danger', *Sociological Forum*, vol 11, no 3, pp 549-62.

Singh Ghuman, P. (2003) *Double Loyalties: South Asian Adolescents in the West*, Cardiff: University of Wales Press.

Smith, M. A. and Rosenthal, D. A. (1995) 'Adolescents' perceptions of their risk environment', *Journal of Adolescence*, vol 18, no 2, pp 229-45.

Thom, B. (2003) *Risk-Taking Behaviour in Men: Substance Use and Gender*, London: Health Development Agency.

FOUR

Risk and the demise of children's play

David Ball

Introduction

In 2002 the Children's Society and the Children's Play Council called on every council and school in Britain to carry out what they called a 'daisy chain audit'. This curious name stemmed from the discovery that somewhere in Britain children had been told not to make daisy chains because of some suspected hazard. The audit's purpose was to expose excessive or unnecessary restrictions on children's play activities.

Contemporaneously, the Play Safety Forum, a group of the main national organisations in England with an interest in safety and children's play,[1] published an important pamphlet called 'Managing risk in play provision' (Play Safety Forum, 2002). This was part of a new campaign to address a growing concern about how safety was being addressed in children's play provision and its effect upon play opportunities. In 2003 a European Play Safety Forum was established with similar goals and agreed a statement of its own in 2005. Even Sir Digby Jones (2005), the Director-General of the Confederation of British Industry, felt drawn to speak out about a culture that 'raises [children] to believe that risk did not exist because of emphasis on rights and an excessive concern for health and safety'.

It is reasonable to ask 'What is going on?' and 'Why has all this been necessary?'. It is surely common knowledge that children have a fundamental right to play as stated in Article 31 of the United Nations Convention on the Rights of the Child, and it is hard to imagine that anyone would seriously wish to deter children from participation in this natural and beneficial activity.

A hint of an answer lies in research commissioned for National Playday in 2002 by the Children's Society and the Children's Play Council. This exposed a growing culture of caution in local authority and private parks and playgrounds in that play equipment was being removed or made less challenging, 'dumbed down' in common parlance, and that children were being prevented from taking part in traditional activities such as doing handstands and playing with yo–yos.

The Children's Society and the Children's Play Council also surveyed over 500 children aged mainly from seven to 11 years to find out their views and experiences regarding play and personal freedom. From this it emerged that children felt they were being prevented from having fun, for example, 45% were not allowed to play with water, 36% were prevented from climbing trees, 27% could not use climbing equipment and 23% were not allowed to ride bikes or skateboards. They reported being frequently bored by what was permitted.

Since 2002 the list of 'don'ts' applied to children has, according to media reports, proliferated to include a rash of other activities from snowballs and conkers to football during school breaks and more besides. One school closed its playground because it was on a (gentle) slope and therefore deemed unsafe. The widely reported threat posed to school trips, allegedly from bureaucracy and litigation, is one more manifestation of a related problem also affecting children. Elsewhere stories of restrictions on school cookery classes, woodwork (the 'tools are dangerous' syndrome), and numerous other once-familiar activities all tell a similar tale, one of a flight, by adults, from anything with an imaginable harmful consequence.

It is important, of course, to ask whether this trend is in the interests of children and what is behind it. Questions have already been raised about the custom nowadays of driving children to school, which, conducted in the interests although not necessarily the actuality of reducing the risk of child versus motor vehicle accidents and avoiding 'stranger danger' (Roberts, 1993), has had a series of unintended consequences upon children's lives. These range from a loss of freedom to reduced opportunities to socialise and a lack of exercise (Hillman et al, 1990), exercise now being seen as healthy and in short supply.

So how has all of this come about? This chapter will consider the provision of children's playgrounds as an example of how society interacts with children, from which it is suggested that more general conclusions can be drawn.

A newly found interest in accidents and the drive for safety

Up to the 1950s, British society had what has been described by Lady Platt of Writtle as a 'robust' attitude to children and risk. It was expected that children had to some extent to learn about risk through experience and that what might loosely be described as mollycoddling ultimately brought more harm than good through producing children who were deprived of experiences and also less able to look after themselves. The most recent half–century, however, has seen a radical change in attitudes. Safety from accidents is now frequently proclaimed as of paramount importance – the number one priority that has to be sought, seemingly, at any cost. Accidents, once regarded as random misfortunes, have, by a curious and complex process, been transformed into preventable misfortunes (for an enlightening account, see Green, 1997). Injury avoidance has become a widespread professional activity, in turn propagating the ethos of voluntary organisations such as the Royal Society for the Prevention of Accidents (RoSPA) and the Child Accident Prevention Trust (CAPT) whose emphasis is upon injury *prevention* as their names suggest.

During this time accidents also became a focus within the health sector, having formerly been regarded as random and unpredictable and hence illegitimate topics of inquiry. Thus, by the middle of the 20th century, professional epidemiologists began to view accident prevention as a public health issue worthy of study, and by the 1960s accidental injuries had come to be regarded as a major public health concern in many western-style countries. In due course the view became commonplace that 'Most accidents are preventable' (DH, 1993, p 9), and targets were being set, for example, to reduce the death rate of young people by at least 25% by the year 2005 (DH, 1992). In 2001 the *British Medical Journal*, in an editorial, went so far as to propose that the word 'accidents' be banned on the basis that almost all injuries are preventable (Anon, 2001), as had Evans (1993) eight years earlier.

The shift in attribution of what were formerly seen as accidental injuries to non-random and hence foreseeable events unleashed a cascade of consequences, not all of which were intended. Once this road is taken, as Sapolsky (1990, p 93) has reflected:

> There is no shortage of advice about risks. Let a potential risk be identified and soon all possibly relevant professions, agencies, and trade groups will offer public positions in order to protect established interests or proclaim new ones. Add the news appeal of risk stories, the availability of advertising dollars to defend and promote products, and the ongoing flood of scientific reports and there is a flood of guidance for the concerned.

In the specific arena of children's playgrounds, and taking off in the 1970s, this meant a free-for-all of advice from government departments, standards agencies, insurance companies, lawyers, regulators, voluntary agencies, special interest groups, manufacturers, professional bodies and media campaigners. Nor was this advice necessarily consistent or evidence-based. Standards published by the British Standards Institution, for example, carried much weight but were not based as one might have thought upon a formal assessment of risk, and it has also been said that they were influenced by narrow commercial interests and anecdotes (Heseltine, 1995). The foreword to British Standard BS 5696 part 2 (1986) on outdoor play equipment also implies, incorrectly, that no detailed statistics existed on playground accidents and so legitimised the judgemental nature of its advice. A later review (King and Ball, 1989) summarised an array of earlier publications on playground risk and accidents, which had seemingly been underused, including one notable article on playground injuries in Sheffield by Illingworth et al (1975), which, despite its having been recognised and cited, was nonetheless regularly misquoted, probably because what it said was not consistent with what was conventionally believed to be true.

Likewise, early government interventions (for example, the Department of the Environment's circular of 31 October 1978 to local authorities [DoE, 1978]) sought to stake out the high moral ground by offering advice to local authorities that they should implement certain risk reduction measures in playgrounds such as 'safer' surfaces, although without specifying at all clearly what form these should take. In fact, nobody knew, and even now, over a quarter of a century later, the effectiveness of the recommended measures remains unproven (Ball, 2004). However, the mere existence of this speculative advice created immense difficulties for play providers since it was taken up rather unquestioningly by the courts, insurance companies and media campaigners as somehow being anchored in established wisdom simply because it was promulgated by officialdom or something that passed for it.

Other important changes too were afoot. As Green (1997) has observed, the second half of the 20th century saw a transformation to a 'risk-based' society in that earlier concepts of 'fate' and 'determinism' were supplanted by notions of risk, which, while uncertain, still had to be managed. Thus, the 1974 Health and Safety at Work Act (HSWA) implicitly introduced the need for all agencies with responsibility for hazards to carry out risk assessments. This requirement became explicit in later legislation such as the Management of Health and Safety at Work Regulations (Health and Safety Commission, 1999). It has been said that one effect has been that today we are in serious danger of being risk managed out of existence in that the growth of strategies to manage risks is displacing valuable, but vulnerable, professional judgement in favour of defendable processes (Power, 2004). We are all engaged in a seemingly irresistible strategy of constant risk management. Even so, this might be acceptable were it being done properly, but the fact that so many problems continue to exist in the safety world strongly suggests that there are serious difficulties, many based on fundamental misunderstandings.

As an indication, even the word 'safety' means wildly different things to different audiences, as set out in Table 4.1. If 'safety' is the goal of risk management, yet means different things to providers of facilities, inspectors, interest groups, insurers, standards agencies, regulators, the public and so on, an element of confusion and chaos is thereby introduced into the risk management process (Ball, 2000a). The implication for play provision and other activities that entail risk is that the process of risk management is in serious danger of generating unintended, and possibly unwanted, consequences, and could even undermine its very purpose (Graham and Weiner, 1995).

How big is playground risk?

An obvious question to ask of any risk is: 'How serious is it?'. Surprisingly, despite the concern that has been expressed over several decades about playground safety, the actual risk of children's play is seldom reported[2] although with some diligence statistics can be obtained. Information on fatalities, on which epidemiology traditionally focuses, is kept by the Health and Safety Executive. During the 19-year period from 1981-99, 17 fatalities were reported as being somehow associated with playgrounds (without any evidence of a trend). However, scrutiny of the causes shows many had little to do with play or playgrounds per se. For example, several involved motor vehicles on school playgrounds and one involved a fall from the roof of a school building. If these and similar cases are discounted, the total of play equipment-related fatalities is five or six, implying a rate of approximately 0.3 per annum, which may be compared to a rate of 500 to 600 accidental childhood deaths per year from all causes in England and Wales. Given that children are believed to spend on average about 50 hours per year in this kind of environment, that is, 1 or 2% of their time, implies that playgrounds are actually relatively safe places compared to other venues that children frequent.

Another way to look at this is in terms of the risk for a given period

Table 4.1: Eight different concepts of the meaning of 'safety', all of which are being used concurrently within the play world

Safety criterion	Zero risk	Safety targets	Standards, CoPs[a] and guidance	Absolute risk	Risk factors	Risk assessment	Cost–benefit analysis	Risk tolerability and ALARP[b]
Typical adherents	Pressure groups	National and international agencies. Major industries	Lower courts, accident investigators, safety inspectors	Actuaries and insurers	Epidemiologists and health scientists	Safety engineers and some inspectors	Government, policy makers, economists	Higher courts, regulatory bodies
Basis of approach	Commitment	Political desire	Expert judgement	Historical data	Evidence	Scientific simulation	Utility theory	Case law (in the UK) and the 1974 HSWA
Strengths	Simplicity, single-mindedness	Clarity of overall policy goal	Should reflect a broad swathe of expert opinion. Tested over time	Helps insurance companies set premia	Scientific basis	Analytical tool. Ability to forecast the unknown	Considers both costs and benefits of safety measures	Considers wider implications of safety measures including cost, practicality and other consequences
Limitations	Associated benefits of activity forgone. Cost of control disregarded	Top-down approach, which may be inconsistent with the sum total of individual safety interventions or wider interests	Validity and motivation of judgements unclear. A bottom-up approach, which may be inconsistent with policy goals	Other priorities are disregarded	Uncertainties, causality and the question of 'how safe is safe enough?'	Uncertainties in assumptions, probabilities and second-order effects (side effects)	Anchored in a particular philosophy. Hidden assumptions and methodological problems, particularly in valuing benefits	Difficulty of striking a balance between competing attributes of a decision, eg the risks and the benefits of hazardous activities

Note: [a] Codes of Practice; [b] As Low As Reasonably Practicable.

Source: Adapted from Ball (2000a). Reproduced with permission of Taylor and Francis Ltd (www.tandf.co.uk/journals)

of exposure because this enables comparisons to be made with other activities. Taking the child population to be about 12 million, and assuming an exposure of, say, 50 hours per year to playgrounds, implies a risk of fatality of approximately 0.05 per 100 million hours of exposure. This is an exceedingly low risk. Comparable figures for adult pastimes range from a high of approximately 200 for aerial sports to 12 for swimming, 2 for soccer and down to a low of 0.06 for golf, all per 100 million hours of exposure (Ball, 1998).

Similar calculations can be made for non-fatal accidents by use of data from the Department of Trade and Industry's Leisure Accident Surveillance System (LASS).[3] An analysis of LASS data indicates that there are about 21,000 childhood Accident & Emergency (A&E) Department attendances per annum in the UK (Ball, 2002) that somehow involve publicly provided play equipment. Using these A&E attendance rates as a proxy for playground accident rates, one can estimate the risk (usually reported as cases per 100,000 hours of exposure) and make comparisons with other activities that have been similarly analysed. For public playgrounds the figure comes out at approximately four cases per 100,000 hours of exposure, whereas for sports the equivalent risks range from 290 for rugby to about 130 for soccer and 80 or 90 for netball and hockey (Figure 4.1). Only for sports like table tennis and golf are lower risks, of the order of one or two, discerned. Likewise, A&E statistics suggest that the risk of injury while simply being at home for young people is about four per 100,000 hours of exposure.

Thus, according to these statistics playground risk is exceedingly small in terms of fatalities, and in terms of lesser injuries is far lower than for most traditional sports which children are encouraged to engage in, and in any case about the same as the risk encountered at home. Given that children are testing their physical abilities in playgrounds, and also have a tendency to run a little wild in those environments, the modesty of this level of risk is surprising.

Of course, it could be argued that playgrounds have been made safer as a result of many campaigns and interventions over the last several decades and that these low risks are the culmination of all that work. However, this is not borne out by the statistics. Figure 4.2 shows the trends in A&E attendances for all playgrounds, public or private, over the period 1988 to 1999 for three of the most common types of play equipment and also by body part injured.

In the case of climbing frames there has been a gradual increase in the number of cases, driven mainly by an increase in the frequency of upper limb injuries. The situation for slides is largely unchanging,

Figure 4.1: Non-fatal injury rate based on A&E attendances

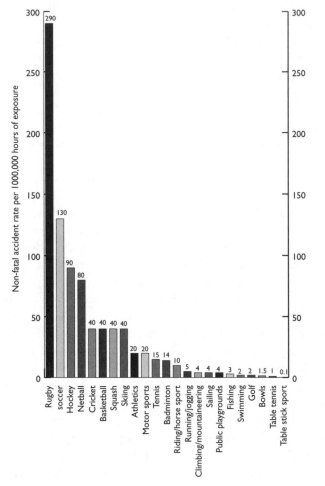

Source: Adapted from Ball (2000b), reproduced with permission of Blackwell Publishing

whereas for swings the number of cases, apart from upper limb injuries, has declined. Taken together, the total number of reported playground injuries on all apparatuses over this 12-year period shows no trend, either downward or upward. However, it is widely believed that there have been other significant changes that need to be factored in, that is, that playground provision and usage has diminished, possibly significantly, over the time period reflected in these statistics. If true, this would imply that the risk per unit time of exposure has actually increased. Unfortunately, sufficiently detailed statistics on how British children spend their time are not available. In passing it is worth noting that the decline in most types of swing injuries, as in Figure 4.2, is

Figure 4.2: Annual numbers (national estimates) of A&E cases associated with climbing frames, swings and slides in terms of body part(s) affected

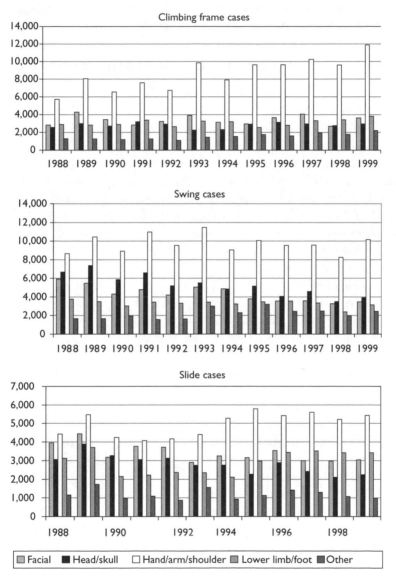

Source: Ball (2002) reproduced with permission of Health and Safety Executive (HMSO)

likely attributable to the gradual removal of swings from playgrounds, these once-popular items having in many cases been taken away on alleged safety grounds. While possibly a success for injury prevention, this represents a loss in terms of enjoyment and aptly demonstrates the potential conflict between safety and other values.

Complexities in the management of playground risks

The plethora of advice on safety of play provision since the late 1970s, the uncertainty over how it should be implemented, and the constant threat of litigation has understandably led many authorities to 'rationalise' their provision. Some have even questioned whether it was worthwhile to provide any facilities at all. Rationalisation has generally meant a reduction in the numbers of playgrounds provided though quality may have improved on those remaining, although there have been suggestions that dumbing down (removal or modification of anything seen as remotely challenging) was also taking place. This was an almost inevitable consequence of the pressure for safety because some of the measures deemed essential, such as safety surfacing, have had the effect of doubling the price of play provision, these products being very expensive to either install or maintain and beyond the budgets set by many councils for children's play. Likewise, the threat of litigation rather encouraged the removal of anything perceived as remotely risky.

Another serious challenge has resided in the issue of 'What is safe?' and 'How safe is safe enough?'. Broadly speaking, two approaches have been used for assessing the safety of playgrounds (Figure 4.3). The most common has been simply to compare the facility with published advice, particularly the recommendations of British and European standards. Thus, assessing safety has tended to be seen as an engineering-style activity since it involved the physical measurement of items of equipment followed by comparison with published standards. One notes, for instance, that solicitors acting on behalf of parties injured on playgrounds frequently request that 'an engineer' be appointed as expert. However, there are issues here because many design features of playgrounds and equipment are not covered by standards, particularly in the case of modern equipment, so judgement is then required. Of greater importance, the provision of play equipment is about balancing the benefits of the equipment against its risk – it is not purely about controlling risk and a more complex judgement is thereby required.

Figure 4.3: Two contrasting approaches to assessing the safety of play facilities

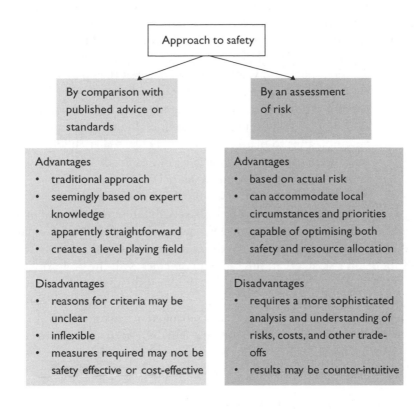

This immediately brings up the question of 'Whose judgement?'. Should it be that of an engineer-cum-inspector, or the play provider, the insurer, or someone else, for example, a specialist in child development? Table 4.1 has pointed out the range of understandings of what constitutes safety. Which should apply? It is likely that from an insurance perspective an actuarial approach would be used since insurers will want to know that, on balance, costs of claims will not exceed the value of the insurance premium. What is noticeable about this approach, however, is that it takes no obvious account of the value of the activity to the child, and the child's perspective is thus substituted by a commercial interest. An engineering-style approach, on the other hand, is more likely to consider compliance with standards even though, as noted, these may not be based on technical assessment of risk. Furthermore, pursuers of engineering-style safety assessments are generally more familiar with workplace environments and, say, building construction sites where those risks that cannot be avoided are seen as an unwanted hazard. No factory inspector in their right mind, for instance, would countenance a wobbly bridge or a climbing net as part of a normal workplace environment. However, for playgrounds the position is quite different. As the Play Safety Forum has said:

> Children need and want to take risks when they play. Play provision aims to respond to these needs and wishes by offering children stimulating, challenging environments for exploring and developing their abilities. In doing this, play provision aims to manage the level of risk so that children are not exposed to unacceptable risks of death or serious injury. (Play Safety Forum, 2002, p 1)

This ethos it should be noticed is sharply different from that of *injury prevention* with its connotations of a quest for zero risk. Instead it talks about *managing risk* and the avoidance of *unacceptable risk*, and pointedly not of 'no risk at all'. In this sense it coincides with the philosophy of the Health and Safety Executive, as encapsulated in their slogan 'Managing risk properly'. But it goes further still when it talks about a need for risk to be present. In this setting, some risk is evidently seen as a positive attribute. This is because 'children need and want to take risks' and because children need to learn somewhere about the reality of risk and the reality of the consequences of occasionally falling foul of it.

There is a powerful argument that this is better achieved in a controlled environment, like a playground or a school, than in some random place. Hence, there is a difficulty for those risk assessors who cross over from the factory environment to children's play unless they are aware of the different balance that needs to be struck between the risks and benefits of an activity. This difficulty could be confronted were those play providers who commission independent risk assessments to set out the philosophy that they wish to be followed. Commonly, however, this is not done. The importance of having a philosophy often passes unrecognised, and the judgements that determine the trade-offs between risk and play value are delegated to some external agency whose value system is not known. Indeed, the existence of this fundamental consideration may be passed over entirely.

But what of the second strand of reasoning shown in Figure 4.3, that of risk assessment? Risk assessment, it should be noted, can also imply different things to different people. RoSPA's playground inspection service (Cook and Heseltine, 2002), for instance, makes use of a risk assessment based on a homespun scoring system, which gives points to items of equipment based on their type, condition and presence or absence of features such as under-surfacing. This is certainly a type of risk assessment and has the advantage of being able to rank and score individual items and whole playgrounds. However, the ranking is predicated upon the suggested scores, yet how these correlate with the real-world risk of injury is unfathomable, certainly to the outsider, and thereby it introduces its own philosophy of decision making, but opaquely.

The RoSPA system also makes an allowance for the level of usage of equipment. That is, if something is popular and therefore much used the system would afford it a higher risk rating, since risk is defined in RoSPA's guide as the product of injury severity and probability of occurrence where the latter incorporates a notion of usage. This would appear to be consistent with RoSPA's ethos of injury prevention, but not with that of managing risk to individuals. The methodology, in scoring playgrounds, is also dominated by the score of the supposed highest risk item, even if it is only one of many. Subtle details such as these, which may not be discernible to play providers, can have a big influence on ratings and hence what is provided. It is arguable, for instance, that one should be concerned about the individual risk per use of an item of equipment, otherwise popular items will be at a disadvantage under this scheme because, through heavy usage, they will necessarily be associated with more injuries. Likewise, if playground ratings are strongly influenced by the deemed riskiest item, this could provide a recipe for removing the more challenging equipment that some children apparently crave.

Alternatively, risk assessment could be conducted strategically. Here this means taking a holistic view of childhood injuries in one's jurisdiction based partly on historical data and assessing the priorities based on statistics and expert knowledge. An approach like this could yield quite different results. For example, every playground that is constructed will necessarily increase the number of playground injuries, so from a narrow and bottom-up perspective any provision could seem undesirable since it would lead necessarily to injuries. However, an overview might show that greater provision would draw children away from more dangerous places, so reducing the overall injury toll in the neighbourhood. As an example, many authorities are wary of providing skateboard facilities because they obviously pose significant risks of injury. But without these facilities skaters almost inevitably end up on the streets and encounter all manner of far worse hazards.

The path ahead

With the introduction of a risk-based approach to safety decision making, as now required by law under the 1974 Health and Safety at Work Act and the Management of Health and Safety at Work Regulations, it has become a requirement for playgrounds to be risk assessed. This situation has now pertained for several decades but the evidence is that there is a need to reconsider how this is done.

Serious concerns about the amount and type of play provision, including its lack of stimulation, are increasingly common (Play Safety Forum, 2002). From time to time, blame for this has been assigned to various parties ranging from inspectors to insurers, solicitors and single-interest safety advisers. Certainly it should be acknowledged that the results of the safety drive over the last few decades are singularly disappointing in that hundreds of millions of pounds have been spent by local authorities and other providers on safety engineering and enforcement measures with little sign of benefit. However, it is not new that costly safety interventions can prove ineffectual as Jarvis et al (1995) and Munro et al (1995) have reported, and what most experts now advocate is a more thoughtful approach (Scuffham and Langley, 1997). But what form could this take and what ingredients should it contain?

The importance of having an explicit philosophy

Arguably first on the list is the need for an overarching philosophy. In the absence of such it is probably inevitable that the goals of play provision will become subjugated to subsidiary objectives such as litigation avoidance, insurability, reputation management, minimum maintenance and so on. This is because there are so many agencies involved one way or another in the provision of children's facilities, all with their own perspective based upon their own pressing needs and values. Thus, unless the play provider has a clear strategy, it is likely that one of these ulterior needs will end up, by default, driving the policy. It can be argued that this indeed is the root of the problem that has beset play provision over several decades.

It is encouraging to observe that there are signs that this need is being acted upon. In England, as already described, the Play Safety Forum of the Children's Play Council has produced its position statement *Managing Risk in Play Provision* (Play Safety Forum, 2002). This should greatly assist every play provider in the task of formulating and maintaining a philosophy. In Wales the Welsh Assembly

Government's (2004) Play Policy Implementation Group has published similarly helpful recommendations, for example Recommendation 19:

> that the Welsh Assembly Government, pursue all avenues to ensure the development of an environment in which the balance between children's play needs and their need to experience risks, is not compromised by inappropriate use of litigation. (Welsh Assembly Government, 2004, p 26)

North of the border, The Highland Council (2004) has issued its own play policy document with similar intentions.

The importance of these and similar documents is that they give play providers backing for the position that some risk is inevitable, even desirable, and that a balanced approach must be taken in deciding how much risk is reasonable in the circumstances. None of the above agencies answer this question of how much risk, and rightly so because the answer should depend to some extent upon local risk management decisions reflecting the needs and values of individual communities.

Understanding risk assessment and risk management

The introduction of risk assessment in Britain owes much to the work of the Robens Committee, which recommended to the British government in 1972 that the proliferation and detail of workplace safety regulation was getting out of hand and that a simpler system spelling out basic duties of employers and employees was needed. This led to the 1974 Health and Safety at Work Act and the implicit requirement for risk assessment. Although this Act simplified matters, it had another consequence – duty holders would be required to act proactively to manage risk and this required an intellectual commitment that, to some extent, the former system had appeared not to need since it was more about compliance with standards and codes of practice, which many managers had learnt to do almost by rote.

This new intellectual challenge was not universally welcomed and it can be sensed that risks are not always being managed as was intended. As Judith Green (1997) has said, the manipulation of risk factors became a talismanic activity in that it was no longer concerned with the actual risk, but with demonstrating that certain required risk management procedures had been duly undertaken. So what can be done? The answer appears to lie in a better understanding of what constitutes risk management. Perhaps the heart of the matter is to realise that while the act of assessing a risk, that is, deciding what the likelihood and severity of an injury is, is a largely technical process, deciding what to do about it, which can be called decision making or risk management, is heavily value-laden and therefore requires policy input and a philosophy.

Thus, given the outputs of a risk assessment, it is necessary to consider what mitigation measures or interventions are available, how effective they might be, how much resource they might consume, and whether the intervention itself might have any undesirable, or desirable, side effects, it now being recognised that many technical measures create risks of their own (Beck, 1992) or detract from the benefits of the activity. Having made this connection, it is quickly apparent that risk management is about trade-offs. It is part of a wider decision-making process that involves multiple objectives, of which safety is but one. This is why these decisions have to be made against the policy framework of the play provider.

Recognising the benefits of activities

Adams (1995), in his analysis of risk management activities, identifies a phenomenon which he terms 'bottom-loopism'. There he refers to risk management activities that are driven by the desire to reduce risk while failing to realise that the reason an activity was undertaken in the first place was for its benefits. The logical conclusion of bottom-loopism for children's playgrounds would be their removal, lock, stock and barrel, since all playgrounds entail some risk. RoSPA, in its approach to risk assessment (Cook and Heseltine, 2002), recognises the importance of the benefits of play equipment and incorporates an assessment of the play value of each site. Failure to consider play value as a legitimate goal will lead to the situation described by Heseltine (1995, p 92):

> We have made playgrounds so monumentally boring that any self-respecting child will go somewhere else to play – somewhere more interesting and usually more dangerous.... The play value in them is so limited that it barely scores on any register of play value.

Of course, setting an appropriate balance between risk and play value presents an intellectual challenge and is more readily attempted against an explicit policy background.

A strategic perspective

Throughout society there is a gradual realisation that the rational approach[4] to the analysis and resolution of problems, while having great strengths, also has deficiencies (Jaeger et al, 2001). These deficiencies can in part be addressed by taking a strategic perspective. Much play provision in Britain is undertaken by agencies with strategic roles, and it therefore follows that a strategic perspective should be engaged as a supplement to the now traditional risk assessment. What this means here is that entire neighbourhoods should be assessed for their risks and the risks posed by, say, playgrounds seen as a part of this whole. In this way it could well emerge that, for example, a greater provision, while increasing the number of playground injuries, would make children safer, healthier and happier overall.

Litigation and the blame society

Probably the best way to address the challenges of the litigation society is to be realistic and open. The reality is that playground providers, like all duty holders, are required to exercise a duty of care. This does not require that risks be eliminated because society, on reflection, recognises that risky activities have to be undertaken in order to receive the benefits. Duty holders have to make trade-offs between the benefits of activities and their dangers, and, as discussed above, children need exposure to some risk in order to have fun and develop their skills and awareness. The law recognises too that the costs and difficulty of applying risk interventions, through its concept of reasonable practicability, have to be factored in to risk management decisions. Therefore, even on the best-run playground, it has to be expected that accidents will occur and the fact that they do occur is no proof that risk management has failed. This in any case should be self-evident because most injuries on playgrounds are connected with the behaviour of children (Pain, 1992) and even whether, in falls, the victim lands head first or feet first (Ball, 2002), neither cause is controllable by providers.

A sensible strategy is therefore one that sets out these principles, shows how risk decisions are made against the principles, and invites public feedback. If a risk manager has made by themselves, or through others, full inquiries into the nature and magnitude of a risk, into the possibilities and consequences of its control including the cost, and taken into account the wider array of public interests, then the manager's decision ought not to be impugned by the courts.

Remaining dangers

Despite the signs of a positive shift to a more thoughtful and balanced approach to play provision, play value and child safety, many deeply ingrained hurdles remain and the playing field may be far from level. The type of play provision selected ultimately involves many individuals with varied professional backgrounds and with different interests. The fear is that the weakest link in the chain – the one that perhaps wants a 'quiet' life or to protect some personal interest such as minimising local cost rather than maximising societal gain – is the one whose interest will prevail. Constant vigilance will be required if this is to be avoided.

Notes

[1] The Play Safety Forum members include the Association of Play Industries, the Child Accident Prevention Trust, the Children's Play Council, the Health and Safety Executive, the Institute of Sport and Recreation Management, the Institute of Leisure and Amenity Management, Kidsactive, the Local Government Association, the National Early Years Network, the National Playing Fields Association, the National Family and Parenting Institute, the National Society for Prevention of Cruelty to Children, PLAYLINK and RoSPA.

[2] Actually, while it might be 'surprising', it is not that uncommon for those proclaiming concern over some safety issue to elect not to use factual data. Daston, for example (quoted in Green, 1997, pp 146-7), says that those offering fire insurance have not always even collected fire statistics and that maritime insurance was for many years positively antistatistical.

[3] These data are now kept by RoSPA.

[4] Rational approach here refers to reductionist analyses, which neglect real-life complexities.

References

Adams, J. (1995) *Risk*, London: UCL Press.
Anon (2001) 'BMJ bans "accidents"', *British Medical Journal*, vol 322, pp 1320-1.

Ball, D. J. (1998) 'Risks and benefits of sports and exercise: part 1 – assessing the risks', *Sports Exercise and Injury*, vol 4, no 1, pp 3-9.

Ball, D. J. (2000a) 'Ships in the night and the quest for safety', *Injury Control and Safety Promotion*, vol 7, no 2, pp 83-96.

Ball, D. J. (2000b) 'Risk of injury – an overview', in M. Harries, G. McLatchie, C. Williams and J. King (eds) *ABC of Sports Medicine*, London: BMJ Books, pp 88-91.

Ball, D. J. (2002) *Playgrounds: Risks, Benefits and Choices*, Sudbury: HSE Books.

Ball, D. J. (2004) 'Policy issues and risk-benefit trade-offs of 'safer surfacing' for children's playgrounds', *Accident Analysis and Prevention*, vol 36, pp 661-70.

Beck, U. (1992) *Risk Society: Towards a New Modernity*, translated by R. Ritter, London: Sage Publications.

Cook, B. and Heseltine, P. (2002) *Assessing Risk on Children's Playgrounds*, Birmingham: RoSPA.

DH (Department of Health) (1992) *The Health of the Nation: A Strategy for Health in England*, London: HMSO.

DH (1993) *The Health of the Nation Key Area Handbook: Accidents*, Leeds: DH.

DoE (Department of the Environment) (1978) 'The need for improved safety in children's playgrounds', Circular to District Councils in England, London Borough Councils, the City of London, the Greater London Council, and New Towns Development Corporations, London: DoE.

Evans, L. (1993) 'Medical accidents: no such thing?', *British Medical Journal*, vol 307, pp 1438-9.

Graham, J.D. and Wiener, J.B. (1995) *Risk Versus Risk: Tradeoffs in Protecting Health and the Environment*, Cambridge, MA: Harvard University Press.

Green, J. (1997) *Risk and Misfortune: The Social Construction of Accidents*, London: UCL Press.

Health and Safety Commission (1999) *The Management of Health and Safety at Work*, Sudbury: HSE Books.

Heseltine, P. (1995) 'Safety versus play value', in M. L. Christiansen (ed) *Playground Safety*, University Park, Pennsylvania, PA: Penn State University, pp 91-5.

Highland Council (2004) *Play Policy*, Inverness: The Highland Council.

Hillman, M., Adams, J. and Whitelegg, J. (1990) *One False Move: A Study of Children's Independent Mobility*, London: Policy Studies Institute.

Illingworth, C., Brennan, P., Jay, A., Al-Rawi, F. and Collick, M. (1975) 'Two hundred injuries caused by playground equipment', *British Medical Journal*, vol 4, pp 332-4.

Jaeger, C. C., Renn, O., Rosa, E. A. and Webler, T. (2001) *Risk, Uncertainty and Rational Action*, London: Earthscan.

Jarvis, S., Towner, E. and Walsh, S. (1995) 'Accidents', in B. Botting (ed) *The Health of our Children: Decennial Supplement*, London: The Stationery Office, pp 95-112.

Jones, D. (2005) 'Children must learn to embrace risk', *The Times*, 3 May.

King, K. L. and Ball, D. J. (1989) *A Holistic Approach to Accident and Injury Prevention in Children's Playgrounds*, London: London Scientific Services.

Munro, J., Coleman, P., Nicholl, J., Harper, R., Kent, G. and Wild, D. (1995) 'Can we prevent accidental injury to adolescents?', *Injury Prevention*, vol 1, pp 249-55.

Pain, D. (1992) *Children's Playground Equipment Related Injuries*, Melbourne: Playgrounds and Recreation Association of Victoria.

Play Safety Forum (2002) *Managing Risk in Play Provision*, London: National Children's Bureau.

Power, M. (2004) *The Risk Management of Everything*, London: DEMOS.

Roberts, I. (1993) 'Why have child pedestrian death rates fallen?', *British Medical Journal*, vol 306, pp 1737-9.

Sapolsky, H. M. (1990) 'The politics of risk', *Daedalus*, vol 119, no 4, pp 83-96.

Scuffham, P. A. and Langley, J. D. (1997) 'Trends in cycle injury in New Zealand under voluntary helmet use', *Accident Analysis and Prevention*, vol 29, no 1, pp 1-9.

Welsh Assembly Government (2004) *Play Policy Implementation Group Recommendations*, Cardiff: The Stationery Office.

FIVE

Children's perceptions of risk on the road

Kenneth Lupton and Mariana Bayley

Introduction

It seems a fundamental right that children and young people should be able to move about safely on our streets, yet, in 2002, 144 children aged between five and 16 years were killed on Britain's roads and 3,950 were seriously injured. Deaths from road accidents represent 11% of all deaths and are the largest single cause of accidental death among schoolchildren. In recent years, in Britain, the number of deaths per head of population among child pedestrians has not compared favourably with other similar northern European countries, such as France or Germany (DfT, 2003). On the other hand, Britain has a low number of deaths among motor vehicle occupants compared to these countries, which implies that while Britain has a good record for protecting motor vehicle drivers and passengers, it has not been so successful in protecting more vulnerable road users such as child pedestrians. To focus attention on this problem, in March 2000, the government set a target for practitioners of a 50% reduction in the number of children killed or seriously injured on Britain's roads by the year 2010, compared to the average for 1994 to 1998 (DETR, 2000).

Casualties arising from road accidents are often categorised according to their mode of transport at the time of the accident. In the main, for children, the relevant classes are pedestrians, cyclists, car passengers and bus passengers but, in addition, there may be small numbers of skateboarders, horse riders, motorcycle riders and even car drivers. Pedestrians and cyclists are the most vulnerable groups since they do not have the protection of a motor vehicle around them and so are more likely to be injured in a collision. Child pedestrians are especially vulnerable due to their lack of skill and experience, and their size, which makes them less visible to drivers and more prone to injury.

Nevertheless, in recent years, the numbers of casualties for all road users including children have been declining, but the reasons for this are complex and involve examining many factors that may contribute to this seemingly encouraging picture.

National road accident statistics need careful scrutiny and only reveal a partial view of the risk unless they are combined with information on the amount of time children spend, or the distances they travel, exposed to the risk of an accident. For example, over recent years parents have progressively reduced their children's exposure to the road environment due to fears over their personal safety, preferring to transport them by car instead. Hillman et al (1990) have suggested that these restrictions on children's independent mobility parallel the decline in child pedestrian casualties, while Roberts (1995) has argued more forcefully that fewer child accidents are a result of fewer children walking on the streets. While a car passenger is less likely to be injured than a pedestrian or cyclist, the limitation of children's physical activity and exploration of their local environment may have undesirable consequences for the long-term health and development of children, and this includes the development of road-crossing skills.

To improve the safety of children, and to persuade parents to feel confident to allow their children back onto the road as pedestrians or cyclists, local authorities have been introducing a range of measures. These include improved road safety education and training for children and parents, and the implementation of engineering and enforcement measures aimed primarily at the reduction of traffic speed in urban areas. While these developments may have reduced the risk for children on the road, they may not pay enough attention to particular problems experienced by children and how risk is perceived and managed by them. Road safety education and engineering design appear to originate from an adult's perceptions of the child's world rather than from the child's actual construction of it. Relatively little is known about the child's perceptions of their environment on the road, how this is constructed and how it fits in with adults' organisation of it.

This chapter reviews national data on road accidents for children, reviews current literature and examines children's own perceptions of risk in the road environment with reference to research carried out by the authors. The study involved schools in North London and Hertfordshire and set out to examine children's interactions and use of the road in the immediate vicinity of their school environment, on their journeys to and from school and places used for play and leisure. Children's concerns and perceptions of risk in the road environment were explored, together with their strategies for dealing with risky situations. The chapter concludes with recommendations based upon current knowledge.

National road accident statistics

In Britain, the police record details of all road accidents that are reported to them by members of the public. If an accident occurs on a public road and results in personal injury then this information is passed on to the Department for Transport (DfT), which compiles national road accident injury statistics. In recent years the annual total number of casualties has been declining, even though the volume of road traffic has continued to grow. The DfT (2003) lists a number of factors that have contributed to this reduction, but summarising it is mostly due to improvements in:

- highway design, based upon a better understanding of the nature of road accidents;
- vehicle design to protect occupants and to minimise injury to other road users;
- the MOT test, introduced in 1961, which ensures the roadworthiness of vehicles;
- the effectiveness of the enforcement of traffic laws, for example, drinking and driving laws and the introduction of the breath test in 1966;
- road safety education, publicity campaigns and improved driving tests;
- the ability of the emergency services to extract victims from damaged vehicles and to provide appropriate treatment for casualties.

These are still important factors in efforts to reduce the number of injuries for all road users. Casualties are usually categorised by age, gender and types of road user, which, for children, are mostly pedestrians, cyclists or motor vehicle passengers. Casualties are also classified by the severity of the injury and these are 'killed', 'serious injury' and 'slight injury'.[1] The next section provides a more detailed breakdown of the casualty statistics for schoolchildren from the recently available national dataset for 2002.

Casualties among schoolchildren in 2002

Table 5.1 shows casualties among children aged between five and 15 in Britain in 2002, categorised by severity of injury and by road user class. To some extent these figures reflect the degree to which children are exposed to the risk of an accident, which is a combination of distance travelled, or time spent, on the road by different transport modes. It shows that more pedestrians and car passengers are injured than cyclists, partly because children make fewer journeys by bicycle. The relatively high number of serious injuries among pedestrians compared to car passengers reflects the vulnerability of pedestrians to injury and the extra degree of protection offered to car passengers by a motor vehicle. This table also provides figures for all road users that includes small numbers of children in other categories, for example car drivers or horse riders.

Child pedestrians are also disadvantaged by their size, which makes them less visible to drivers. The police record whether a driver failed to see a pedestrian because they were masked by a stationary vehicle. Younger or smaller children are more likely to be masked; for example, in 2002, 57% of five- to 10-year-old casualties were masked compared to 38% of 11- to 15-year-olds.

Table 5.2 shows the number of casualties who were pedestrians or cyclists categorised by gender and age. More than twice as many children aged 10 to 15 were injured as those aged five to nine, and more than twice as many boys were injured as girls. The gender difference is most evident among cyclists where more than five times as many boys were injured as girls. These figures tend to reflect the fact that older children are allowed more freedom to travel unsupervised than are younger children and that boys are allowed more freedom than girls. However, the figures may also reflect the fact that older children and boys are more likely to take risks on the road (Foot et al, 1982). A more comprehensive comparison between different groups would include estimates of the distance travelled, or time spent, by each mode and would also include data for leisure journeys. It would also include data relating to the volume and type of traffic to which children are exposed. For example, Bly et al (1999) found, after

Table 5.1: Casualties by road user class and severity for schoolchildren aged five to 15 in 2002

Road user class	Killed	Serious	Slight	Total
Pedal cyclists	22	564	4,151	4,737
Pedestrians	60	2,447	10,179	12,686
Motor vehicle passengers	56	808	11,247	12,111
All road users	144	3,950	30,017	34,111

Source: DfT (2003).

Table 5.2: Pedestrian and cyclist casualties by age and gender among schoolchildren aged five to 15 in 2002

Age band	Pedestrians		Cyclists		Totals
	Boys	Girls	Boys	Girls	
5 to 9	2,854	1,414	938	236	5,442
10 to 15	4,869	3,545	3,027	533	11,974
Totals	7,723	4,959	3,965	769	17,416

Source: DfT (2003).

conducting a questionnaire survey of children in Britain, France and Denmark, that children in Britain are exposed to higher volumes of traffic travelling at higher speeds than their European counterparts.

National statistics allow for the identification of high-risk groups and provide the impetus for research and for road safety initiatives. However, the relationship between injury and risk propensity is not straightforward and the following section outlines some of the factors that need to be considered in examining accident statistics, especially those relating to high-risk groups.

High-risk groups

Road accident statistics show that boys are consistently overrepresented and some studies have suggested that this is because boys are allowed to spend more time on the road than girls. Hillman et al (1990) found that boys are more likely to be allowed to cross roads, go to leisure places, travel to school, cycle on the road and to use public transport without adult supervision. Numerous studies have reported a difference in risk-taking behaviour between boys and girls (for example, Foot et al, 1982), but that boys generally show greater knowledge of roadside objects and safe and dangerous places to play (Ampofo-Boateng and Thompson, 1989). However, despite this increase in knowledge, boys' propensity for taking risks and spending time on the road results in a higher number of injuries.

Numerous research studies have demonstrated a link between deprivation and an increase in the number of injuries resulting from road accidents. A constellation of social characteristics has consistently been reported as affecting the number of accidents, such as overcrowding, living in older housing, previous injury, single parenthood and competing demands placed on a parent's time (Christie, 1995). Some researchers have concluded that the socioeconomic effect is also related to exposure. Bradshaw (1995) found that twice as many children of parents in skilled manual occupations walked to school as did children of parents from professional groups with the mediating factor being the level of car ownership. Bradshaw also found that many parents drove their children to school if they perceived a threat from adult strangers. In addition, some children may be more likely to be exposed to dangerous road environments. After investigating high casualty rates among Asian children in Birmingham, Lawson (1990) concluded that these children were at risk because they tended to live in densely populated inner-city areas with narrow streets and high levels of on-street parking.

Exposure to traffic, as mentioned, has appeared to be linked with overrepresentation in accident statistics, however, the role of exposure is paradoxical. Demetre (1997) has argued that safe practice on the road can only be achieved if children have had sufficient independent exposure in traffic environments beforehand. Withdrawing children from the road as pedestrians may deny them the opportunity to learn crossing skills, built upon road safety education provided in schools.

Road safety education

Road safety education forms an important part of the initiative to reduce road accidents among schoolchildren. Psychological research has had a significant impact upon education and has focused on the fields of developmental, cognitive and perceptual–motor abilities. In a comprehensive study, Thomson et al (1996) summarise the following sequence of skills that a child requires to cross the road safely:

- detect traffic presence and distinguish between relevant and irrelevant stimuli;
- assess the trajectory and arrival time of vehicles;
- coordinate information about vehicles approaching from different directions;
- assess the time available to cross with an acceptable margin of safety.

In a later publication the same authors (Foot et al, 1999) add another stage, before the visual timing stage, of recognising safe or dangerous crossing locations, for example, not crossing near a blind bend or near a parked car where a pedestrian might not be seen. The authors also suggest that, because of the complexity of the road environment, these skills are learned more successfully by practical training on the road rather than by traditional classroom methods.

Other researchers have investigated whether or not children who have been injured are lacking these skills or whether skills training leads to a reduction in the number of accidents. In fact, there is no evidence to support either. West et al (1999), while recognising the importance of skills training, found that many child pedestrian accidents resulted from impulsive behaviour. The authors also discovered links between accident involvement and self-reported antisocial behaviour, which included theft, violence and vandalism. Based on this evidence their recommendation was that there should be community-wide interventions to encourage children at risk to develop safe attitudes and to place a higher value on their own safety.

The role of parents

Parents have an important role in road safety education and many believe that the primary responsibility for road safety education rests in the first instance with parents, a view found to be shared by parents themselves (Sadler, 1972). However, there is evidence to suggest that sometimes parental supervision of children can increase vulnerability rather than enhance it. For example, Sandels (1975) noted that often adults were observed crossing roads without first checking that a small child's attention had not wandered elsewhere and was ready to cross with them. One of the factors mediating this lack of awareness appears to be unrealistic parental expectations. Dunne et al (1992) found that parental expectations of children's pedestrian skills were overestimated for all ages from five to 10 years but most significantly for the youngest children. As children grew older the gap between parental expectations and children's actual pedestrian skills closed.

Social and environmental issues

An environmental or ecological alternative to the skill-based approach focuses on aspects of the physical road environment and attempts to change the behaviour of pedestrians by modifying or introducing specific road safety measures. However, children's interactions with elements of the physical features of the road often occur within the context of their social world where there are competing demands for their attention.

The demands placed on children to become safe pedestrians may conflict with their need to explore their environment, find opportunities for play and to engage in social activity. Indeed, being in the company of other children often appears to increase children's vulnerability on the road. In a study examining the higher casualty rates among children in Britain compared to France and the

Netherlands, Bly et al (1999) found that British children were accompanied by other children more often than French children, who were more likely to be with adults or children over 16 years of age, and Dutch children, who travelled on their own more often. As noted by Van Vliet (1983), the world of shops, parks, streets and open spaces is used differently by children than it is by adults. For children, it is often used to meet and socialise with other children, to exchange information and to observe, and to develop a sense of, their local community as they approach adulthood.

Until recently, the ways in which children find a balance between their social needs, road safety and the complexity of the road environment had not been fully explored. Subsequent sections of this chapter report on a study carried out by the authors that attempted to redress this balance. The aim of the research was to reveal how children's perceptions of the road environment affect their crossing behaviour and highlight issues to be addressed by road safety education or by the design and positioning of appropriate safety measures. The study entitled 'Children's Perceptions of the Road Environment: The Implications for Highway Design' was funded by the Engineering and Physical Sciences Research Council and the Department for Transport in their Future Integrated Transport Programme and carried out by members of the Transport Management Research Group at Middlesex University.

Children's perceptions of the road environment

Relatively little is known about the child's perception of their environment on the road, how this is constructed and how it fits in with what is essentially an adult's organisation of it. This study considered children's independent mobility, their perceptions of risk in the road environment, their views on drivers and the function of highway engineering measures designed to improve safety. Twelve schools were chosen for the study, six were located in inner-city environments in London and six were located in more rural environments in Hertfordshire. Six were junior and six were secondary schools. The schools were chosen to provide a range of road-crossing facilities and socioeconomic backgrounds indicated by the number of children entitled to free school meals.

The research design was essentially qualitative and group interviews were carried out with 24 single-sex groups of children, aged between eight and 15 years. A total of 122 children were interviewed. The group discussions were based on a semi-structured interviewing technique. An interview guide was constructed, which listed the areas of interest to be covered, but with enough flexibility to allow variation on when and how a question was asked, and exploration of issues arising during the session. A non-directive style was adopted, using open-ended questioning, in which the children were encouraged to talk freely and allowed to choose descriptive categories significant to them, rather than having them imposed as in structured interviewing or questionnaires. The study aimed to capture children's interactions and use of the road in the immediate vicinity of their school environment on video and to use examples from the video footage as triggers to open up discussions with children on the issues arising. This study is reported more fully in Lupton and Bayley (2002) and Lupton et al (2002).

There are a number of factors that affect the kinds of risks children highlight when playing or travelling in the road environment generally and, specifically, when they are negotiating road crossings. These factors are considered in the next section, illustrated by quotes from the children who participated in the study.

Independent mobility

> I play out the front on my bike sometimes or my scooter and I'm only allowed from one end of the road to a certain tree and I'm allowed to the corner shop with my big brother and I play with my friends. (Female, aged 8)

> There is not much that worries us because we, like, stick together. (Male, aged 10)

> I wouldn't be allowed to go to, I haven't asked my mum to go anywhere by myself because there's no point asking. If you've got company with you then she will, probably. (Female, aged 14)

The aspiration to be able to travel and to explore their environment without adult supervision was important to most children. The degree to which they were allowed to do so varied considerably: some children were allowed virtually no freedom due to parental concerns over safety and for some older children the only limitation appeared to be the cost of public transport. Generally, mobility increased with age and boys were often allowed more freedom than girls. Independent mobility appeared to be reviewed continuously and was negotiable with their parents or carers throughout most young children's lives. Destinations were usually restricted to those locations where previously parents had assessed the potential dangers and which were familiar to both parents and children. Some journeys were allowed if the child was accompanied by an older sibling but most children wanted to travel with friends of their own age and did not want to travel alone. When travelling with their peers most children felt safer since they were better able to deter threats from other children or unwanted attention from adults:

> You can just get on a bus to the next stop and you are not having to walk miles or get your parents to come and pick you up, or take you. (Female, aged 14)

Children mentioned walking and travelling by bus as their most frequent modes of transport and older children in rural schools often travelled by train. Distance, cost and the availability of public transport were limiting factors for older children. However, children in London who were entitled to free bus passes or cheaper fares often preferred independent travel by bus to being given lifts in their parents' car. Cycling tended to be regarded as a leisure activity more than a means of transport, which was due to concerns over security if a bicycle was left unattended.

Risky behaviour

> I nearly got run over by a car because I was talking with one of my friends, and we were crossing the road, and we never actually realised. (Male, aged 8)

Children were invited to reflect on occasions when they might feel at risk or put themselves at risk on the road. On the whole, they perceived themselves liable to be more distracted and at risk in the company of other children. Children were well aware of the potential for social activity to result in behaviour that could compromise their safety on the road. A number of children recounted situations where they were so engrossed in conversation, or in a hurry to join friends on the other side of the road, that they paid less attention to crossing. Most junior schoolchildren appreciated the risks of playing in or near the road. If the game involved running after or catching other children, they recognised that this could create high excitement that could distract them from their vigilance. Ball games were considered risky because cars might swerve to avoid the ball and children might be overanxious to retrieve their ball from the road, without paying enough attention to traffic conditions:

> We do things like try and wear bright colours and sometimes do things like stick signs in the mud, saying 'Kill Your Speed Not a Child' and things like that. (Male, aged 10)

Paradoxically, it is important to note, however, that some children living in deprived urban areas played by the roadside because it was one of the few environments in which they felt they could play relatively safely. For these children the local park was out of bounds because of perceived danger from gangs, drunks and adult strangers, but they were still determined to exert their right to play even if it meant playing by a busy road:

> If there's a really, really busy road, when you get the red light you run across the road quick. (Male, aged 14)

Some secondary schoolchildren, mostly boys aged 12 to 13, reported incidents where they had overestimated their ability to run, or cycle, through tight gaps in the traffic. Their propensity for risk appeared to be compounded by a lack of crossing opportunities in heavy traffic. A small number of children enjoyed the sense of risk, for example, negotiating small gaps in the traffic or inducing drivers to stop:

> Some people play dares and stuff, they say, like, 'I dare you to cross the road' and all that when there's a car coming. But I just ignore it because I know if I get hit then that's it really. (Male, aged 11)

Some children recalled situations where other children had encouraged them to take undue risks and, as a result, preferred to cross alone. They had developed a strategy for negotiating their own safety, possibly with the social cost of feeling left out by friends:

> If there are just two people then they won't stop as much as if there are like seven or eight. (Male, aged 10)

However, many children felt safer crossing the road in a group of children since they believed drivers were more likely to stop for a group and less confident children thought that the group could relieve them of the responsibility for crossing the road. Other children perceived that crossing in a group was a way of exercising control over drivers. The greatest influence on children's crossing behaviour appeared to come from their parents, either by explicit instruction or by children simply copying their parents' behaviour. However, children often noted that they received mixed messages from parents who did not always follow their own instructions, such as teaching a child to use a pedestrian crossing but not using it themselves.

When discussing the causes of accidents more generally, blame was divided between children and drivers. Children thought that, compared to adults, they were less likely to think before they acted, to rush more and were more easily distracted, particularly by friends. They did not accept full responsibility for accidents, however, as the main source of danger on the road was perceived to be careless or reckless drivers.

Views on drivers and pedestrian crossings

> Sometimes I can just tell by looking at a car what sort of person they are. Like if it's a really flash car and you know like and they are driving pretty fast you know they are trying to get somewhere. Or if they are like playing their music really loud you know they are not paying attention to what's going on. (Male, aged 10)

> Nothing can be a hundred per cent safe because, even zebra crossings, because they are not exactly breaking the law and because it doesn't say you have to stop or else you go to prison and so they don't have to stop for you. (Female, aged 10)

> Men go really fast, and once you stop at the zebra crossing they will just go whoosh ... and then you know, they are really late for work and they are really in a rush. That is the way they feel. So, you know, they should think again, if they run over a person, they are going to be even later. (Female, aged 14)

Children complained about young male drivers and drivers who were impatient or careless and, in particular, drivers who failed to stop at pedestrian crossings. The conclusion that some children reached about drivers who failed to stop was that they thought children were unimportant, or that they were unable to see children because they were too small. Instances of poor driver behaviour were reported more frequently by children who lived and played in deprived areas. For young children, deciding when to cross the road involved dealing with the uncertainty of drivers' actions, which were not always predictable:

> I think the most dangerous things on the road is like cars that don't tell you the truth. (Female, aged 8)

Junior schoolchildren, aged eight to 10 years, were often unsure about drivers' intentions and some felt that cars should stop when a person was crossing, but others suggested that it was better to wait for the car to stop and then cross. These feelings of uncertainty about drivers' intentions sometimes caused some children to run or move quickly on the crossing itself, as they were not confident that drivers would stop even when children were already on it. Two children reported that they preferred not to use zebra crossings at all, but to cross anywhere, to remove all ambiguity about drivers' perceived intentions. Most children thought that crossings were enhanced by the provision of additional measures to control drivers' behaviour such as speed cameras, lower speed limits, traffic calming or the presence of police officers. Overall, children preferred mandatory measures for drivers, for example, light–controlled crossings were preferred to zebra crossings where the priorities were believed to be less clear.

Children often emphasised the protective function of roadside furniture. For example, guard railing, which is put in place to inhibit crossing movements, was often described as a crash barrier but it was also recognised that it was too flimsy for this purpose. Children often had similar views about traffic signs, keep–left bollards and also parked cars. Apart from offering them no protection, children who use these features in this way are placed at greater risk if they become less visible to drivers.

Conclusions and recommendations

Road safety education, supported by schools and local and central government, is the focus of efforts to reduce the number of injuries on the road among child pedestrians. In the past, education has often concentrated on the cognitive skills that children require to cross the road, but relatively little has focused on the influence of children's social behaviour. Being engrossed in play or conversation with other children appears to increase children's vulnerability by distracting them from safe crossing procedures. During our research it was found that children were well aware of the rules of road safety but importantly also had insights into aspects of their own behaviour that placed them at risk, including the distraction of friends. While they did not condone this behaviour, many children believed that some risk was inevitable in negotiating roads and that adult drivers should make allowances for children's behaviour and not to expect children to behave as adults. Endeavours could be made to teach children how to manage traffic conditions while in the company of friends or in different social situations. This is a relatively under-researched area and requires a higher profile in road safety education.

Children often made vehement criticism of a minority of drivers who were careless, impatient or could not be trusted to stop at pedestrian crossings. These drivers were often perceived to be dismissive, or unaware, of the particular problems that children face. Part of the aim of road safety education is to teach children to behave more safely, but fewer efforts are made to make drivers more aware of children's behaviour and the difficulties they encounter in making road-crossing decisions.

While the law recognises the vulnerability of children, it could do more to protect them from careless drivers. Currently, much attention is focused on changing driver behaviour by implementing a variety of speed reduction measures, but more could be done to remind drivers about the unpredictability of children especially when they are in the company of other children. There may also be scope for increasing driver awareness of children and the problems they face through media campaigns, driving tests and Driver Improvement Schemes, where drivers can be referred by the police after being summoned for a traffic offence.

Local authorities often install traffic calming measures, including 20mph zones, in residential areas and near schools where children are most likely to be found. Such measures were generally popular with children as was any measure that provided children with protection from traffic. However, roadside furniture is designed for adults and it is assumed that road users will understand its function. Children often perceived that some measures, such as guard railing, had a protective function where none was intended by the designer and this affected the way that they interacted with these measures. Potentially, this assumption could place children at greater risk if they seek refuge behind street furniture and become less visible to drivers.

Compared to other countries, Britain has been successful in producing a road network that is safe for vehicle occupants, but unsafe for child pedestrians and cyclists. In some ways that is not surprising since, in the past, children have not received a high priority in the highway design process. As roads become increasingly congested they become more difficult to cross and this can often encourage children, especially boys, to make risky crossing decisions, such as running through tight gaps in the traffic. The challenge for designers is to provide crossings that are perceived to offer children greater protection, make children more visible to drivers and to provide them with more crossing opportunities.

Acknowledgements

The authors would like to thank the staff of Hertfordshire County Council and the London Boroughs of Barnet, Enfield and Haringey for their help with this research, which was funded by the Engineering and Physical Sciences Research Council's and the Department for Transport's Future Integrated Transport Programme.

Note

[1] The definitions of the severity of injuries from DfT (2003) are:

- *Killed*: Human casualties who sustained injuries which caused death less than 30 days (before 1954, about two months) after the accident. Confirmed suicides are excluded.
- *Serious injury*: An injury for which a person is detained in hospital as an 'inpatient', or any of the following injuries whether or not they are detained in hospital: fractures, concussion, internal injuries, crushings, burns (excluding friction burns), severe cuts and lacerations, severe general shock requiring medical treatment and injuries causing death 30 or more days after the accident.
- *Slight injury*: An injury of a minor character such as a sprain (including neck whiplash injury), bruise or cut which is not judged to be severe, or slight shock requiring roadside attention. This definition includes injuries not requiring medical treatment.

References

Ampofo-Boateng, K. and Thomson, J. A. (1989) 'Child pedestrian accidents: a case for preventative medicine', *Health Education Research*, vol 5, no 2, pp 265-74.

Bly, P., Dix, M. and Stephenson, C. (1999) *Comparative Study of European Child Pedestrian Exposure and Accidents*, London: DETR.

Bradshaw, R. (1995) 'Why do parents drive their children to school?', *Traffic Engineering & Control*, vol 36, no 1, pp 16-19.

Christie, N. (1995) *The High Risk Child Pedestrian: Socio-Economic and Environmental Factors in their Accidents, TRL Project Report 117*, Crowthorne: Transport Research Laboratory.

Demetre, J. D. (1997) 'Applying developmental psychology to children's road safety: problems and prospects', *Journal of Applied Developmental Psychology*, vol 18, no 2, pp 263-70.

DETR (Department of the Environment, Transport and the Regions) (2000) *Tomorrow's Roads: Safer for Everyone: The Government's Road Safety Strategy and Casualty Reduction Targets for 2010*, London: DETR, available at: www.dft.gov.uk

DfT (Department for Transport) (2003) *Road Casualties in Great Britain: Main Results: 2002*, London: The Stationery Office.

Dunne, R. G., Asher, K. N. and Rivara, F. P. (1992) 'Behaviour and parental expectations of child pedestrians', *Pediatrics*, vol 89, no 3, pp 486-90.

Foot, H. C., Chapman, A. J. and Wade, F. M. (1982) 'Pedestrian accidents: general issues and approaches', in A. J. Chapman, F. M. Wade and H. C. Foot (eds) *Pedestrian Accidents*, Chichester: John Wiley and Sons.

Foot, H. C., Tolmie, A. J., Thomson, J., McLaren, B. and Whelan, K. (1999) 'Recognising the hazards', *The Psychologist*, vol 12, no 8, pp 400-2.

Hillman, M., Adams, J. and Whitelegg, J. (1990) *One False Move: A Study of Children's Independent Mobility*, London: Institute for Policy Studies.

Lawson, S. D. (1990) *Accidents to Young Pedestrians: Distributions, Circumstances, Consequences and Scope for Countermeasures*, Basingstoke: AA Foundation for Road Safety Research and Birmingham City Council.

Lupton, K. and Bayley, M. (2002) 'Children – how they interact with the street environment', *Traffic Engineering & Control*, vol 43, no 6, pp 224-8.

Lupton, K., Colwell, J. and Bayley, M. (2002) 'Aspects of children's road crossing behaviour', *Proceedings of the Institution of Civil Engineers Municipal Engineer*, vol 151, no 2, pp 151-7.

Roberts, I. (1995) 'Editorial: Injuries to child pedestrians', *British Medical Journal*, vol 310, pp 413-14.

Sadler, J. (1972) *Children and Road Safety: A Survey Amongst Mothers*, London: HMSO.

Sandels, S. (1975) *Children in Traffic*, London: Elek.

Thomson, J. A., Tolmie, A., Foot, H. C. and McLaren, B. (1996) *Child Development and the Aims of Road Safety Education*, Department of Transport Road Safety Research Report No 1, London: Department for Transport.

Van Vliet, W. (1983) 'Exploring the fourth environment: an examination of the home range of city and suburban teenagers', *Environmental Behaviour*, vol 15, no 5, pp 567-88.

West, R., Train, H., Junger, M., Pickering, A. and West, A. (1999) 'Psychological factors in child pedestrian accident risk: the link with problem behaviour', *The Psychologist*, vol 12, no 8, pp 395-7.

SIX

New technology and the legal implications for child protection

Alan S. Reid

Introduction

Electronic communication is a modern, pervasive phenomenon, enabling anyone to work, play and communicate 24 hours a day. Third generation mobile phones, combined with digital media convergence, has enabled the fixed internet to break free from the physical confines of the desktop to become truly wireless and portable.

This interactive, interconnected and instantaneous world promises immense societal benefits for young people. They can play virtual games, interact socially to define, refine and express preferences and learn about the world around them, enhancing their personal development. Mobile phone and internet use is ubiquitous among young people, with instant messaging and texting now part of mainstream culture. The societal advantages are tempered by significant risks. Cyber-stalking, cyber-bullying, happy-slapping, child abuse and abduction, racist and hate speech, gambling and pornography are indicative of the online dangers preoccupying parents, guardians and legislators (Bocij and McFarlane, 2003).

This chapter discusses the legal issues surrounding the availability and use of e-communication technologies. It discusses the dangers associated with e-communication and options available to mitigate these risks. It argues that risk assessment must strike a balance between overcautiousness and foolhardiness. Effective technical, legal and regulatory measures must be appropriate to the level of risk, proportionate, inclusive and holistic in their approach. Educational initiatives must raise awareness of the risks and inculcate a culture of individual responsibility. The eventual creation of an information technology (IT)-aware society will ensure that new technology is enthusiastically embraced, not feared or distrusted.

The risks of the internet: the three C's

Children and young persons are inquisitive by nature and readily adapt to new technology, thus they have enthusiastically embraced e-communication. Online, they face risks associated with the three C's: content, contact and commerce.

Children face a proliferation of adult-based materials, including pornographic and violent imagery, websites promoting illegal drugs, hate speech and racism, abusive language amounting to bullying, harassment and intimidation and inappropriate chat-room conversations (Magid, 2003).

Contact by a paedophile or a bully is a perennial concern for young people. Universal internet access increases the likelihood of unwanted contact, dissemination of paedophiliac imagery and encouragement of children to take and send images of themselves or of other children (Carr, 2004). The anonymity and remoteness of the internet make it easy for paedophiles to pretend to be much younger in order to befriend and ultimately abuse a child. Children may unthinkingly divulge personal information or may unwittingly provide information useful to a paedophile, such as their location, through their e-communications.

Commercial dangers for young persons include pop-up ads and messages advertising games, competitions, gambling and expensive downloads. Such activities may be exploitative, preying upon their vulnerability, naivety and suggestibility.

Society has a collective interest in limiting children's access to such content. The available responses range from legislative initiatives, private industry initiatives, educational initiatives and technological controls (Williams, 2003). The nature and extent of the threat posed determines the level of response required and must balance the need for protection with the aim of maintaining freedom of communication while avoiding any subjectivity.

Legislative initiatives

The 2003 Sexual Offences Act contains a number of provisions specifically designed to address paedophiliac activity. The most important provision is the Section 15 offence of meeting a child following sexual grooming (Gillespie, 2006). On indictment, the offender can be imprisoned for up to 10 years. The offender is placed on the Sex Offenders Register and a civil law Restraining Order may be requested. This order effectively bars paedophiles from using computers or mobile phones for a set period. Enforcement of such an order may prove problematic in this era of truly anonymous internet access. The nebulous and diffuse nature of child abuse necessitates that the Section 15 offence does not attempt to define grooming but rather concentrates upon post-grooming behaviour of the defendant (Gillespie, 2006). The offence is satisfied where the defendant meets or communicates with a person under the age of 16 on at least two occasions, then intentionally meets that person or travels with the intention to meet that person anywhere in the world and intends committing a sexual offence against that person. The Act is technology neutral, applying to offline and online communication. Section 15 has been subject to strong criticism, being characterised as a 'thought' crime or inchoate crime in that the accused may be arrested before they have committed an actual sexual assault on the child. However, the provision is designed to minimise the risk to a child by permitting proactive intervention by the police to arrest the individual at a stage prior to fulfilment of the plan. The provision is unlikely to catch innocent individuals who converse with a child since the cumulative *actus reus* and *mens rea* requirements are that the accused not only communicates with the child on at least two occasions but that they then meet the child or travel with the intention to meet the child and, further, they intend to commit a sexual offence against that child. Similarly, the offence does not criminalise mere thoughts, since liability is only engaged when the paedophile moves beyond mere preparation for the offence, taking active steps to travel (Ormerod, 2005, p 636).

More generally, the 2003 Act provides for a range of preventative measures. For example, persons convicted of a sexual offence may be subject to a Notification Order and possibly a Sexual Offence Prevention Order. This latter order will list a range of prohibited activities, breach of which will constitute a criminal offence. If an individual is deemed to be a potential sexual threat to anyone, they can be made the subject of a Risk of Sexual Harm Order and if a paedophile intends to go abroad, a Foreign Travel Restriction Order can be imposed.

The Act also introduced a number of offences relevant to the virtual world of instantaneous communications. First, under Section 10, it is an offence to cause or incite a child to engage in sexual activity. Second, it is an offence under Section 12 to cause a child to watch a sexual act, both offline and online. Third, a person will commit an offence under Section 14 where they arrange or facilitate commission of a child sex offence. In respect of child prostitution and child pornography, Sections 48 and 50 criminalise conduct that is intended to cause, incite, arrange or facilitate such activities. The Act amends the age range for child pornography upwards such that images of 16- and 17-year-olds now come within the definition of child pornography, in part a recognition of the growing international consensus that a child should be defined as a person under the age of 18 (Stone, 2004, p 319). Interesting questions of personal autonomy are raised by this provision. For example, an exemption to the child pornography offence provides that it is not an offence for the civil partner of a 16- or 17-year-old to take risqué pictures of them. Further, it may be argued that some extremely mature 16- and 17-year-olds may resent the paternalistic slant of the legislation since they are now prohibited from engaging in glamour modelling as a career choice. Nevertheless, the new rules can be viewed as a useful brake on the increasing objectification of young girls and boys. It is a truism that, in these circumstances, the law is operating to protect young persons from themselves as much as from predatory and manipulative adults.

In addition to the specific provisions concerning child pornography, the 1959-64 Obscene Publication Acts criminalise the publication of obscene images and possession for gain of such materials. Images are deemed obscene where they have the tendency to deprave and corrupt those who are likely to see, hear or view the matters complained of. At this juncture, it has to be noted that recourse to the obscenity laws has been in decline in the past quarter of a century, with a corresponding increase in the number of prosecutions for child pornography offences (Home Office and Scottish Executive, 2005, p 7). This inverse relationship is attributable to the inherent subjectivity of the 'deprave and corrupt' test when compared to the objective, strict liability test of possession of child pornography.

In a recent development, the Home Office and the Scottish Executive have suggested the creation of a new offence of possession of 'extreme pornographic material' defined as material including scenes or realistic descriptions of bestiality, necrophilia and serious sexual violence (Home Office and Scottish Executive, 2005). This would criminalise mere possession, operating in a similar vein to the law against child pornography. This proposed offence would be of general application, however, in the case of paedophiles, it would have the potential to indirectly protect children. The offence would apply in the situation where a paedophile possesses extreme pornography with a view to displaying the images to a young person for the purpose of either satisfying their own sexual gratification or desensitising the young person for grooming purposes.

The internet has undoubtedly facilitated possession of extreme pornography. The risk of detection and potential humiliation or embarrassment was high when an individual wishing to view this type of material had to visit a sex shop, order physical copies through mail order or telephone sales or become friendly with like-minded individuals. In the age of digital convergence, this material is easily obtainable anonymously through internet search services, membership of secretive chat-groups and through peer-to-peer networks.

There is a substantive difference between child pornography and adult pornography. Child pornography is universally condemned as illegal, with an overwhelming majority of states outlawing the production, possession and proliferation of such material. Conversely, adult pornography is permitted in a wide number of countries as a legitimate commercial endeavour. The societal impact of such freely available adult pornography is notoriously difficult to quantify and makes governmental action in this field almost impossible. There appears to be a growing trend in society towards more violent and aberrant adult pornography. If the new offence were introduced, it would create a three-tier taxonomy of pornography, with child pornography and extreme pornography illegal and adult pornography still subject to the obscenity test. Such a change would bring greater clarity to the law and would be a welcome addition to the extant range of sexual offences.

The relative ease, availability and anonymity of communicating electronically can create a dangerous synergy in the minds of certain individuals who wish to engage in paedophiliac or other illegal activity, such that they may be more willing to engage in online illegal activity than with more traditional forms of communications. Section 127 of the 2003 Communications Act proscribes improper use of a public electronic communications network, including conduct that is 'grossly offensive or of an indecent, obscene or menacing character'. Conviction can bring a sentence of up to six months' imprisonment and/or a fine up to £5,000.

Law enforcement measures

Effective legislative initiatives must be accompanied by adequate law enforcement provisions. The British government has taken this seriously, with three organisations actively engaged in the fight against online abuse, namely the Serious Organised Crime Agency (SOCA), the Child Exploitation and Online Protection Centre (CEOP) and the Task Force on Child Protection on the Internet. SOCA, a non-departmental public body, is tasked with preventing and detecting serious organised crime. The increasingly lucrative nature of activities associated with child abuse, child trafficking and child prostitution have attracted the interest of organised crime. SOCA has been given a budget of £457 million for the year 2006/2007 (SOCA, 2006).

CEOP came into being in April 2006 and is affiliated to SOCA. It brings together police personnel, industry representatives, government and child welfare experts and has a budget of £5 million and a staff of over 100 personnel. CEOP has five objectives: first, to identify, locate and protect young people from sexual exploitation; second, to engage and empower children through information and education; third, to protect children and young persons; fourth, to enforce the law; and, fifth, to enhance existing responses to online sexual exploitation and abuse through designing a safer online environment. The CEOP website (www.ceop.gov.uk) allows individuals to report illegal activity to the police and contains both child-orientated and parent- and guardian-orientated advice on how to stay safe online.

CEOP is also a significant partner in the Virtual Global Task Force (VGTF), a collaborative venture between law enforcement bodies in the US, Canada, the UK, Australia and Interpol. The VGTF has similar tasks to both the Home Office Task Force on Child Protection on the Internet and CEOP. It attempts to make the internet a safer place, to identify, locate and help children at risk and to bring perpetrators to justice. One of the most significant VGTF initiatives is Operation PIN, whereby a fictitious child abuse website has been created. People who access this site are ultimately directed to a website that informs the viewer that they have tried to access illegal content and as such their details have been collected and passed to the relevant law enforcement authorities. Police from the VGTF countries also engage in 24-hour monitoring of internet chat-rooms to deter paedophile grooming. If the communication is gauged to be potentially dangerous, officers will intervene and alert both parties that their conversation is being monitored.

The Task Force on Child Protection on the Internet is a Home Office initiative, aiming to 'make the UK the best and safest place in the world for children to use the internet' (http:\\police.homeoffice.gov.uk). It is a partnership between the internet industry, the police, government and child welfare bodies, designed to promote co-regulation of the internet. Examples of such cooperation include the development of a kite-marking scheme for child-friendly chat-rooms, development and promotion of education and awareness campaigns and fostering enhanced cooperation between the police and Internet Service Providers (ISPs).

This new triangulated framework of British law enforcement raises a number of questions. First, how important a priority will child abuse and sexual exploitation be for SOCA and how much of its £457 million budget will be earmarked for the suppression of paedophiliac activity? Large-scale, commercial production of child abuse imagery will be of great interest to the agency, but what will be the position where the abuse is of a smaller magnitude? Under the old regime, illegal online activity fell within the remit of the National High Tech Crime Unit, which brought together police officers and IT specialists. Under the new regime, the 'seriousness' of the activity will be the main criterion for action. Seriousness in this context will be determined by the scale of the illegal operations and the extent to which the activity is highly organised and not the seriousness of the crime for the individual. It is not hard to imagine a situation in which a small number of paedophiles work together in a geographically restricted locality to abuse children. Will they be deemed to be sufficiently 'serious' and 'organised' to trigger the attentions of SOCA?

As yet, there is no indication of the breakdown of the SOCA budget and it is extremely difficult to anticipate the level of resources available in the fight against the sexual exploitation and abuse of children. One indicator of the relative importance that will be assigned to these crimes is that CEOP has been allocated a budget of £5 million and a potential staff count of 100. This would appear a wholly inadequate allocation of resources for the fight against child pornography. It is essential that greater financial and human resources are allocated to the fight against online paedophiles.

CEOP is operationally independent of SOCA, although ultimately accountable to it (SOCA, 2006). It has to be questioned why CEOP has been separated from the corporate structure of SOCA. It may be cynical to suggest that this could allow SOCA to distance itself from CEOP in the event of underperformance and further make it easier to (re)allocate resources that were ring-fenced for CEOP to other operational areas in the event of CEOP's failure.

In addition to these concerns, it appears that the work of CEOP and the Task Force share a great deal of overlap. The membership of both bodies is drawn from a range of public and private organisations, and both are entrusted with promoting safer internet use and promulgating appropriate guidance. Common sense would dictate that there is only room for one organisation in this field and it may be that the Task Force will be subsumed into CEOP.

Notwithstanding the above criticisms, it is clear that the UK government is committed to reducing the potential harm associated with e-communications. It is important that the objectives of child protection are effectively promoted by all law enforcement agencies. Finite resources must be used efficiently and duplication of effort must be avoided at all costs.

Hotlines and ISP liability

The traditional approach towards harmful and illegal digital content is to prohibit the display of such content. More recently there has been a move towards the development of illegal content hotlines, whereby internet users are encouraged to contact a website and leave details of any illegal content discovered. The most famous hotline system is that of the British Internet Watch Foundation (IWF). The success of the IWF partnership model has led to the development of a network of hotlines across the European Union (EU) and internationally. At the EU level, INHOPE (the International Association of Internet Hotlines) exists to coordinate and facilitate cooperation between national hotlines.

The IWF is a British charity, first established in 1996. It works in partnership with government, law enforcement and ISPs and has three main functions, namely: minimisation of the availability of illegal internet content; fostering of trust and confidence in the internet; and providing assistance to service providers and law enforcement. As regards minimising the availability of illegal content, the IWF concerns itself with child abuse images hosted anywhere in the world, obscene content hosted in Britain, and British websites that incite racial hatred (IWF website, www.iwf.org.uk).

In conjunction with the IWF hotline, internet users may also notify law enforcement of illegal content directly via the CEOP (www.ceop.gov.uk) and VGTF (www.virtualglobaltaskforce.com) websites, respectively. The IWF reports illegal websites to the appropriate law enforcement agencies nationally and internationally and operates a 'Notice and Take Down' system for ISPs. ISP liability in the UK is governed by the 2002 Electronic Commerce (EC Directive) Regulations. These regulations provide that ISPs are not liable for content available through their service network if they are merely transmitting information, temporarily storing content or innocently hosting material. In the case of both the caching and hosting defences, ISPs will only be absolved from liability where they act expeditiously to remove or to disable access to information once they receive notice of the existence of the offending material. Under the hosting defence, the ISP must also prove that it did not have actual knowledge of the offending material.

IWF success in combating British-based illegal imagery has been spectacular, with a massive reduction in the percentage of British-hosted images from 18% in 1997 to just 0.4% in 2005 (IWF, 2005, p 13). Nevertheless, there are concerns with this system of identifying illegal content, in particular with respect to obscene material hosted on British websites. These concerns relate to the use of hotlines in general and with the work of the IWF in particular. The IWF is a not-for-profit organisation and is not an integral part of the law enforcement framework. Thus, there is ambiguity surrounding the role, responsibility and accountability of the IWF. More generally, criticism of hotlines and Notice and Take Down procedures has centred upon the subjective nature of the work and their perceived chilling effect upon freedom of expression (Sutter, 2000; Akdeniz, 2001). Essentially, a private organisation has assumed the very emotive, sensitive and public role of state censor, interpreting and adjudicating upon whether various offences have been committed (Hedley, 2006, p 143). The IWF works very closely with law enforcement organisations nationally and internationally, so there is a high degree of consistency of approach towards the definition and interpretation of what is illegal, especially as regards child pornography. However, there is a particular concern as regards obscene imagery. As stated earlier, obscenity law within the UK is heavily subjective since the test is whether the material tends to deprave and corrupt. The ever-present risk of legal liability for ISPs accompanied by the lack of a formal 'put back' procedure creates an overly cautious ISP environment, whereby distasteful, disgusting or unpalatable content is routinely removed.

Interference with freedom of expression is an attack upon one of the essential foundations of democracy and thus must be strictly defined and only permitted in a narrow range of circumstances (Harris et al, 1995, p 373). Restrictions must be prescribed by law, must pursue a legitimate objective, be necessary in a democratic society, or satisfy a pressing social need and be proportionate to that legitimate objective. British obscenity laws have been confirmed by the European Court of Human Rights as being in compliance with Article 10 of the European Convention on Human Rights. However, effectively delegating the task of interpreting what constitutes obscene material online to a private organisation that adopts a cautious stance may fall foul of the margin of appreciation afforded to the UK since it disproportionately impacts upon freedom of expression. Domestically, the IWF's role in determining obscenity may be challengeable since freedom of expression is now granted a high level of judicial protection by virtue of the 1998 Human Rights Act.

Technological measures

There is a qualitative difference in the magnitude of risk attaching to illegal online content and content merely harmful to children and young persons (Akdeniz, 2001, p 304; O'Connell, 2005). Classically illegal content violates criminal law, for example child pornography, while harmful content falls short of criminality but is inappropriate for children and young persons, such as adult pornography and adult-themed websites. Defining harmful content is a highly subjective task. The lack of European and international consensus in defining harmful content plus the greater risk posed by illegal content has meant that legislation in this field has concentrated upon the fight against child pornography, with attempts to prohibit dissemination of harmful content floundering in constitutional and human rights challenges. European governments tend to favour non-legislative measures to combat harmful content and have been keen to leave the regulation and control of harmful content to ISPs and proactive 'netizens', with an emphasis upon technological measures, such as age verification software, filtering technology and content rating (Watson, 1996; Sutter, 2000).

Contrary to the perception among the general public, most adult-orientated material is not freely available, since purveyors of such services wish to ensure that full access to their material is conditional upon payment. In addition, public policy dictates that the law should restrict young people's access to addictive pastimes such as gambling and adult-material websites. The new liberalised gambling regime created by the 2005 Gambling Act attempts to strike the correct balance between liberalisation and protection of vulnerable persons. For example, Part 4 of the Act, which is due to come into force in September 2007, explicitly recognises that large numbers of young people under the age of 18 wish to gamble and provides for a number of limited exceptions to the general rule against underage gambling, such as for the national lottery, football pools and electronic gaming machines. Therefore, the new rules on majority as regards gambling have moved from the old binary approach to a more gradated approach and are an attempt to be less paternalistic while still achieving a high level of protection for vulnerable persons.

More generally, the law concerning majority is inconsistent and incoherent in the UK both in terms of the range of the activities concerned and the approaches of the separate legal systems within the UK. It is anomalous that at age 16, young people can join the armed forces, get married (with parental consent in England), leave school and engage in gainful employment and yet cannot vote, buy alcohol or drive a car and do not have full contractual capacity to enter into significant financial obligations. The alternative option, whereby the young person assumes full capacity overnight on attaining the appropriate age is also fraught with difficulty since the young person may be overwhelmed by the array of new opportunities and legal vices. As a matter of principle, the gradated approach to capacity and responsibility is the most appropriate, however, it can also be extremely confusing for young people since the law is sending out mixed messages in respect of personal autonomy. It is important that the rights progressively made available to young people as they mature advance consistently and coherently.

A relatively simple and cost-effective way to limit young people's access to such websites is through age verification software. The technology deployed to verify age relies on two vital criteria which children do not satisfy: registration on the electoral roll and possession of a credit card (Smeaton et al, 2004). As with most technological measures, the weakest link in the system arises not from technology but from human error and/or human frailty (Fox, 2003, p 190).

It is clear that service providers, financial service organisations, ISPs and Mobile Phone Network Operators must cooperate with each other to ensure not only that age verification systems are implemented as a matter of course but also that these systems are used correctly and effectively, incorporating robust employee vetting procedures. In future, access control mechanisms will increasingly rely upon biometric data validation. The use of encrypted biometrics such as iris recognition or fingerprint scanning creates its own unique problems of privacy interference and identity theft, nevertheless, it is accepted that such systems do offer a higher level of security and user authentication accuracy than at present.

Where unwanted online material is not put beyond reach of the average internet user by means of pay to view access controls, then filtering may be useful. Filtering software systems search for prohibited words, images, texts and URLs and occur at the server or service provider level or are installed on the internet-enabled device (Cradden, 2003). Filtering has to be adopted at both levels since network- or server-level controls can be easily circumvented by logging onto another access provider or changing SIM cards on a mobile phone.

Filtering suffers from a number of weaknesses. First, although filtering is a technical screening system, it is still reliant upon human intervention for its effectiveness, including regular software updates that introduce new listings of inappropriate websites. This necessarily involves value judgments being made by humans and this increases the likelihood of inaccuracies or omissions. Second, filters are blunt instruments and can create disproportionate effects. Filters either under-block, such that offensive material evades detection, or over-block whereby innocuous websites are locked out. Third, the entire filtering process may lack transparency since the methodologies used, the filter parameters and the operational results are not divulged to the user (Thomson, 2004). Filtering software must, as a minimum, inform the user when the site is blocked, why the site has been blocked, who requested the block and the legal consequences of further attempted access.

Creating content-specific internet top-level domain names, which identify the subject matter of the website, is a simple development that could reduce the incidence of accidental surfing onto harmful sites (McCarthy, 2006). ISPs, Mobile Phone Network Operators and search service providers could control access to these sites more accurately and effectively since it would be easier to evaluate the nature and content of the site and then disable access. Such a regime may reduce the number of innocent sites inadvertently blocked (McCullagh, 2004).

Content rating is an adjunct to filtering and classifies online content according to a range of subjects and themes, for example, sex, drugs, violence or humour. Content classification is undertaken either by the content creator or an independent third party (Weinberg, 1997, p 1; Balkin et al, 1999, p 12). Concerns over content rating relate to the subjectivity of the process. In self-rating, the content creator may intentionally under-classify to ensure that the site is placed in a 'safe' category, to increase visitor numbers. In third-party rating, the organisation may over-classify material to protect itself from potential legal liability claims. In addition to this potential chilling effect upon freedom of expression, rating undermines user control and autonomy and is rather obtuse as regards the classification taxonomy (Weinberg, 1997, p 3; Walker and Akdeniz, 1998, p 15).

Notwithstanding these limitations, the increasing convergence of digital media may mean that rating becomes increasingly attractive to regulators and governments alike. Rating is not a new concept and has been practised in the broadcasting and audiovisual sectors for decades. Modern rating systems include that of the European computer games industry (PEGI [Pan European Game Information]) and that of the Independent Mobile Classification Body (IMCB), a subsidiary of ICSTIS, the premium rate services regulator in the UK. If rating is to prove successful, there is a need for more rating and quality labels that can be consistently applied across all media platforms. The increasing availability, commercialisation, maturity and societal significance of the internet will create a tremendous spillover demand for regulatory intervention of the type commonly found in other media environments.

Self-regulation

Increasing governmental zeal for regulatory oversight of the internet means that adoption of soft law voluntary codes of conduct has been a key feature of internet governance. Industry self-regulation operates most effectively where the members of the industry accept that there is a comparative advantage to be gained through voluntary adoption of the code. In the case of the internet, one such advantage is increased user numbers. As the reputation of the internet industry improves, more people will venture online. The industry acts out of enlightened self-interest, since voluntary adoption of a code of conduct satisfies the twin imperatives of pre-empting governmental intervention in the field and promotes the financial imperative of increasing corporate success in an era of increased acceptance of Corporate Social Responsibility (CSR) norms.

Ethically and socially aware consumers and customers are an integral element of any successful self-regulatory regime. Their attitudes, expectations and preferences will determine the extent to which companies have the will to self-regulate their activities and to adopt unilateral, bilateral or multilateral action to restrict the availability of illegal and harmful content. Service providers who are the most effective at limiting exposure to harmful, unwanted or illegal conduct will generate increased revenue through expansion of their customer base. CSR encourages the corporation to move beyond the baseline of compliance and proactively adopt a superior ethical and social standpoint. This superior stance is ultimately rewarded through increased customer share, satisfaction and retention.

Examples of codes of conduct include that of the Internet Service Provider Association (ISPA) and the Code of Practice for the self-regulation of new forms of content on mobile phones. Codes of conduct emphasise the promotion of ethical and responsible behaviour by industry. In the case of adult entertainment service providers, organisations must reconcile maximisation of profit with wider stakeholder and CSR obligations. Mobile phone companies and ISPs may increase their competitiveness, brand recognition and reputation through proactive measures to control and restrict the availability of such content.

Education and awareness-raising

If self-regulation and CSR are to produce meaningful and tangible results in reducing the incidence of illegal and harmful content on the internet, consumers must be fully informed of the risks posed and be given information and advice on the tools available to reduce those risks. Media literacy is a pivotal component of European and British regulation of information society services.

In the UK, the Office of Communications (OFCOM) is the primary regulator responsible for communication and information society services and is under a specific obligation to promote and increase media literacy (Weinstein, 2003, p 162). This obligation encompasses education about the availability of new technologies, its benefits and how to use it, the dangers for vulnerable sectors of society and also the limitations of new technology. In fulfilling its functions, OFCOM is also obligated to take into account the vulnerability of children and others who need and deserve special protection. As part of its remit, OFCOM must also publish consumer information and advice.

OFCOM can discharge its obligation of media literacy itself or it can direct others to raise media literacy (Weinstein, 2003). OFCOM must therefore directly engage with other actors in the communications industry to achieve its policy objectives. Thus, the communications sector in the UK is governed in a co-regulatory manner. There is a wealth of information providers in the e-communications sector. Organisations like the IWF and INHOPE, and websites such as Stop Text Bully (www.stoptextbully.com), Chat Danger (www.chatdanger.com, INSAFE (www.saferinternet.org) and Think U Know (www.thinkuknow.co.uk) provide useful advice for internet users on online dangers.

The Task Force on Child Protection on the Internet has also been instrumental in providing detailed guidance and advice on staying safe online. Examples include good practice guidelines in respect of search service providers, guidelines for educators in using real-life examples to illustrate online dangers and guidelines for moderating chat-rooms, instant messaging, bulletin boards and discussion forums. Moderation, the process whereby communications are filtered for harmful or illegal content, can be undertaken by human actors or by the adoption of technological tools designed to block access by way of keywords. The guidance is cognisant of the fact that moderation is not foolproof and indeed in the case of human moderation, the job of moderator may be attractive to paedophiles as a way of gaining access to communications channels. Thus, the advice concentrates upon informing parents and guardians of the limitations of technological moderation and ensuring that human moderation providers implement robust vetting procedures. The guidance also promotes the provision of clear information to users of internet and mobile phone services regarding the safety tools available and whether personal information will be publicly accessible. The guidance also states that mechanisms for reporting abuse are to be clear, accessible and user-friendly.

At the European level, since early 2006, free information for parents, teachers and children has been available from Europe Direct, the EU's telephone and e-mail information service, in addition to the INSAFE EU web portal, dedicated to information about safer internet use.

In providing information for children, it is essential that websites are designed with young people in mind. They must not be too childish, condescending, patronising, heavy-handed or serious. The advice must be targeted at specific age groups since a 'one size fits all' approach is likely to be counterproductive. Young people will more willingly accept and assimilate advice if they can 'uncover' information about the latest technology for themselves. Empowerment is the key to successful information provision.

Models of good practice and information provision provide a framework to deliver better and safer services, to empower users and children, provide clear information, warnings and advice and thereby strengthen public confidence. However, this presupposes that the information provided by the state, industry and independent organisations is clear, relevant and up to date. It cannot be assumed that this is always the case. For example, conventional advice from both government and non-governmental organisations has stressed the availability of parental control and supervision, through placing the PC in a family room (Carr, 2003, p 5). Obviously, this is not possible with an internet-capable mobile phone. Government initiatives must stress the new dangers posed by mobile phones and must highlight the private and atomistic nature of mobile phone use.

Conclusion

The fixed and mobile internet offers tremendous possibilities for human interaction, entertainment and education. Anonymous accessibility to the internet, however, poses particular dangers for young people. They face physical and virtual dangers from adults, other children and exposure to inappropriate, illegal or harmful multimedia content. Responses to these dangers must be proportionate, effective and integrated. The commercial viability of the internet must not be undermined by draconian restrictions, but utilisation of the network must be undertaken in a way that guarantees an adequate level of security and protection for vulnerable sectors of society. This requires a balance between different, and sometimes conflicting, stakeholder interests.

Effective regulation requires a multi-agency approach that includes the internet industry, content providers, government and law enforcement and which takes into account the views of young people, parents and guardians. Legislative initiatives, technological tools, responsible self- and co-regulation and awareness-raising can all play their part in minimising the risks to children and young persons. In short, there is no quick fix to the problem of online danger.

References

Akdeniz, Y. (2001) 'UK government and the control of internet content', *Computer Law and Security Report*, vol 17, no 5, pp 303-17.

Balkin, J., Noveck, B. and Roosevelt, K. (1999) *Filtering the Internet: A Best Practices Model*, available at: www.law.yale.edu/infosociety

Bocij, P. and McFarlane, L. (2003) 'The internet: a discussion of some new and emerging threats to young people', *Police Journal*, March. vol 76, pp 3-13.

Carr, J. (2003) *Children Charities Coalition for Internet Safety – Response to Consultation on the Draft Code of Practice for the Self-Regulation of New Forms of Content and Experiences on Mobiles*, available at: www.nch.org.uk/itok/chis/MobilesConsultation.doc

Carr, J. (2004) *Child Abuse, Child Pornography, and the Internet*, January, available at: www.nch.org.uk/uploads/documents/children_internet_report_summ.pdf

Cradden, J. (2003) *Irish Firm Launches 3G Porn Blocker*, 2 May, available at: www.electricnews.net/news.html?code=9356853

Fox, M. (2003) 'Controlling unlawful internet gambling through the prohibition of bank instruments', *International Company and Commercial Law Review*, vol 14, no 5, pp 187-93.

Gillespie, A. (2006) 'Indecent images, grooming and the law', *Criminal Law Review*, May, pp 412-21.

Harris, D. J., O'Boyle, M. and Warbrick, C. (1995) *Law of the European Convention on Human Rights*, London: Butterworths.

Hedley, S. (2006) *The Law of Electronic Commerce and the Internet in the UK and Ireland*, London: Cavendish Publishing.

Home Office and Scottish Executive (2005) *Consultation: On the Possession of Extreme Pornographic Material*, ISBN 0 7559 1206 3 (web only publication), available at: www.scotland.gov.uk/Resource/Doc/ 57346/0017059.pdf

Internet Watch Foundation (2005) *2005 Annual and Charity Report*, available at: www.iwf.org.uk/documents/ 20060306_iwf_annual_report_2005_-_high_res.pdf

Magid, L. (2003) *Child Safety on the Information Highway*, National Center for Missing and Exploited Children, available at: www.safekids.com/child_safety.htm

McCarthy, K. (2006) *ICANN Chokes Off .xxx Porn Registry*, The Register, 11 May, available at: www.theregister.co.uk/2006/05/11/ icann_kills_xxx/

McCullagh, D. (2004) *Google's Chastity Belt Too Tight*, CNET News.com, 23 April, available at: http://news.com.com/ Googles+chastity+belt+too+tight/2100-1032_3-5198125.html

O'Connell, R. (May 2005) *Defining and Understanding Harmful Content*, UCLAN Cyberspace Research Unit, 20 May, available at: www.saferinternet.org/ww/en/pub/insafe/news/articles/0505/ defining.htm

Ormerod, D. (2005) *Smith and Hogan's Criminal Law* (11th edition), Oxford: Oxford University Press.

Smeaton, M., Poole, A., Chevis, A. and Carr, J. (2004) *Study into Underage Access to Online Gambling and Betting Sites*, Joint NCH, GamCare and Citizencard Report, available at: www.gamcare.org.uk/pdfs/ StudyReportFinal.pdf

SOCA (Serious Organised Crime Agency) (2006) www.soca.gov.uk

Stone, R. (2004) *Textbook on Civil Liberties and Human Rights* (5th edition), Oxford: Oxford University Press.

Sutter, G. (2000) 'Nothing new under the sun: old fears and new media', *International Journal of Law and Information Technology*, vol 8, no 3, pp 338-78.

Thomson, B. (2004) *Doubts over Web Filtering Plan*, BBC website, 11 June, available at: http://.news.bbc.co.uk/1/hi/technology/ 3797563.stm

Walker, C. P. and Akdeniz, Y. (1998) 'The governance of the internet in Europe with special reference to illegal and harmful content', *Criminal Law Review*, Special Issue, December, pp 5-19.

Watson, D. (1996) 'Internet censorship: cleaning up the global metropolis', *The Library Association Record*, vol 98, no 10, pp 498-9.

Weinberg, J. (1997) *Rating the Net, 19 Hastings Communication and Entertainment Law Journal 453*, available at: www.copacommission.org/papers/rating.htm

Weinstein, S. (2003) 'The medium is the message: the legal and policy implications of the creation of OFCOM in the age of convergence', *Computer and Telecommunications Law Review*, vol 9, no 6, pp 161-73.

Williams, N. (2003) *Children, Mobile Phones and the Internet*, Childnet International, available at: www.iajapan.org/hotline/2003mobilepro-en.html

SEVEN

Parenting and risk

Rachel Hek

Introduction

This chapter focuses on the ways risk is defined and applied in relation to social work with families. First, policy and practice in relation to child welfare will be considered. This will highlight how risk is viewed and identified by government policy makers and social care service providers. Second, the experiences of families who have been pulled into the child welfare system will be considered through an examination of research that looks at their views – in particular drawing on work carried out by the National Evaluation of the Children's Fund (NECF). Parents' and children's views will be contrasted with those of service providers, and with policy, in order to examine if and how they coincide.

Parton (1996, p 98) points out that risk has become central to social work with families:

> Increasingly, social workers and social welfare agencies are concerned in their day to day practice with the issue of risk. Risk assessment, risk management, the monitoring of risk and risk taking itself have become common activities for both practitioners and managers. Similarly, estimations about risks have become key in identifying priorities and making judgments about the quality of performance and what should be the central focus of professional activities.

He suggests that the concept of risk gained purchase in social work alongside the rise of individualism throughout the Thatcher years and following the collapse of 'welfarism'. Parents are seen as a risk to their children, either through 'omission' (for example, neglect or lack of control) or 'commission' (for example, physical cruelty or sexual abuse). Children present a risk to society if parents do not control them, when they become labelled as antisocial. State intervention into family life has always been double-edged, playing both 'care and control' functions; providing for those deemed to be 'deserving' of help and controlling or reforming the behaviour of the 'deviant' or 'undeserving' poor (Banks, 2006). This tension has grown as resources shrink alongside seemingly ever-increasing levels of need. Although writing some time ago, Parton's analysis remains relevant: 'Risk has become the key criterion for targeting scarce resources, protecting the most vulnerable, and making professionals and agencies accountable' (Parton, 1996, p 104).

The development of child welfare policy in the UK

The problems that child welfare policy in the UK seeks to deal with are socially constructed, and change over time (Fox-Harding, 1996; Corby, 2000; Stainton-Rogers, 2001; Ferguson, 2004). In the early 19th century, in response to the notion of the 'ideal' childhood perpetuated by the middle classes, children began to be seen as vulnerable and 'at risk' of exploitation. A range of laws concerning child labour and formalised schooling emerged (Foley et al, 2001). Organisations such as Save the Children and Dr Barnardo's developed, dedicated to 'rescuing' children from bad environments. The introduction of the Poor Law and workhouses labelled and pathologised working-class families. Notions of deserving and undeserving poor took hold. By the late 19th century there was extensive state intervention and social workers increasingly took over from parents as decision makers and protectors of children (Fox-Harding, 1996).

Following the Second World War, 'welfarism' encouraged pooling of resources and social responsibility. Family-based support services were predominant in social work until the 1970s (Parton, 1985). The ethos was one of prevention, non-punitive attitudes and a casework approach informed by psychoanalytic ideas (Corby, 2000).

The inquiry into the death of Maria Cowell in 1974, and other highly publicised child protection cases in the 1970s and 1980s, shifted focus onto child abuse and child protection; social work became more procedural and 'risk' orientated. During this period, there were 46 inquiries into child deaths (Corby, 2000). This was a time of contradictions for social workers, characterised by the contradictory popular reaction of 'too little too late, too much too soon'. Risk assessment and increased monitoring of families became more prevalent. Preventative work with children in their own families, informed by a structural understanding of the causes of child abuse, gave way to an emphasis on the removal of children from individually 'bad' families.

The Cleveland Inquiry changed the focus of child welfare policy yet again (Parton, 1997). There had been a public outcry at the large number of children taken into care following suspected but often unproven sexual abuse. The focus shifted back to one of support for families and voluntary approaches to the protection of children. Greater legal rights were given to parents, less discretionary power to professionals, more emphasis was placed on interagency working, and procedures and guidelines were amended. This also spurred on the implementation of the 1989 Children Act and the first publication of *Working Together to Safeguard Children* guidelines (DH, 1991), which has since been updated.

The 1989 Children Act contributed to the refocusing of children's services from the investigation of abuse to provision of family support services for children 'in need'. However, there continued to be a focus on children for whom social services departments already had responsibility and who were seen as being 'at risk', at the expense of children with lower levels of perceived need (Smith, 1999; NECF, 2004; Morris, 2005). Eligibility and funding issues made refocusing child welfare services difficult, as did further inquiries during the 1990s into organised abuse and abuse of children in the care of local authorities.

Current child welfare policy

The first explicit family policy in the UK was set out by the New Labour government during the 1990s, and since 1997 social exclusion and youth crime have been identified as major policy priorities. A range of initiatives has been developed aimed at children 'at risk' of social exclusion, which focus on reducing risk factors and promoting protective factors for individual children and their families. These policies and initiatives recognise the impact of structural factors – such as high crime rates, low-paid employment, family breakdown – on children's future life chances (SEU, 2004).

However, in spite of policy targets aimed at alleviating child poverty and improving opportunities for children, 'welfare-to-work' policies and the drive towards adoption for children in care suggest a wish to relieve the state of obligations and, in turn, expenditure. The current definitions and applications of support, intervention, prevention and risk are therefore complex (Morris, 2005). New Labour initially focused on supporting families, but this moved to a focus on the concept of parental responsibility. In the discussion paper *Supporting Families* (DH, 1999) the socialisation of the young is presented as the responsibility of the 'family unit'. In the 2001 Labour manifesto, Blair talked of 'hard-working families' providing children with opportunities. Henricson (2004) points out that there has been no specific review of family policy since 1998 and argues that this should be done alongside a more explicit statement of what the government means by rights and responsibilities of parents and how these are balanced against the rights of children. This focus on children and families, social exclusion, families' responsibilities and the link with 'risk' can be tracked through initiatives, procedures and inquiries introduced over a five-year period (SEU, 2000).

The Children and Young People's Unit (CYPU) was launched in 2000 to ensure that government policy on children was 'joined up' across the age ranges; the strategy was to prevent social exclusion and tackle poverty through both universal and targeted services. The CYPU became responsible for the administration of the Children's Fund, which had the aim of identifying children and families 'at risk' of social exclusion and promoting opportunities for them through the provision of preventative services (NECF, 2003). The *Framework for the Assessment of Children in Need and their Families* (DH, 2000a) emphasised the importance of a holistic approach to assessing children and specifically acknowledged the importance of preventative services in supporting children and families experiencing problems, stress and poverty. *New Directions for Children's Services: Background briefing for preventative strategy announcement* (DH, 2002) required local authorities to draw up local preventative strategies identifying effective support structures and services early enough to address the problems before statutory intervention or acute services became necessary.

In 2001, the public inquiry into the death of child abuse victim Victoria Climbié opened. The chair, Lord Laming, pledged that it would mark a turning point in the protection of vulnerable children. The inquiry report (Laming, 2003) made 108 recommendations, many similar to previous inquiry recommendations, and these also influenced thinking about preventative services and the tone of developments in children's services.

The Department of Health announced that it would pilot Children's Trusts, bringing together health, education and social services into new organisations under the expected control of local government. The Green Paper *Every Child Matters* (DfES, 2003) outlined this and other aspects of the changing emphasis in relation to children's services. Importantly, however, despite the use of the term 'prevention' the tone of the document moved away from notions of children 'in need' towards children potentially 'at risk'. The 2004 Children Act and *Every Child Matters: Change for Children* (DfES, 2004) have placed children 'at risk' of social exclusion at the centre of the emerging childcare policy agenda. Children who had previously been provided with services as children in need (1989 Children Act, Part III) began to be described as children 'at risk' of social exclusion.

The 2004 Children Act and *Every Child Matters* (DfES, 2004) identify five broad outcomes for children. These are staying safe, being healthy, enjoying and achieving, contributing to society and economic well-being. They aim to provide children and young people with useful support when they need it, to promote better information sharing and a common assessment framework, to provide for lead professionals to ensure clear accountability, and to establish multidisciplinary teams based around universal services. This constitutes a preventative agenda that is 'outcome focused' rather than 'need focused' (NECF, 2004). However, this raises questions about what is meant by a 'preventative agenda'. Some children and their families are seen as 'at risk' of social exclusion, but they also continue to be viewed as a risk to society and as such their behaviour needs to be controlled. Current legislation and guidance places responsibility on parents for children's 'bad' behaviour. Parents who fail to control their children may be subject to a range of punitive measures such as parenting orders, parenting contracts and Anti-Social Behaviour Orders (ASBOs). Linley and Jordan (2005) highlight the contradictions with other legislation, guidance and research that suggest the best way to prevent such risks is to work in partnership with parents (DH, 2000a; Quinton, 2004).

Family experiences of being seen as 'risky'

Research with parents shows that they need and want support to help them fulfil their role and provide effective boundaries for their children (Parentline Plus, 2005). Quinton (2004) identifies key messages about what works in the delivery of family support services. Parents want service providers to treat them as adults and partners in problem solving. They value being listened to and having their views respected in relation to the support they need in caring for their children. They value the flexibility and 'lack of stigma' that voluntary sector services provide, and group activities that enable parents to meet with other parents, reducing social isolation. The Family Policy Alliance (2004) emphasises the need for adequately resourced, accessible and sustainable services to support children and parents when they need it, addressing problems when they first emerge. Linley and Jordan (2004) and Parentline Plus (2005) point out that punitive measures against parents can have detrimental effects on family relationships. They may deter parents from asking for support in the early stages of problems, so these are more likely to descend into crisis. Linley and Jordan (2004) point to a lack of adequate resourcing of family support and a lack of will to see parents and children as experts on their own lives. They argue that many families receive support not when they ask for it, but only when their situation has become so serious that child protection concerns have arisen.

This highlights the tensions in policy that promotes family support on the one hand, while, on the other, implements potentially unsupportive and punitive measures in relation to child protection and youth crime. Practitioners are required to deliver preventative services, but are also told to make demands of parents who may already be under stress, and to place punitive sanctions on children.

A number of research projects have investigated how families experience child protection investigations and care proceedings. Parents had extremely negative views of child protection interventions (Farmer and Owen, 1995; Cleaver and Freeman, 1995). They often recognised that they were having difficulties, but felt wrongly labelled as 'risky' by professionals (Freeman and Hunt, 1998). Cleaver and Freeman (1995) found that ethnicity, religion and class had a bearing on how parents were seen and treated. Parents felt that help was often focused on the child, rather than being holistic, and said that they needed input for themselves in order to make positive changes (Freeman and Hunt, 1998). Cleaver and Freeman (1995) found that when supportive interventions were made for the whole family, parents changed their views of social workers and welcomed the input they had initially been hostile to. It is interesting to note parents' concern about the lack of holistic policies in the light of government policy that is moving towards a narrower focus on children rather than the family as a whole. Parents also highlighted the lack of attention by professionals to structural risks in their lives such as poor housing, poverty and domestic violence (Freeman and Hunt, 1998).

Domestic violence has been highlighted by mothers as a particular area of concern, with social workers providing inadequate support and often minimising the risk to them and their children (Farmer and Owen, 1995; Brandon and Lewis, 1996; Humphreys, 2000). However, at the same time, women talk of being 'blamed' and seen as 'a risk' to their children if they fail to leave the situation of violence. In one study, women said that they had been 'threatened' by social workers with having their children accommodated (Maynard, 1985). A further study found that, on average, women have to contact 11 agencies before they get the help they need to protect themselves and their children and in the case of black or minority ethnic women this figure rises to 18 (Hanmer and Saunders, 1993). There is also a stark contradiction between what mothers say about risk and current family policy that deems 'lifelong parenting' a parental 'responsibility', forcing women and children to maintain contact with violent partners. Child contact sessions after separation are particularly dangerous, with further violence taking place in up to 94% of these sessions (Hester and Radford, 1996; Hester and Pearson, 1998).

The views of Children's Fund service users about risk

Between 2003 and 2006, the National Evaluation of the Children's Fund (NECF) has worked across 16 case study sites in England with children and families who use its services. These are aimed at all children in an area and also include 'targeted' services for particular groups of children (refugee and asylum-seeking children, disabled children, Gypsy and Traveller children, black and minority ethnic children, children at risk of becoming involved in crime and antisocial behaviour). The NECF worked in each of the areas for about six months and visited the Children's Fund projects about once a month during that time. The overall aim of the research was to evaluate the impact of services on outcomes for children, and to ascertain families' views on what difference the Children's Fund projects have made to their lives.

As part of the NECF team, the author talked to children and their families using a range of Children's Fund services and projects, such as before- and after-school clubs, youth clubs, nurture groups and evening, weekend and/or holiday activities. Children and families were visited in a range of settings: at home, at school or at the Children's Fund projects. Research involved a range of methods to facilitate informal discussion with children and parents about what they considered important in their lives, including individual interviews, group interviews and participation in activities, such as games and arts and crafts.

Parents and children identified a number of risks they feel they are exposed to and the support that helps them live with these risks day to day. These risks are partially recognised at governmental level and through the implementation of locally based preventative strategies. However, there is a substantial difference between the way that these risks are viewed in policies and the way that families talk about them.

While parents identified individual, relational and structural risks, these policies focused on the first two. The following short case studies illustrate families' experiences of dealing with risk.

P and his mother, A

P is an 11-year-old boy whose mother (A) is white British and father is black Caribbean. He lives with his mother and two brothers, and although his father has left the family home he sees him on Sundays. P and A say that they would be safer and happier as a family if P's father still lived with them.

P has already been in trouble with the police for stealing and harassing people in the street. P and A are concerned about the neighbourhood and say that the estate they live on is dangerous. P's older brother (15 years old) had been shot in the leg on his way home from youth club. They both say that P will get pulled into criminal behaviour and drug use and see no way out of this situation as they have no hope of being rehoused in a different area:

> I can sit here now and say my 11-year-old son, in another two years, is going to be either smoking weed or he's either going to be taking cocaine and I'm just – it destroys me, but there's nothing I can do, I am just destroyed. (A)

They talked about racism in the area. P spoke of racist gangs looking for black or Asian people to attack. A spoke of constant harassment, including daily verbal abuse, petrol bombing and having the front door kicked in. Both P and A felt that there was no point in reporting incidents to the police whom they saw as at best ineffective and at worst racist:

> My son was beaten and all his clothes were torn off of him, you know, and the police came round and they said to me, you know, 'oh well,' you know, 'another racist attack'. (A)

P talked about bullying and although he feels able to stand up for himself he worries about his younger brother. He feels a responsibility to help other younger children, even when this places him at risk.

> Whenever there's trouble with my brother I stop them hitting him, because he's in Year 3. A Year 6 boy went for a Year 3 boy and I had

to stop him ... I do stop people because there's these like ... there's 10 people were beating up this boy, they were kicking him and then they chased him and then I was stopping them, I pushed one back and then they all started coming, so I couldn't do nothing. (P)

P has aspirations to be an engineer, but already feels that he will not have the opportunity to achieve this. He finds school hard and spoke of feeling labelled because of his behaviour. He thinks this will stop him doing well:

Everyone said I had a mental problem. People at school [said it]. But I don't really know why. I know I was bad in my school ... and I never would work or wouldn't listen, I was kicked out of school every day ... that's why. (P)

P and A see lack of opportunities in all areas of their lives as placing them at risk. A pointed to the risks for P and other local children if the club on the estate, which is funded by the Children's Fund, shuts down:

Well funding ... definitely, funding. I cannot believe that they can't give them more help.... The little club ... if we start to lose things like that, because they can't run it ... the children are not safe enough ... they're going to lose out ... we're going to lose the little bit of facilities that we've got. (A)

This case illustrates the multiple risks this family faces. P and his mother identify individual within-person or relational risks and see individual help and support as important, particularly ongoing counselling support. However, they also highlight many structural risks that need to be recognised and addressed if their lives and relationships are to improve. This family are clear that lack of facilities, racism and lack of opportunities contribute to crime and the lack of safety in the area. They stress the importance of the Children's Fund project and worry that this will stop as a result of lack of continuing funding. P and his mother are very clear about what risk and prevention mean to them; they say that without a holistic long-term approach, P will have no real alternative to becoming involved in the general culture of the area.

B and her grandmother, E

B is a nine-year-old white British girl. She has lived with her grandmother (E) since she was a baby, as her parents were unable to look after her. She has been in trouble with the police for throwing bricks through windows and harassing people in the street:

> I was breaking windows and people came out and said 'don't break me windows', and I sweared at them and that. (B)

B said that bullying is a regular occurrence in her life. She finds school difficult, and thinks that this together with the bullying contributes to her behaviour. She also knows this makes her vulnerable:

> They just teased me. I had coloured hair. Three boys came up to me and I was just walking over, and they came up and like pushed me and I just got mad. (B)

> Some lessons what I don't like, that's why I always get mood. I don't like the lessons ... I get in a strop and I'll run out the classroom and go in the toilets. I'll go in the toilets and that and I lock meself in and I'll run out of school. (B)

B also identified limited activities and opportunities outside of school as being a factor in her getting into trouble out of school. She often spends time with older young people and takes part in activities that she knows will get her into trouble:

> We just play; we pick stones up, and have stone fights. (B)

> People I knew were making me do it ... and saying if you don't do it I'll batter you and stuff like that.... It was older people who I don't hardly know. Saying 'go on, go on, do it'. (B)

B said she is worried about this, and the risk of getting into trouble with the police. B's grandmother is also worried about B getting into trouble as she grows up in the area, and about the possibility of her getting sucked into 'the system' (for example, police, social services).

> They can get themselves into trouble with the police, and from the police you get them going to court and you get them into the system, or they're out of the parents' control, you put 'em away. You put the

child away in a home; they ... might see worser things than what they actually seen in own home ... might learn more ... might learn how to get a screwdriver and open your car ... might learn about drugs. (E)

Both B and E feel that the greatest risk to them is the withdrawal of support services that have helped them make changes in their lives and that they rely on. They were both clear that they needed support on an ongoing basis:

I want her [Children's Fund project worker] to talk to me more, like she used to come once a week every Wednesday.... I'm changing now. But now I've got a bit worse because she's gone. (B)

I think even to support the person ... does need quite an extension than what they're giving ... 12 weeks we've got, it's good, but you're only just getting to know that person ... and you think, oh it's great, I can talk to [the project worker] and then it's gone, so who do you talk to then ... I miss her myself ... but the kids miss her terrible, they're going back to their old routine at school.... I just can't cope with that happening. Because it were everything that she had done good were turning back to normal (E)

The risks that this family identify are multiple, and again are not purely individual within-person or relational. This family again point to lack of facilities and opportunities in the area as contributing to crime, and B particularly feels peer pressure to behave in a certain way, and fears for her personal safety if she does not conform. This family state that without the support of the Children's Fund project they would not be able to manage the risks they currently face, and feel that the support they need is long term.

T and his mother, S

T is a 13-year-old white British boy. He lives with both of his parents. He has been in trouble at school and at home due to angry and uncontrollable behaviour. His mother (S) has also hit him as she was unable to cope with his behaviour.

The concerns for both T and S are around dealing with T's angry and uncontrollable behaviour, which results from bullying in the neighbourhood and at school. S described him as not fitting in with other young people, particularly boys. She said that he likes activities and subjects not usually associated with teenage boys. She said that some of the bullying is homophobic in nature. They both feel that this has spilled into many areas of their lives. S found dealing with T's behaviour very difficult and lost control, physically assaulting him. She identified this as a risk to their relationship and to T's safety.

Both T and S are concerned about safety in the local area, and are particularly worried by groups of older teenagers. S also identified a lack of activities for young people as a problem. T finds school work challenging and needs support with this. Both T and S are worried about lack of opportunities if he does not get extra help in school.

The risks identified by this family relate to bullying, in particular homophobic bullying and prejudice, and the lack of personal safety and the behavioural issues this leads to for T. Although T and his mother locate difficulties in their relationship and within T as an individual, they recognise the impact of wider structural factors on these. Both T and his mother feel that the lack of facilities and opportunities increase aggressive and antisocial behaviour by young people in the area. They also highlight the lack of opportunities and the risks of reduced life chances if T does not receive appropriate educational help.

The views of children and families about help to relieve the risks they identify

The children and parents involved in the NECF research gave some clear feedback about what they think works for them.

The importance of relationships with Children's Fund project staff

Children, young people and parents talked about how positive relationships with Children's Fund project workers helped them to make the most of learning opportunities and allowed them to express their opinions. Children's Fund project workers seek children's and parents' views and involve them in projects and decision making. Children's Fund projects also provide important positive adult role models for children and young people. However, families also said that they feel they have little impact on policy at a higher level. One mother talked about the positive role of the project workers in relation to her son:

> My son is very fond of the project workers. It's nice for him because one worker is a black man that he can look up to ... they know what he's talking about, they've given him support, it's nice, because he hasn't got it at home ... because my boys are mixed race. They've got him to open up a little bit.

Good one-to-one relationships with a worker provide a strong and successful adult role model. They offer children the notion that aspirations and involvement are possible and provide someone who children are able to trust and can talk to if they are experiencing bullying and feel unsafe.

The importance of safe spaces for children

Parents said that projects provided safe places for their children to go, and that this had helped their children feel more confident, and to 'come out of themselves'. A mother talked about the importance for her sons of the chance to expand their opportunities:

> They've taken the boys for lovely days out, they've had some great little adventures out, where they take them off the estate ... I don't normally have the money to do things like that, because I'm on Income Support and things and sometimes the money's a little bit tight. I mean he loves it ... it shows him that there's more outside that I can't really show him.

Children said that projects allowed them to make new friends, or develop friendships with people they had known before, and that this helped them feel more secure in the local area. Activities provided by the projects were seen as enjoyable and helpful and as providing space and opportunities to get on with school work and learning. Young people often said that projects had given them the chance to be involved in activities or trips they would not otherwise have had access to.

The interventions children and families highlighted here indicate how, through providing individual support and opportunities, the Children's Fund projects offer partial responses to some of the risks of exclusion. The projects can offer a safe environment for children, some respite for stressed parents who have little other support and widen children's horizons and aspirations.

Parents and carers suggested that projects helped to raise the self-esteem and confidence of their children, as well as practical and independence skills. Parents also said that 'holistic' services helped them feel less isolated and more able to cope with their children, as the following quotes illustrate:

> It's just stopped me from feeling like an alien.

> They just sent me a load of information and they made me feel like I wasn't on my own because up to that point I was just, there was no one knew, you know.

Parents saw evidence of improvement in their children's engagement with activities and more social interaction as a result, as the following quote from a mother illustrates:

> … and this other little boy came to play and A [her son] normally would just walk off and wouldn't have that, but he let this other little boy do what they was doing and that was a real breakthrough, he would never have accepted this before.

Support for the whole family allows for individual and relational risks to be attended to; this in turn allows children and parents to develop the confidence to engage with other people and to take up opportunities.

The NECF findings confirm those of the studies mentioned earlier (Family Policy Alliance, 2004; Quinton, 2004). In general, families believe their coping mechanisms or resilience can be built up through the provision of services for the entire family. Although some of these views have been used to inform good practice, service users' views are often not fully taken into account, or related changes are slow in coming.

Other views on services

Families also identified the following as important:

- accessible services, preferably located in one place and where they can see the same worker in order to avoid having to go through their stories again and again;
- professionals who recognise the families' view of their needs, who explain rights and entitlements clearly, who have correct information about a range of services and can assist families to access these;
- professionals who listen to and respect families' views, wishes, culture and skills and who accept that families have a degree of expertise about their own situations;
- professionals who allow families to be involved in planning and decision making and to retain control in this process;
- professionals who review support regularly to ensure that it continues to be relevant and useful.

Conclusions

Parenting is of central concern to the New Labour government; and the stated aims of current initiatives, to reduce poverty and prevent social exclusion, are clearly important for families. The concept of parenting is increasingly linked with the concept of risk when outcomes for children are discussed in the social care arena. This is a complex and multifaceted debate and this chapter has shown how thinking in this area shifts regularly.

The current policy position recognises that children and families may be seen as 'at risk' of social exclusion through poverty, crime, disability, ethnicity and so on. It is clear from the studies discussed that the identification of risk is a difficult task that must include listening to parents and children. It is important that all parents and children are listened to, not just those seen as 'deserving', or the most marginalised families who are already facing the most punitive interventions will become further disenfranchised.

The NECF case studies illustrate the specific ways that parents and children define risk in their lives. They identified risk as being located not just within an individual or family, but as a mixture of structural and relational factors. Parents and children see these risks as impacting heavily on their lives and affecting the opportunities and trajectories they are able to take up. The key risks identified are:

- unsafe neighbourhoods – children and parents are worried about violence, availability of drugs and crime;

- racism/homophobia – children and parents identify racism as a risk for them, and often see it as an aspect of the other concerns they raise (for example, bullying, unsafe neighbourhoods, a factor in the lack of opportunities);
- bullying at school – children identify the impact that this has on their confidence and ability to do well at school. Parents often indicate that they feel schools are unable to deal with this problem, and that bullying leads their children into other problems (for example, 'dropping out' of school, becoming involved in crime);
- lack of opportunity to find 'pathways' out of their current situations, due to structural inequalities. In particular, children and parents highlight the importance of local Children's Fund projects and individual workers in their lives. They also identify the risks for them if the funding for such projects is not ongoing.

Many of the risks identified by the families in relation to the task of parenting are also identified by service providers within the Children's Fund. However, for them, the lack of ongoing funding and the enormity of overcoming child poverty and unsafe neighbourhoods often lead service providers and policy makers to concentrate on individual input. This is more likely to lead to a view of children being seen as 'at risk' within their families, rather than 'at risk' due to structural issues. It is interesting to note that bullying, often comprising a racist element, is mentioned as a risk by many of the children. This risk impacts on their self-image and ability to take up opportunities on offer, and potentially leads to involvement in 'problematic' behaviour. However, during this research service providers did not identify this as a 'risk' that children may be concerned about.

From the NECF research it is clear that families and young people have views about the potential benefits projects such as those funded by the Children's Fund can bring to them and the way that such services should be delivered. As a general theme, parents and children see their lives in the round. They talk about wanting workers who listen to them, are there for them and respond to their needs as they arise. Parents and children want services that benefit the whole family and that provide support for the long term. They also link what they want on an individual or family level with what they feel would help their situations at a structural level. They are clear about the effects on them and those around them of poverty, deprivation and the lack of facilities and resources. Families feel strongly that they should be listened to about their own situations, that often individual workers in local projects do this, but that their views are only heard 'tokenistically' at a higher level. Other research with children and families supports these messages; families highlight the importance of accessible services where workers listen, respect their views and value their input on their own situations. Families also say that they want services that provide for all their needs and that check if what they are providing is useful (Linley and Jordan, 2004; Quinton, 2004).

All of these messages from families support moves towards holistic and long-term approaches. Finally, many of the 'risk' factors children and parents point to are structural as well as individual. Addressing issues such as bullying in schools, unsafe neighbourhoods or poor social housing provision will involve a wider range of initiatives than can be supported by local social services departments, or single initiatives such as the Children's Fund. It will also require the long-term funding of a family support approach.

References

Banks, S. (2006) *Ethics and Values in Social Work* (3rd edn), London: Palgrave.

Brandon, M. and Lewis, A. (1996) 'Significant harm and children's experiences of domestic violence', *Child & Family Social Work*, vol 1, pp 33–42.

Children Act 1989, London: HMSO.

Children Act 2004, London: HMSO.

Cleaver, H. and Freeman, J. (1995) *Parental Perspectives in Cases of Suspected Child Abuse*, London: HMSO.

Corby, B. (2000) *Child Abuse: Towards a Knowledge Base*, Buckingham: Open University Press.

DfES (Department for Education and Skills) (2003) *Every Child Matters*, Norwich: The Stationery Office.

DfES (2004) *Every Child Matters: Change for Children*, Nottingham: DfES.

DH (1991) *Working Together to Safeguard Children: A Guide to Interagency Working to Safeguard and Promote the Welfare of Children*, London: The Stationery Office.

DH (1999) *Supporting Families*, London: The Stationery Office.

DH (2000a) *Framework for the Assessment of Children in Need and their Families*, London: The Stationery Office.

DH (2000b) *Assessing Children in Need and their Families: Practice Guidance*, London: The Stationery Office.

DH (2002) *New Directions for Children's Services: Background Briefing for Preventative Strategy Announcement*, London: The Stationery Office.

Family Policy Alliance (2004) *Submission by FPA to the Commission on Families and Well-being of Children*, London: Family Policy Alliance.

Farmer, E. and Owen, M. (1995) *Child Protection Practice: Private Risks and Public Remedies*, London: HMSO.

Ferguson, H. (2004) *Protecting Children in Time*, London: Palgrave.

Foley, P., Roche, J. and Tucker, S. (eds) (2001) *Children in Society: Contemporary Theory, Policy and Practice*, London: Palgrave.

Fox-Harding, L. (1996) *Family, State and Social Policy*, London: Macmillan.

Freeman, P. and Hunt, J. (1998) *Parental Perspectives on Care Proceedings*, London: The Stationery Office.

Hanmer, J. and Saunders, S. (1993) *Women, Violence and Crime Prevention*, Aldershot: Avebury.

Henricson, C. (2004) *Government and Parenting: Is there a Case for a Policy Review and a Parent's Code?*, York: Joseph Rowntree Foundation.

Hester, M. and Pearson, C. (1998) *From Periphery to Centre: Domestic Violence in Work with Abused Children*, Bristol: The Policy Press.

Hester, M. and Radford, L. (1996) *Domestic Violence and Child Contact Arrangements in England and Denmark*, Bristol: The Policy Press.

Humphreys, C. (2000) *Social Work, Domestic Violence and Child Protection: Challenging Practice*, Bristol: The Policy Press.

Laming, Lord (2003) *The Victoria Climbié Inquiry: Report*, London: The Stationery Office.

Linley, B. and Jordan, L. (2004) *Submission by the Family Policy Alliance to the House of Commons Education and Skills Committee*, London: Family Policy Alliance.

Linley, B. and Jordan, L. (2005) *FPA Response to Statutory Guidance on Making Arrangements under S11 CA2004*, London: Family Policy Alliance.

Maynard, M. (1985) 'The response of social workers to domestic violence', in J. Pahl (ed) *Private Violence and Public Policy*, London: Routledge.

Morris, K. (2005) 'From 'children in need' to 'children at risk' – the changing policy context for prevention and participation', *Practice*, vol 17, no 2, pp 70-6.

NECF (National Evaluation of the Children's Fund) (2003) *Early Messages for Developing Practice*, London: DfES.

NECF (2004) *Collaborating for the Social Inclusion of Children and Young People*, London: DfES.

Parentline Plus (2005) *Youth Matters: Response from Parentline Plus*, London: Parentline Plus.

Parton, N. (1985) *The Politics of Child Abuse*, London: Macmillan.

Parton, N. (ed) (1996) *Social Theory, Social Change and Social Work*, London: Routledge.

Parton, N. (1997) *Child Protection and Family Support: Tensions, Contradictions and Possibilities*, London: Routledge.

Quinton, D. (2004) *Supporting Parents: Messages from Research*, London: Jessica Kingsley.

Rutter, J. (2003) *The Experiences and Achievements of Congolese Children in Camden Schools*, London: London Borough of Camden.

SEU (Social Exclusion Unit) (2000) *Report of the Policy Action Team 12: Young People*, London: HMSO.

SEU (2004) *Report of the Policy Action Team 12: Young People*, London: HMSO.

Smith, T. (1999) 'Neighbourhood and preventative strategies with children and families: what works?', *Children and Society*, vol 13, pp 265-77.

Stainton Rogers, W. (2001) 'Constructing childhood, constructing child concern', in P. Foley, J. Roche and S. Tucker (eds) *Children in Society: Contemporary Theory, Policy and Practice*, London: Palgrave, pp 26-33.

EIGHT

Meeting the needs of children whose parents have a serious drug problem

Neil McKeganey and Marina Barnard

Introduction

For years drug abuse treatment and child protection services in the UK have operated under the belief that drug addiction does not necessarily undermine a parent's ability to look after their children. As recently as 2003, for example, the Scottish Executive was issuing guidance to services working with addict families saying that 'parental substance misuse alone is neither a necessary nor a sufficient cause of problems in children' (Scottish Executive, 2003, p 13). In May 2006 that, rather comforting, view was blown apart when the Justice Minister, the Health Minister and the Education Ministers in Scotland all put their name to the statement that 'Serious and chaotic drug abuse is incompatible with effective parenting' (Scottish Executive, 2006, p 5). Published as part of the *Hidden Harm: Next Steps* report, that statement indicates a hardening in the attitude of some of those in government to the problem of parental drug addiction and, in particular, the impact of parental drug use on children.

In this chapter we look at what is known about the ways in which parents' drug use may influence the lives of their children and the challenges faced by those seeking to meet the needs of these children. Before doing so we should add a word on terminology. Throughout this chapter we use the term 'addict' or 'dependent drug user' to refer to individuals who have a serious drug problem. These are individuals who are using heroin, often on a daily basis, frequently by injection and who are experiencing a range of problems associated with their drug use. We are not referring here to individuals who may be using a range of other drugs, such as cannabis, on an occasional or repeated basis without any obvious impact on their own lives or the lives of their children.

The impact of parental drug use on children

In 2003 the Advisory Council on the Misuse of Drugs published the results of a two-year inquiry into the impact of parental drug use on children. Titled *'Hidden Harm': Responding to the Needs of Children of Problem Drug Users*, the report outlined the estimate that there may be something of the order of 350,000 children in the UK with one or both parents dependent upon illegal drugs (ACMD, 2003). Striking as that figure is, the authors of this report acknowledge that the true figure could be even higher. When one considers that the heroin problem in the UK really took off in the early 1980s, it is striking that it was not until 2003 that a government report focusing specifically on the impact of parental drug use was produced. For most of the years over which the UK heroin problem has grown, the children of dependent drug users have been largely invisible to both services and policy makers.

There are likely to be many reasons why we have tended to ignore this issue. One possible reason may have been the perception on the part of many of those working within the drugs treatment world that their primary focus is upon the individual drug user, rather than those within the drug user's family. In addition, the focus of drug abuse policy and provision itself since the late 1980s has been orchestrated by two major concerns. First, in the late 1980s and early 1990s, too much of service providers' and policy makers' attention was taken up with the need to reduce drug users' risks of acquiring and spreading HIV infection. Second, from the late 1990s onwards, the primary concern exercising policy makers has been to reduce drug-related offending. Set alongside these major concerns, the focus upon children and families affected by drug abuse has attracted relatively little attention.

In addition, there has also been something of a reluctance on the part of the research community to focus upon addict families – perhaps in part as a result of an excessive sensitivity that such studies may be seen as an example of middle-class researchers judging the family life of others living in much less comfortable circumstances. Whatever the reason, the outcome has been that, for the most part, children within addict families have been largely ignored and rarely seen. Indeed, we have tended only to become aware of the impact of parental drug abuse on children when cases of young children living within addict households have been covered in the media as a result of their suffering serious harm (O'Brien et al, 2003). In the next section we draw upon data from one of the few UK qualitative studies to look at the impact on children of living with parents with a serious drug problem.

Living with drug dependence: parent and child perspectives

This section draws upon research in Scotland carried out by Professor Marina Barnard and Joy Barlow to look at the various aspects of dependent drug use that may have an adverse impact on parents' ability to look after their children. The research involved qualitative interviews with 62 problem drug-using parents and 36 children whose parent or parents were dependent upon illegal drugs (Barnard, 2006).

Maintaining a drug habit is for many problem drug users a demanding, expensive, dangerous and unpredictable business. Drugs impose exacting routines centred on the need to fund, find and use drugs, often two to three times a day. Children born and raised in families where one or both parents have drug problems inevitably become part of this dynamic. The effort of trying to meet the demands of a drug habit while, at the same time, attending to the equally rigorous demands of childcare is a large part of the explanation as to why these children are at serious risk of neglect and abuse. These children are not for the most part exposed to danger because they have parents who do not love them; it is because the needs of the drug habit so preoccupy the daily round that there is little left over to give the children. One of the parents interviewed in the Barnard and Barlow research succinctly made this point in the following way:

> It's not bad people that become addicts and it's not bad people that don't care about their kids that it's just people that an addiction has got a grip of and that that is more powerful than anything, even the love that a parent would have for their children, it just overrules even that. (Parent: Alexa)

The level of children's involvement in their parent's drug problem is bound up with the stability of the parent's drug use and the extent to which there are other protective adults, such as grandparents, who may be able to shield the child from exposure to all the unpredictability and danger associated with drugs. Drugs do not have to mean that a parent cannot provide a safe and caring home but to do so requires that their influence is minimised, which means that their use is stable and regular and not at the forefront of the day's routines. Where drug use is unstable and children are not shielded from this, then there is a good chance that they will have an impact on the lives of the children concerned.

The compulsivity of drugs

One of the most significant features of problem drug use is its compulsivity. It was described variously by parents as 'taking everything away from them', as 'driving them', as making them selfish and self-absorbed. A narrowly focused preoccupation with getting and using drugs was almost universally described and can be heard in the following interview extract:

> If you're taking the heroin, that's your master, know ... I don't know anybody that's been able to do it yet; take the drug and look after their family and things like that ... that's the bottom line, it just doesn't work, I've never known it to work anyway. I've seen it all over the years and I don't think there's anybody that's managed it. (Parent: Frank)

Numerous of the parents interviewed described how drugs had to have precedence within their life if they were to function at all. So that if it came to a choice between paying for drugs or buying nappies or food, the immediate priority would be to buy the drugs. Once this need was appeased then attention could turn to meeting the child's needs. This prioritising was rationalised in terms of the incapacity brought on by the drug withdrawals, which, once averted, would create the space to attend to the child. This ranking of the parent's need for the drug over and above the needs of the child has an inescapable brutality that can be quite difficult to hear, but it was central to the ways in which parents spoke about their relationship with drugs as can be heard in the following extract:

> 'Cos you only care about yourself, you think you care about everybody else but number one comes first and that's yourself and if you're lucky, if you've got anything left, they get it, but you would take it off them to give to you ... I mean at the time I wouldn't admit that, but now I would. (Parent: Jocelyn)

The physiological and psychological sense of dependency upon drugs that these parents reported meant that they routinely made choices that compromised their responsibilities towards their children's welfare.

Competing routines

The degree to which the routines of funding, finding and using drugs were intrinsically at odds with the routines of feeding, bathing, supervising, playing and generally caring for children can be illustrated by looking at just one aspect of maintaining a drug habit. Every time that drugs need to be bought, parents face a choice: do I take the child with me or do I leave the child at home? If the child is taken on the journey to buy drugs there is the uncertainty as to whether the journey will have been successful. If the drugs are not at the agreed destination then the journey must be resumed. Having reached the place where drugs can be bought the parent has to face the decision of whether to take the child inside or leave the child outside probably unsupervised:

> 'Cos a few times like, before I started dealing myself, I used to have to take him with me to go and buy and that's one thing I hated, d'you know what I mean, dragging the wean with you. Into these houses that nobody knows and they're all lying about full of it and you're like that 'phew....' but he [son] must've known, know what I mean, and then I've took him halfway along Easterhouse and down to Carntyne and trekking away up here. You'd walk for miles. Just to get something. If this person didn't have it, you'd walk to Easterhouse. If they didn't have it, you'd walk to the other side of Easterhouse. If they didn't have it, you'd go to Cranhill. I've actually walked nearly the whole of Glasgow. (Parent: Julia)

In this description one gets a sense of the relentless search that took place irrespective of what the child needed or wanted. The only positive one can draw from this is that the child was at least in the mother's care while she searched for the drugs. On the other hand, would it be a better decision to leave the child unsupervised on the basis that at least this way they would be home and their exposure to illegality (among other things) would be reduced? The obvious problem here is that where young children are left unsupervised there is the danger that something will happen to the child, as in the following case:

> I left David [three-year-old son] in the flat himself and I
> went to the next flat to, know [buy drugs]. What had
> happened was I was lying sleeping and David woke up
> before me and I had a box of matches in his baby bag. But
> I woke up and the baby bag was on fire. He'd got the
> matches, right, so but I managed to get it out, which I
> thought was out, right, and then I thought … David was
> sitting, he'd no clothes or anything on, know how he'd got
> up and took his clothes off and running about mental and
> I was still lying there sleeping…. I was like that I'll need to
> jump over to this next flat to get a bag, to get myself squared
> up so I was like that to David, right David you sit and
> watch telly, Mammy'll be back in a minute and I went out,
> so I must've been away about 10 minutes and see when I
> came back over … walked in the living room, eh, I couldn't
> have put the fire out right in the bag and the room was full
> of smoke, it was…. And David was sitting on the chair
> watching the telly and his wee eyes were all watering and
> oh the smoke … I could've killed ma wean. (Parent: Alexa)

This parent was convinced that she had not left her children
unsupervised for any length of time and perhaps she had not. However,
as the following mother recounted, keeping an accurate grasp of passing
time was difficult:

> … and scared because I left her in herself, even like during
> the day I would go away to score and I would think I
> would only be five minutes, know, and I probably wouldn't
> know this as well unless she [daughter] told me. One time
> my cousin came round to see me and she sat with the
> wean an hour and a half and that's how long I took but I
> didn't ever think I was that long, d'you know what I mean
> and she had to sit in for hours sometimes. (Parent: Morgan)

Of course, parents who have children in nursery or school are able to
use this time to secure and use drugs. However, the business of finding,
funding and using drugs would not always calibrate neatly with the
school day. Children might be left late in nursery or, more troublingly,
as in the following case, left to fend for themselves outside while
waiting for the parent's return:

> Say I went out, you know, during the day and you'd every
> intention to be back in time for him coming in from school,
> now he was only five and six, right, now some nights I
> wasn't getting back 'til six o'clock so that wean was coming
> home from school, nobody in, so he was putting his wee
> schoolbag and things underneath the hedge and going away
> and playing about the streets until I came home. And it was
> a case of I'd be away looking for my fix and couldn't go
> home until I'd got that, knowing fine well that that wean
> was up the road playing about, waiting on me coming
> back. (Parent: Hailey)

The important point in so far as this child's welfare is concerned is
that he frequently came home to a locked, empty house irrespective
of the weather, or season, or how hungry he might be. And moreover,
no one knew he was there; as his mother noted, anything could have
happened to him.

Some parents spoke of leaving the child with friends but as these
were often other drug users one has to question the likelihood that
children would be any safer in their care. Take, for example, a situation
where a non-drug-using aunt walked in on her baby niece left in the
care of a near stranger:

> One of the other times I went up, it was on a Saturday one
> weekend. I popped up unexpectedly and there was a strange
> guy in with Grace and he was sitting feeding her. When I
> asked where my sister was he said that she was away on a
> message [shopping]. I mean I didn't know him or anything
> so I just got the wean ready and took her. (Aunt: Natalie)

In the interviews with parents there were instances of children being
physically abused while left in the care of problem drug-using friends
and in two cases children were sexually abused.

One might perhaps argue that most of the problem for children
resides in the illegality of drugs. Were these drugs legalised, there would
be none of this unpredictability over supply and removing the
criminality would, among other things, mean that the cost of drugs
would be regulated. The first most obvious point is that alcohol is
legal and yet parental alcohol misuse is prominent in registrations of
child abuse and neglect cases across the UK and internationally
(Kelleher et al, 1994). Drug and alcohol problems are not reducible to
their legal status; it is the dependent nature of the relationship with

these substances that is the problem for children because in the midst of their parents' chaotic, uncontrolled use, their own needs, wants and wishes all come a long way second. A further, related, point is to consider the physiological and psychological effects of dependency. Problem drug use is characterised by mood swings that are closely connected to the body's metabolism of the drug. When withdrawing from drugs, parents are liable to be highly irritable, anxious and bad-tempered. The children interviewed in this study reported these to be tense, difficult times marked by argument and physical threat. It was at these times that they were least likely to have their needs met:

> I couldn't look after Sarah when I was strung out, I had to have drugs in me. I'd be shouting and bawling at her and a couple of times I even sort of a hit her, know I was violent. I wouldn't get her dressed or anything until I had my drugs in me, but it was a real struggle, you know to get up off the chair … so she was left to her own devices sort of a, you know, wander about the house with just underwear on, or her nightie, from the night before. (Parent: Hilary)

However, once the drug had been taken, while there might be some respite, it was not necessarily more likely that their needs would be attended to since the parent might then be physically incapacitated, at least in the first throes of its effect. These metabolic oscillations brought on by the use, or non-use, of opiate or other drugs were intrinsic to the lives of these children and part of what made their lives so unpredictable and puzzling, at least in the early years when young children would be unlikely to understand the cause of these dramatic mood swings:

> As long as I had my drugs I was happy, so everything was all happy round about, that's the way I remember it but it probably wasn't. Probably chaotic for the wean, you know. I'm thinking like 'och I'm fine' you know what I mean, once I was full of it, brand new and all that, but the wean must've known like the mood swings were going up and down, one minute Mammy's wanting to play with you all happy and the next minute she's 'GRRR', screaming at you, running you up the hall and throwing you in your room, know what I mean, and shut the door, 'STAY THERE, 'til I get something', know what I mean and then once you got it you were like that [calm] and the wean

must've been 'how is she alright now? About an hour ago she was wanting to kill me'. (Parent: Julia)

Once a parent had secured and used drugs there could be problems being sufficiently compos mentis to supervise children effectively. A number of parents spoke of serious lapses in attention, which had almost resulted in their children being harmed. This included nearly dropping babies or inadvertently setting clothes or furnishings alight with unattended lit cigarettes and, in one case, a forgotten chip pan burst into flames while the mother was fully under the effects of drugs:

> She [young daughter] would say 'watch, Mum, you've got a fag' and stuff like that and maybe I'd be sitting too close to the fire, 'watch, Mum' and like one time I went and fell asleep and I went and left a chip pan on and the place ... the whole house full of smoke and the kitchen was on fire and she was the one that woke me up.... Know, the fire brigade and the ambulance and that said 'you were very lucky to get out of that' but she didn't move from the bed until she woke me up and I kept wakening up and going 'it's alright, just go back to sleep' and she was screaming the place down, but I got her out. (Parent: Morgan)

Children's exposure to drug-related criminality

The illegalities associated with drug misuse are inevitably an integral feature of the lifestyle for parents. While parents might try to shield their children from exposure to the underworld of drug supply and its associated criminality, some contact was unavoidable. Furthermore, the high costs of buying drugs perhaps two to three times a day and the difficulties of meeting these costs through legitimate means, given the near universally reported unemployment among this sample of parents, meant that parents would have to engage in illegitimate means of income generation. Shoplifting, prostitution and drug dealing were the most likely crimes to be reported in this study. Children were either directly involved, for example, when parents took young children shoplifting using the pram to hide stolen goods and as a foil to deflect attention from their stealing, or they might be involved indirectly – where parents were using prostitution as a means of income and the child was present in the house, but not the room necessarily, where clients were brought. They were directly involved when drug dealing took place in the house as can be heard in the following mother's description of the situation her (then 18-month-old child) was exposed to:

> I mean the two of us [parents] were doing the same, leaving the needles lying about and people were coming in and saying 'is it alright if I have a hit?' And 'aye, no bother, batter in, on you go' and that's just not right.... Sometimes even the house would be full. (Parent: Angela)

Drug dealing is illegal and fraught with danger. If raids by police were not enough to contend with, there were raids made by other drug users to steal drugs by force or to collect unpaid drug debts. These were frightening and often violent events, which children in these data were party to on a number of occasions. These must have been deeply traumatic. The following, not isolated, case describes a situation where the child was used as a pawn:

> Then, the house that I was staying in, the fella was selling heroin and we got robbed at knifepoint. Now the kids were there when this happened ... the fellas that were robbing us, we knew them. This was 14 up [14th floor of a tower block] this happened, where we stayed, and they knew that there was heroin 18 up as well and they asked me to go up and chap [knock on] the door so the girl would open the door and I said 'no', so they grabbed my son Ethan with the knife and they got him to run up and chap the door but I ran with Ethan and I was saying you know 'get your hands off ma baby' and all that and there was screaming going on and everything was going on and wee Ethan was screaming and I'm pulling Ethan and they were pulling Ethan and I'm saying 'get your hands off my son' and the wean chapped the door and I've grabbed him and ran right down the stairs with him. (Parent: Nicky)

The drama of these children's lives is perhaps the most easily grasped dimension of the problems they face in growing up. The instability, the danger, the hunger, the lack of routine; these are tangible and to an extent measurable deficits. However, to our minds the emotional and social developmental costs of living with parental drug problems, while much less easily appreciated, are also those most likely to have scarred these young lives most deeply. The next section uses accounts both from parents and children to describe the hidden harm.

The hidden harm

> When my Mum is using drugs it just makes me feel as if I
> am here myself – not got anyone else here. (Child of drug-
> using parents: Jenny, aged 15)

Virtually all of the children and young people interviewed in this
study shared the sense that their needs and interests had all been
sidelined by their parents' preoccupation with drugs. They might
understand addiction as a kind of illness and as a powerful force but
they were hurt, confused and angered by the degree to which it took
their parents' attention and resources. Drugs excluded them from what
they took to be their rightful place at the centre of their parents' lives.
They could not rely on their parents to provide for them and this
most mundane lack was important in signalling their lesser place relative
to drugs. Take, for example, the following girl's account of making up
stories to her friends about her family life:

Respondent:	I used to make up stories about when I was younger and all that in school.... Aye, I just used to ... I just blocked all that out, totally.
Interviewer:	And why did you do that?
Respondent:	'Cos I heard everybody else talking about when they were wee and their Mas used to take them here and they would do this and they'd be talking to their Mums and they were saying 'aye, when you were a wee lassie you used to do this', kinda thing, and you were dead quiet so I just used to make it all up. (Child of drug-using parent: Jan, aged14)

Her fictitious family life is so modest, it is just a family doing things
together, but so far from her own family experience that she had to
make it up. Something of the same can be heard in the following
mother's account of her son's appreciation of the ordinary now that
she has stabilised on methadone:

> He [nine-year-old son] goes places; me and him joined
> the Sports Centre together, we go there, know, we got to
> the swimming and things, he goes to dancing every week

> ... and what he'll say to my Mum is 'oh Nanna I'd hate to
> go back to staying the way we stayed when we were in
> Govanhill'. And he remembers it all. He'll say, em, 'you
> used to think it was great Ma when you came home and
> you would give me like a pound or two pound and say
> "right, to the chippy and get yourself something"'. He says
> 'but I didn't want the chippy, I wanted you to be in for me
> coming home from school and making ma dinner', you
> know. (Parent: Brenda)

Having your dinner cooked for you, having boundaries on behaviour;
these most mundane aspects of childcare were routinely cited by these
children and young people as being important markers of the care
they wanted and needed. The distance between these expectations
and the lives they lived in the shadow of drugs was great. As children,
however, they were very largely powerless to do much about it, as the
following young girl makes clear:

> You can't do nothing about it, you can't go ... leave home
> or nothing, you just can't say 'that's not right', you can't be
> doing that, 'I'm not for any of that', you can't say that ...
> 'cos like a 10-year-old saying that, you wouldn't say that.
> (Child of drug-using parent: Susan, aged 14)

The dependence of children and, relatedly, their fear of separation
from their parents serve to lock them into silence over their
circumstances. Most of these children and young people avoided any
mention of drugs in their lives, which served to keep the harm hidden.
However, it was also the case that other adults, often in the caring
professions, had on occasion strayed into their lives but they had on
the whole not seen them, usually because the focus had been on the
adult. One young man described the small army of drug and social
workers who had passed through his family door but had never engaged
with him as a child. His interpretation 'I thought no one cared – after
all, you all knew but did nothing to help' is a salutary reminder of how
children can remain invisible, even when we think we see.

Meeting the needs of children within drug-dependent families

Within these data extracts it is very easy to see the deeply negative
impact that parental drug addiction can have upon young children.

Whenever stories of child neglect involving addict parents appear in the press there are likely to be calls made for the removal of children from the care of dependent drug-using parents. Clearly, it is neither desirable nor possible to remove all or even most of the estimated 350,000 children within the UK with one or both parents dependent on illegal drugs. As a result, there is little doubt that whatever the greater recognition of the impact of parental drug use on children, still the majority of these children will remain with their addict parents. In the course of determining how and at what point to intervene within drug-dependent families, social work and other staff will be called upon to make judgements in relation to some of the thorniest issues they are likely to face in their careers, namely how much adversity is it tolerable for children to experience at the hands of their addict parents?

It is easy to make absolute judgements in this area – easy and pretty near pointless. It is also easy to exercise the wisdom of hindsight when something goes wrong. Whenever a social worker is confronted by a child who may be experiencing serious harm from parental drug use they will inevitably assess that child alongside other children whose need may be even more urgent. In making a judgement about how bad things are for children, social work and drug treatment staff have to assess the addict parents' drug problem and the danger posed to their children. There is a temptation, however, for drug treatment services to be reassured by addicts' claims that they are making progress. But even if addicts reduce their illegal drug use, their children can still be suffering enormously. Social work and other staff need to continually ask themselves whether the improvements they are seeing in the addicts are being translated into benefits for the child. Paradoxically, those children whose parents are recovering from their drug addiction may be even more traumatised than those children whose parents' drug use remains much more consistent. Why might this be the case? We know that recovery from dependent drug use often involves significant periods of relapse. If a child starts to glimpse the parent behind the drug use and starts to build a more healthy relationship with the adult during a period of recovery, it is likely to be much more upsetting for the child when, as often happens, the addict slips back into a pattern of chaotic drug use. Upsetting or not, relapse is an ever-present feature of the recovery process.

If social work and drug treatment staff are going to help children in addict families they need to treat addicts' claims of improved behaviour with a degree of healthy scepticism. They also need to make sure that they see and speak with the children involved. But here there is a further major problem. Interviewing children about parental drug misuse is extraordinarily difficult. In the Barnard and Barlow research, children found it extraordinarily hard to talk about the impact of their parents' drug use on their lives. For many of the children, their parents – neglectful or not – were still the adults that they looked to for support and care and they were fiercely loyal to them. Social work staff will need, then, to be enormously skilled to get an accurate picture of what these children may be going through. Frequently they will need to interpret not the flow of words but the silences within the children's accounts to get a picture of what they are going through. This is a world, then, more glimpsed than forensically examined, within which reassurances, broken trust and great anxiety will shape children's faltering narratives.

If services are going to intervene earlier, as many have said they should, this will in itself present social work staff with a further serious challenge: they may be intervening not on the basis of clear evidence of serious harm that has already occurred to children, but on the probability that children are going to experience such harm at some point in the near future. And these judgements may have to be justified in court proceedings. In the past, drug users and their families have rarely challenged the legality of social work decisions to remove children temporarily or permanently. But if the number of children being removed were to increase, there is no certainty that these challenges might not occur in the future.

Judgements about prospective harm are very difficult. But workers also have to assess what benefits support, or even removal, can offer. At the moment these complex judgements are being made on the basis of very little clear evidence as to the different likely outcomes for children either being left with or removed from their addict parents. It is often said that the outcomes for children in residential care are often the least good. The challenge for all of those working in this area, however, is to ensure that we can offer the most vulnerable of these children a quality of care that is better than the neglect or chaos they will have been experiencing while living with their drug-addicted parents. Research in this area, as in so many others, has been seen as a bit of a luxury – something that one can do without while responding to the crisis that is unfolding. If we are asking social work staff and others to make these life-changing decisions, we should ensure that they have access to the best evidence as to when to intervene, how to intervene and the likely outcomes of their interventions within families. At the moment that evidence is sorely lacking.

References

ACMD (Advisory Council on the Misuse of Drugs) (2003) *'Hidden Harm': Responding to the Needs of Children of Problem Drug Users; The Report of an Inquiry by the Advisory Council on the Misuse of Drugs*, London: Home Office.

Barnard, M. (2006) *Drugs in the Family: The Impact on Children and Families*, London: Jessica Kingsley Publishers.

Kelleher, K., Chaffin, M., Hollenberg, J. and Fischer, E. (1994) 'Alcohol and drug disorders among physically abusive and neglectful parents in a community-based sample', *American Journal of Public Health*, vol 84, no 10, pp 1586-90.

O'Brien, S., Hammond, H. and McKinnon, H. (2003) *Report of the Caleb Ness Inquiry*, Edinburgh: Edinburgh and Lothians Child Protection Committee.

Scottish Executive (2003) *Getting out Priorities Right: Policy and Practice Guidelines for Working with Children and Families Affected by Problem Drug Use*, Edinburgh: Scottish Executive.

Scottish Executive (2006) *Hidden Harm: Next Steps, Supporting Children – Working With Parents*, Edinburgh: Scottish Executive.

NINE

Lives at risk: multiculturalism, young women and 'honour' killings

Veena Meetoo and Heidi Safia Mirza

Introduction

Following the media coverage of several murders of ethnicised[1] young women, risks associated with gender-related violence in minority ethnic communities in Britain are high on the public and political agenda (Gill, 2003; CPS, 2004). Why are the risks faced by young ethnicised women being highlighted by national and local mainstream agencies now? In this chapter we aim to unpack how risks that some young women face are constructed and heightened in the current climate of risk in relation to multiculturalism and Islamophobia in Britain. We argue that young women from some minority ethnic communities living in the UK are exposed to particular forms of risk. As gendered subjects they experience greater risk within both the cultural relativism of the British multicultural discourse and the private–public divide that characterises the domestic violence discourse. Multiculturalism, which is underpinned by notions of 'respecting diversity and valuing cultural difference', has for the most part engendered non-intervention when dealing with domestic violence rooted in cultural and religious practices in the private sphere of the home. However, in this chapter we also suggest that young women's risk is heightened because they 'slip through the cracks' of the multicultural discourse. Since 11 September and the 7 July bombings in Britain, young ethnicised women have become highly visible, but now they are contained and constructed in the public consciousness within a discourse of fear and risk posed by the presence of the Muslim alien 'other'.

It is said that we are living in a 'risk society', however in the case of ethnicised young women and honour killings we have to be cautious of what risks are being selected for public attention and what risks are being marginalised. It is argued that risk theory pays insufficient attention to the role played by gender, age, social class, 'race', ethnicity and nationality in constructing differing forms of risk knowledge and experiences (Adam and van Loon, 2000). Lash (1993) suggests that we need to consider the way in which people respond to risk as members of cultural subgroups rather than as atomised individuals. He asserts the importance of understanding group membership, traditional conventions and social categories in structuring our moral values, assumptions and practices in responses to risk. Thus, in this chapter we use honour killings as a means to highlight the way domestic violence *as a global risk to all women* has become racialised in the British multicultural context and examine the consequences of this.

The cultural context of honour killings

Honour killings have been defined as 'the killing of women for suspected deviation from sexual norms imposed by society' (Faqir, 2001, p 66). Honour killings are extreme acts of violence upon a woman when an honour code is believed to have been broken and perceived shame is brought upon the family. Women can also carry the risk for the shame of male violations of their sexual honour and have been killed because they have fallen pregnant as victims of incest and rape. Being suspected of sexual deviancy such as pregnancy outside marriage or adulterous behaviour is also seen as enough to justify punishing a woman. What marks so-called honour killings is that it is not just the husband or partner that may carry out the act, but also sometimes the community and other family members such as mothers, brothers, uncles and cousins.

Gendered violence is not normally perceived as a global risk although systematic violence against women and in particular honour killings have been widely reported. The United Nations (UN) estimates that 5,000 women are being killed each year in the name of honour (UNFPA, 2000). Honour killings have been documented in Bangladesh, Brazil, Ecuador, Egypt, India, Israel, Italy, Jordan, Morocco, Pakistan, Sweden, Turkey, Uganda and the UK (Sajid, 2003). While more than 100 women are killed by their partners in England and Wales every year, the Metropolitan Police estimates that there have been approximately 12 honour killings across Sikh, Muslim and Christian communities (Gupta, 2003). Southall Black Sisters, a campaigning group for the rights of minority ethnic women, deal with over 2,500 cases of domestic violence a year and report over 20 honour killings in the UK since 2001 (RWA, 2003). While many of these reported cases come from the Pakistani, South Asian and Kurdish communities, African and Caribbean women are also affected by crimes of honour (RWA, 2003). In this sense the experience of violence or that of honour is not confined to women in Asian communities, or the preserve of Muslim communities. However, in the UK, honour killing as a specific phenomenon is perceived by the media and government agencies as a crime that is practised only among certain minority ethnic groups. Thus, honour killing as domestic violence has become ethnicised within the British multicultural context.

Media reports frame the popular discourse on honour killings in Britain. These reports are often sensationalised, focusing on the individual family and their barbarity and senselessness. They also suggest that it is often younger women in their late teens and early twenties who are victims of this crime. At this age young women's emerging sexuality comes under increasing regulation and control by the family and wider community. It is the young woman's sexual purity and honour that is seen to define the status and regard with which the family is held in the community. One such case is that of Heshu Yones who at age 16 was murdered in 2002 by her Kurdish father in West London as he feared she was becoming too westernised. Rukhsana Naz, age 19, was murdered by her brother and mother in 1998 because she was expecting an illegitimate child. To the mother, Rukhsana was guilty of insult to the honour or 'izzat' of her family. She was held down by her mother and strangled by her brother. There is the well-known case of Zena Briggs. Zena declined to marry a cousin in Pakistan and ran away with her English boyfriend. Her family hired professional 'bounty hunters' and hitmen from within their community to track down both her and her boyfriend. A television documentary was made and the couple are still in hiding after several years.

Hannana Siddiqui of Southall Black Sisters argues that using the term 'honour' is a misnomer. 'The crimes themselves are dishonourable: they are merely justified by the perpetrator, and wider community, in the name of honour' (RWA, 2003, p 6). In this sense, honour crimes are essentially a justification for male violence and essentially about domestic violence. However, only in relation to religious and ethnic communities is the concept of honour invoked as motivation for domestic violence, or a reason why women are unable to escape domestic violence. The concept of honour plays a part in perpetuating violence against women in two ways. On the one hand, it is used by the perpetrator as an excuse or a mitigating factor when they commit acts of violence against women. As Siddiqui argues, 'The State thinks that honour crimes are about cultural beliefs that they should not criticise. Implicitly this means the state accepts honour as a mitigating factor and condones crimes perpetrated in the name of it' (RWA, 2003, p 6). On the other hand, from the perspective of the women themselves the concept works differently. What is particular about the concept of 'honour' and the fear of 'shame' is that it isolates women and this results in preventing them seeking outside help when affected by domestic violence. Women fear punishment for having brought shame on the family or community honour, and they can suffer anything from social ostracism, to acts of violence, or, as in the cases cited here, murder itself.

Focusing on culturally specific forms of domestic violence is often seen as very controversial ground. As a counter to the racist assertion that black and Asian men are more barbaric, Gupta (2003) argues that it is important to take a global perspective on domestic violence and see honour killing as part of a wider global patriarchal phenomenon of violence. The problem of femicide is not particular to one culture or religious group or community. Women are beaten and murdered across the globe for similar reasons. Gupta argues that domestic violence cuts across class, 'race', religion and age. Patriarchal structures use violence extensively to subjugate women in different forms in relation to class, 'race' and ethnicity – it is not an issue of racial or ethnic differences.

By highlighting domestic violence issues in specific cultural and religious ethnic communities in the UK are we at risk of stereotyping these communities as backward and barbaric? Does this place a disproportionate gaze on the 'other' woman – racialising her, separating out this form of domestic violence as a special cultural phenomenon needing special cultural sensitivity? These questions lie at the heart of understanding the tensions between recognising gender oppression and preserving multicultural difference. This debate has been raised in relationship to other practices such as female genital mutilation and forced marriages, where the sanctity of (male) community rights is privileged over the bodily rights of individual (female) victims when the cultural context is brought to bear (Beckett and Macey, 2001).

Domestic violence, gender and the contradictions of British multiculturalism

How then do professionals and social services relate to young women at risk of violence, abuse and death in the context of the discourse of multiculturalism in Britain? Perhaps most importantly in the case of honour killings, is the way in which multiculturalism is predicated upon a laissez-faire approach to gendered cultural difference.

Multiculturalism in the UK is a contested term meaning different things to different people (Hall, 2000). It is often used loosely in political discourse to affirm the distinctness, uniqueness and individual validity of different cultures, groups or communities, and also recognises the importance of acknowledging and accommodating these differences and distinctness (Fisher, 2004). The Commission on the Future of Multi-Ethnic Britain (Runnymede Trust, 2000) highlighted a need to move towards a multicultural post-nation in which Britain would be a 'community of communities', in which we have shared values, but also the autonomy of cultural expression to wear the Muslim Hijab headscarf or eat Halal meat. State intervention, policy and professional discourse in the UK are predicated upon a loose and historically haphazard notion of what Hall (2000) has called 'multicultural drift'. Here multicultural policies have been piecemeal and based on concessions, extensions and exemptions such as scheduling exams to avoid key festivals for various religious groups, Sikhs being exempt from wearing helmets, and slaughterhouses for Jews and Muslims (Harris, 2001).

However, multiculturalism as it has evolved in the British context is also deeply racialised (Hesse, 2000). While liberal multiculturalism is popularly and politically conceived as celebrating diversity and 'tolerating' different cultural and religious values between groups, the notion of mutual tolerance is fragile. Multiculturalism in this sense is 'skin deep', and it works only if the demands of visible and distinct ethnic groups are not too 'different' and not too rejecting of the welcoming embrace of the 'host' society (Ahmed, 2004). In the face of growing racist political rhetoric, Islamophobia and anti-asylum and immigration policies in the UK, we are witnessing a retreat from multiculturalism and a move towards 'civic integration'. As part of the civic integration agenda newcomers have to swear an oath at ceremonies, meet the toughening of the English language requirement when acquiring British citizenship and accept mandatory citizenship and democracy education at English schools (Joppke, 2004). In the context of racial unrest and ethnic segregation in the mainly Muslim Northern Towns in Britain in 2001, 'social cohesion' and 'civic integration' has become the new discourse on multiculturalism (Bhavnani et al, 2005). Social cohesion emphasises 'building bridges' between segregated communities through interfaith and cultural understanding, legitimating the link between citizenship and nationhood as essential for multicultural coexistence. Integration and active citizenship are now seen as the solution to economic inequality, political representation and structural segregation in housing and education, which are the core issues of racial unrest.

However, gender differences within the multicultural discourse both now and in the past have yet to be recognised (Okin, 1999). In the 314-page *Commission on the Future of Multi-Ethnic Britain* report (Runnymede Trust, 2000), women get a three-page mention (Mirza, 2003). The Community Cohesion report (Home Office, 2001) fails to look at the specificity of gendered social action (Bhavnani et al, 2005). A gender-blind multicultural discourse means that women remain invisible, locked into the private sphere where the gender-oppressive cultural and religious practices are still played out. To understand the invisibility of gender and violence in multicultural discourse we need to look at the way in which ethnicity has become reified and essentialised in the western construction of difference (Fisher, 2004). Yuval Davis (1997) calls this process of reification 'ethnic fundamentalism'. Here ethnic group identity becomes defensive, constructed in fixed 'immutable collectivity boundaries'. The inherent cultural reductionism in multiculturalist discourse not only assumes cultural homogeneity among local communities, with each one spatially segregated, but it also means we cannot talk about racial difference and hierarchies of cultures as it is politically incorrect (Stolcke, 1995). As a consequence of this culturalist tendency in political discourse, the exclusion of minority ethnic groups, and especially women, is legitimated through insensitive multicultural policies that locate them in marginal spaces, on the periphery of decision making both politically and in terms of policy (Bhavnani et al, 2005). Such reductionism fails to see the intersectionality of structural inequalities that affect all women, including an understanding of the interrelationship between global patriarchy, racism and domestic violence (Williams Crenshaw, 1994).

Liberal multiculturalism in the UK has functioned to privilege 'race' and ethnicity over gender, in that the focus on racialised position rather than gender has paradoxically given rise to some acute cases of women's exclusion from services (Burman and Chantler, 2004). Women from minority ethnic communities can lack protection because organisations are fearful of being seen as racist when taking a positive stance in relation to culturally specific problems such as honour crimes. Elders and patriarchal leaders of many minority ethnic communities have used the liberal discourse of multiculturalism as a means of localised empowerment although claiming to be the vanguards of women's traditional honour codes. They often act as gatekeepers between minority and majority communities. As Johal (2003) argues, if the state colludes with community leaders, what kind of protection can women expect from the state?

Sanctuary and services: risk, social policy and the multicultural malaise

In a climate of increasing personal responsibility for risk, how then do professionals and services relate to young women at risk of violence, abuse and death in the context of the discourse of multiculturalism in Britain? In social policy more generally the individual has become more accountable as social problems are reconstructed as individual choices and responsibilities (Kemshall, 2002). When risk is used in relation to particular ethnic groups, it has been deployed in terms of identifying which ethnic groups are more at risk from, say, cultural habits and diets for which the individual is responsible (Nazroo, 2003). The danger of this individualisation, as well as racialisation, of ethnic groups, is that social inequalities remain hidden and collective responses de-legitimated. So risks often replace references to inequalities associated with social class, 'race' and gender and their manifestations more locally (Adam and van Loon, 2000).

In the case of domestic violence, honour killings and the risk faced by young ethnicised women, the tendency to individualisation and accountability in the discourse on risk, along with a laissez-faire multicultural approach to dealing with violent gendered cultural practices within the private domestic sphere of the ethnicised family, can exacerbate non-interventionism. An overly sensitive multicultural approach can often lead to negative action or inaction and can replicate structures of oppression within communities. Based on primary research with healthcare physicians, Puri (2005) cites cases where general practitioners breached confidentiality by telling the family of the woman of her injuries. One general practitioner did not know how to handle a patient's 'cultural baggage' and allowed the patient's husband to stay for his wife's physical examination. As Burman et al (2004) argue, community networks are usually seen as a support mechanism in minority ethnic communities but for some women in violent and life-threatening situations, they can be followed and caught through their community networks, which may make them reluctant to approach community organisations.

Black and minority ethnic women's groups have been central in raising awareness and tackling problems related to domestic violence, sexuality and cultural and religious conservatism within specific communities and groups (Gill and Rehman, 2004). For over 20 years organisations such as the Newham Asian Women's Project (NAWP), Southall Black Sisters (SBS) and the Refugee Women's Association (RWA), to name but a few, have contributed to placing minority ethnic women's issues on the agenda. Thus, various services have been developed as a result of struggle by these groups. A multicultural approach to service provision has meant more involvement of different communities, and this has taken the form of multi-agency work. But despite these struggles by women's groups, male community leaders are still influential within the communities. Ali Jan Haider, a Muslim social worker, relates how male family and community elders personally threatened him and his family when he helped a 21-year-old woman and her five children escape domestic violence and placed her in a refuge. The young woman, when aged 16, had come to the UK from the rural Mirpur district of Pakistan and had been subjected to persistent physical and mental abuse at the hands of her husband and her in-laws for several years. He explains the consequences of his actions:

> ... the community interference began in earnest. I had a phone call from a local Asian councillor asking me if I could explain why I had taken mum and children away and broken up this respectable family. I then had phone calls and visits from countless community elders including a local religious leader. He did not waste any time castigating my actions and telling me what I had done was sinful. He told me how I should be personally held responsible for the family's loss of face, and the distress I had caused them. (Haider, 2003, p 4)

Haider explains the complex interrelationship and confusion between the Muslim religion and Pakistani culture on the one hand and the practice of the social services and his white and non-Muslim colleagues on the other. This confusion often leads to inaction and resistance, preventing Muslim women from seeking out help when they most need it.

Gender, Islam and the racialisation of risk

Post-11 September, risks associated with gender-related violence are on the public and political agenda.[2] However, this raises the question, 'what is behind this growing concern for the hitherto invisible and marginalised "ethnic woman"?'. Mary Douglas (1992) suggests that some risks are selected for concern in particular times, and constructed and legitimated for public attention. She argues that risks are chosen for their usefulness to the social system. Beck (1992) also argues that risk is malleable and open to social definition and construction. He was aware that the elite, such as the media, scientists, politicians and the legal profession, can define and legitimate risk. The mass media have a big part to play in public perception of risk. It is a filter in the way lay people and experts receive news and interpret events (Gabe, 1995). Questions should repeatedly be asked such as whose definition of risk is accepted, and how has the perception of risk been constructed? How are some risks selected for concern and how are they legitimated for public attention? In the case of violence to young ethnicised, and in particular Muslim, women, the question arises as to why their risks are selected for attention over others right now?

While the increased attention given to honour killings in the media has opened up the issue of individual human rights for these women, it has also had the effect of exacerbating Islamophobia and fear of the 'other'. Honour killings have become associated with Islam and the risk of terrorism in our midst. Thus, honour-based crimes need to be seen within the current climate of Islamophobia. Fekete (2004) has written of the climate of claimed global threat to security from Islamic extremism. We are living in a time when it is not just a case of fear from 'outsiders' but also from those within. Resident Muslim and Asian citizens within western countries are now under the spotlight. The current discourse on 'others' is about the threat that multicultural policies pose to core values, cultural homogeneity and social cohesion. To minimise the risk of threat we now have increased citizenship laws and security legislation, the introduction of compulsory language and civic tests for citizenship applicants, and codes of conduct for trustees of mosques.

Honour killings when reported in the British press are often sensationalist, which puts the gaze on the 'other' (Majid and Hanif, 2003). The young woman is constructed as either a romantic heroine, struggling for the benefits of the 'West' against her cruel and inhuman father and family, or a victim, succumbing to her backward and traditional 'eastern' culture (Puwar, 2003). Parallels can be drawn to colonial times where women's bodies were part of the debate over the civilising mission. The British abolition of sati, the practice of widow burning in India, was a case of the heroic white male colonists 'saving brown women from brown men' (Spivak, 1988, p 299). In current discourse, the gaze, as ever, is on the woman. As heated public debate on the matter of Muslim women wearing the face veil demonstrates (Bunting, 2006), her vulnerable yet overdetermined body has become symbolic in the battle against Islam and the barbaric 'other' (Dwyer, 1999). But unlike in colonial times, the woman is not 'saved' within the concurrent competing discourses of Islamophobia and multiculturalism. The visibility of community and group cultural practices conveniently contributes to the further construction of the 'other's' barbaric customs and cultures (Said, 1985).

While honour killings are real in *effect*, in that women are brutally murdered, they are also constructed as an ethnicised phenomenon within the racialised multicultural discourse and are, as such, also an *affect* of this discourse. In this regard the media reports have a real consequence. They contribute to putting women at risk through sensationalising these crimes through their style and content of reporting, which results in voyeuristic spectacle (cries of 'how dreadful!') followed by multicultural paralysis and inaction ('nothing to do with us! It is part of their culture').

Sensationalist images and analysis are frequently used in the media, as are generalised and simplified explanations of honour crimes (CIMEL/Interights, 2001). By not acting in conjunction with human rights activists, women's groups and academics, the mainstream media collude to undermine the subjectivity and agency of the marginal ethnicised woman. In what Mohanty (1988) has called the 'latent ethnocentrism' of the West, the women are presented as voiceless, stereotyped, racialised victims rather than active agents working to determine and engage their rights as individuals. Such sexualised objectification of ethnicised women disavows the relationship of gender, power and patriarchy within the negative social construction of Islamophobia.

Conclusion: minimising gendered and racialised risk through human rights

If risk is democratising in its universal effects (Beck, 1992) then why do the old modernist categories of 'race', ethnicity, age, gender and social class still play such an important part in understanding people's responses or non-responses to risk? In this chapter we argue that risk for some is not recognised depending on who you are. The risk of gendered violence is not perceived as a global threat like other risks. Furthermore, for women, gendered violence has become ethnicised in the context of the cultural relativism inherent within the discourse of multiculturalism.

Phoenix (1996) suggests that there is a normative absence/pathological presence response with regard to women from ethnicised communities. Indeed, ethnicised women are caught up in a collision of discourses. They are visible and yet pathologised as victims in relation to the negative media attention in the current discourse of Islamophobia. However, these women at the same time are largely absent in the normative discourse on domestic violence in the West (Carby, 1982). Many young women from minority ethnic communities are at risk of not being fully protected by the state as equal citizens as they are invisible. Within the discourse of multiculturalism, women 'fall between the cracks'. In this discourse 'race' and ethnicity are prioritised and gender differences and inequalities are rendered invisible. However, the killing of women must never be seen as a cultural matter, but always as a human rights issue (Salim, 2003). The power struggle between community leaders and women's groups within a multicultural policy framework needs to be reassessed in terms of with whom agencies should be working and consulting. Questions such as who is getting marginalised and by whom should be asked repeatedly.

The state's response to domestic violence in minority ethnic communities has been slow, as experienced first-hand by women's organisations such as the Southall Black Sisters where the police until recently have lacked interest or even been hostile to such cases. Women's campaigning organisations have highlighted how immigration law continues to sideline women who may be fleeing a violent domestic situation, as gendered risk is not recognised as grounds for asylum (RWA, 2003). The burden of proof is so onerous on women who have been raped, sexually threatened or forced to marry that they would often rather face death or incarceration than be publicly shamed (FCO, 2000).

If honour killings and forced marriage as forms of domestic abuse and violence are constructed as ethnicised problems, it can create not only multicultural marginalisation but also racist backlash. While the intersectionality of 'race', class and gender power dynamics produces culturally specific manifestations of domestic violence that are important to acknowledge and address in local service delivery, the responses and funding should be mainstreamed into informing domestic violence interventions more generally. Policies such as not putting non-English-speaking women into white-run refuges because of a perceived lack of 'cultural fit' can leave desperate women without care or shelter (Williams Crenshaw, 1994). At the same time it is important to black and Asian women's empowerment to be in a domestic violence project that enables their equal participation and values their decision making (Gill and Rehman, 2004). The climate that multiculturalism has produced in relation to racism is one of 'walking on eggshells' where cultural differences are respected, often without question, for fear of not offending communities and ethnic groups. In these situations young minority ethnic women can suffer from a lack of protection because organisations that deal with their protection are fearful of being seen as racist, or feel they lack the cultural expertise, or cannot access ring-fenced specialist funding.

In 1995 the Beijing Platform for Action resulted in the declaration that culture, tradition and religion could not be used by the state to avoid its obligation to protect women (Kelly, 2005). At a roundtable held to address the issue of honour crimes held by CIMEL (Centre for Islamic and Middle Eastern Law) and Interights (2001), it was recommended to raise honour crimes as a human rights violation before as many UN human rights bodies as possible. An effective human rights approach would include concerns from each country about sexuality, patriarchy and sexual autonomy. With the appropriate enforcement of the Human Rights Act in the UK in 2000, it could be possible to move away from the 'gender trap' of cultural relativism inherent within liberal democratic discourse on multiculturalism, and challenge the false dichotomy between community and women, where women are placed outside of the community. Such an approach would call for a redefinition of community, citizenship and the individual and in so doing we can begin to address the injustice of culturally endorsed domestic violence and so honour the memory of the young women who have been so brutally killed.

Notes

[1] We use the term 'ethnicised women' in preference to the official and much-contested term 'black and minority ethnic women' (Bhavnani et al, 2005). While the latter term denotes the social construction of difference through visible racial (black) and cultural (ethnic) markers, it does not emphasise the *process* of racial objectification implied by the former term, which, we suggest, frames the women's experience. Thus, *being or becoming* 'ethnicised' brings into play the power relations that inform and structure the gaze of the 'other'. Despite women's agency and activism, women deemed as the 'other' are often 'ethnicised' or typified by the media and state agencies in terms of their perceived (backward) cultural and religious practices.

[2] When war was declared on Afghanistan in 2001 in response to 11 September, Cherie Blair and Laura Bush, the wives of the UK Prime Minister and US President, took up the issue of 'Taliban oppression of women and children in Afghanistan' (*The Telegraph*, 2001). Holding

special meetings in 10 Downing Street to 'give back a voice' to Afghani women, Cherie Blair chose to spotlight the 'shocking and inspiring stories' of the women and raise charitable funds for the cause (*The Guardian*, 2001).

References

Adam, B. and van Loon, J. (2000) 'Repositioning risk: the challenge for social theory', in B. Adam, U. Beck and J. van Loost (eds) *The Risk Society and Beyond: Critical Issues for Social Theory*, London: Sage Publications, pp 1-31.

Ahmed, S. (2004) *The Cultural Politics of Emotions*, Edinburgh: Edinburgh University Press.

Beck, U. (1992) *Risk Society: Towards a New Modernity*, London: Sage Publications.

Beckett, C. and Macey, M. (2001) 'Race, gender and sexuality: the oppression of multiculturalism', *Women's Studies International Forum*, vol 24, no 3/4, pp 309-19.

Bhavnani, R., Mirza, H. S. and Meetoo, V. (2005) *Tackling the Roots of Racism: Lessons for Success*, Bristol: The Policy Press.

Bunting, M. (2006) 'Straw's storm of prejudice', *The Guardian Unlimited Weekly*, 13 October.

Burman, E. and Chantler, K. (2004) 'There's no place like home: emotional geographies of researching 'race' and refuge provision in Britain', *Gender, Place and Culture*, vol 11, no 3, pp 375-97.

Burman, E., Smailes, S. L. and Chantler, K. (2004) '"Culture' as a barrier to service provision and delivery: domestic violence services for minoritized women', *Critical Social Policy*, vol 24, no 3, pp 332-57.

Carby, H. (1982) 'White women listen! Black feminism and the boundaries of sisterhood', in Centre for Contemporary Cultural Studies, *The Empire Strikes Back: Race and Racism in 70s Britain*, London: Hutchinson, pp 212-33.

CIMEL (Centre for Islamic and Middle Eastern Law)/Interights (2001) *Roundtable on Strategies to Address 'Crimes Of Honour': Summary Report*, Occasional Paper No. 12, November, London: Women Living Under Muslim Laws (WLUML), available at: www.wluml.org/english/pubs/pdf/occpaper/OCP-12.pdf

CPS (Crown Prosecution Service) (2004) 'London honour killings six a year', available at: www.cps.gov.uk/london/cps_london_news/honour_crimes_conference/

Douglas, M. (1992) *Risk and Blame: Essays in Cultural Theory*, London: Routledge.

Dwyer, C. (1999) 'Veiled meanings: young British Muslim women and the negotiation of difference', *Gender, Place and Culture*, vol 6, no 1, pp 5-26.

Faqir, F. (2001) 'Intrafamily femicide in defence of honour: the case of Jordan', *Third World Quarterly*, vol 22, no 1, pp 65-82.

FCO (Foreign and Commonwealth Office) (2000) *A Choice by Right: Working Group on Forced Marriage*, available at: www.fco.gov.uk

Fekete, L. (2004) 'Anti-Muslim racism and the European security state', *Race and Class*, vol 46, no 1, pp 3-29.

Fisher, L. (2004) 'State of the art: multiculturalism, gender and cultural identities', *European Journal of Women's Studies*, vol 11, no 1, pp 111-19.

Gabe, J. (1995) *Medicine, Health and Risk: Sociological Approaches*, Oxford: Blackwell.

Gill, A. (2003) 'A question of honour', *Community Care*, 27 March, available at: www.communitycare.co.uk/articles/

Gill, A. and Rehman, G. (2004) 'Empowerment through activism: responding to domestic violence in the South Asian Community in London', *Gender and Development*, vol 12, no 1, pp 75-82.

Guardian, The (2001) 'Cherie Blair pleads for Afghan women', 20 November.

Gupta, R. (2003) 'A veil drawn over brutal crimes', *The Guardian*, 3 October.

Haider, A. J. (2003) 'Domestic violence: an Islamic perspective', Paper presented to the conference 'Tackling Domestic Violence in the Asian Community', Cardiff, September, Alijanhaider@hotmail.com

Hall, S. (2000) 'The multicultural question', in B. Hesse (ed) *Un/Settled Multiculturalisms: Diasporas, Entanglements, 'Transruptions'*, London: Zed Books, pp 209-41.

Harris, C. (2001) 'Beyond multiculturalism: difference, recognition and social justice', *Patterns of Prejudice*, vol 35, no 1, pp 13-34.

Hesse, B. (ed) (2000) *Un/Settled Multiculturalisms: Diasporas, Entanglements, Transruptions*, London: Zed Books.

Home Office (2001) *Community Cohesion: A Report of the Independent Review Team, chaired by Ted Cantle*, London: Home Office.

Johal, A. (2003) 'Struggle not submission: domestic violence in the 1990s', in R. Gupta (ed) *From Homebreakers to Jailbreakers*, London: Zed Books, pp 28-50.

Joppke, C. (2004) 'The retreat of multiculturalism in the liberal state: theory and policy', *The British Journal of Sociology*, vol 55, no 2, pp 237-57.

Kelly, L. (2005) 'Inside outsiders: mainstreaming violence against women into human rights discourse and practice', *International Feminist Journal of Politics*, vol 7, no 4, pp 471-95.

Kemshall, H. (2002) *Risk, Social Policy and Welfare*, Buckingham: Open University Press.

Lash, S. (1993) 'Reflexive modernisation: the aesthetic dimension', *Theory, Culture and Society*, no 10, pp 1-23.

Majid, R. and Hanif, S. (2003) *Language, Power and Honour: Using Murder to Demonise Muslims*, October, Wembley: Islamic Human Rights Commission, available at: www.ihrc.org

Mirza, H.S. (2003) "All the women are white, all the blacks are men – but some of us are brave': mapping the consequences of the invisibility for black and minority ethnic women in Britain', in D. Mason (ed) *Explaining Ethnic Differences: Changing Patterns of Disadvantage in Britain*, Bristol: The Policy Press, pp 121-38.

Mohanty, C. T. (1988) 'Under western eyes: feminist scholarship and colonial discourses', *Feminist Review*, no 30, pp 65-88.

Nazroo, J. (2003) 'Patterns and explanations for ethnic inequalities in health', in D. Mason (ed) *Explaining Ethnic Differences: Changing Patterns of Disadvantage in Britain*, Bristol: The Policy Press, pp 87-104.

Okin, S. M. (1999) Is multiculturalism bad for women?, in J. Cohen, M. Howard and M.C. Nussbaum (eds), *Is Multiculturalism Bad for Women?* , anthology, Princeton, NJ: Princeton University Press.

Phoenix, A. (1996) 'Social constructions of lone motherhood: a case of competing discourses', in E. Bortolia Silva (ed) *Good Enough Mothering?*, London: Routledge, pp 175-90.

Puri, S. (2005) 'Rhetoric v. reality: the effect of 'multiculturalism' on doctors' responses to battered South Asian women in the United States and Britain', *Patterns of Prejudice*, vol 39, no 4, pp 416-30.

Puwar, N. (2003) 'Melodramatic postures and constructions', in N. Puwar and P. Raghuram (eds) *South Asian Women in the Diaspora*, Oxford: Berg, pp 19-42.

Runnymede Trust (2000) *The Parekh Report: Commission on the Future of Multi-Ethnic Britain*, London: Profile.

RWA (Refugee Women's Association) (2003) *Refugee Women's Association: Refugee Women's News*, June and July, no 23.

Said, E.W. (1985) *Orientalism: Western Concepts of the Orient*, Harmondsworth: Penguin.

Sajid, I.J. (2003) 'Honour killing: a crime against Islam', October, Muslim Council of Britain, available at: www.mcb.org.uk/downloads/honour_killings (accessd 08 March 2004).

Salim, S. (2003) 'It's about women's rights and women's rights are human rights', Speech for Kurdish Refugee Women's Organisation at the 'Stop Violence Against Women Honour Killing Conference', 28 October 2005, London.

Siddiqui, H. (2003) 'It was written in her kismet: forced marriage', in R. Gupta (ed) *From Homebreakers to Jailbreakers*, London: Zed Books, pp 67-83.

Spivak, C. G. (1988) 'Can the subaltern speak?', in C. Nelson and L. Grossberg (eds) *Marxism and the Interpretation of Culture*, London: Macmillan Education, pp 271-313.

Stolcke, V. (1995) 'Talking culture: new boundaries, new rhetorics of exclusion in Europe', *Current Anthropology*, no 36, pp 1-24.

Telegraph, The (2001) 'Cherie Blair in campaign to liberate Afghan women', 17 November.

UNFPA (United Nations Population Fund) (2000) *The State of the World Population: Chapter 3: Ending Violence Against Women and Girls*, available at: www.unfpa.org/swp/2000/english/press_kit/summary.html

Williams Crenshaw, K. (1994) 'Mapping the margins: intersectionality, identity politics, and violence against women of color', in M. Albertson Fineman and R. Mykitiuk (eds) *The Public Nature of Private Violence*, New York: Routledge, pp 93-118.

Yuval Davis, N. (1997) *Gender and Nation*, London, Sage Publications.

TEN

Risk embodied? Growing up disabled

Lesley Jordan and Rosemary Sales

Introduction

Growing up disabled imposes wide-ranging risks on young people and their families. Disabled young people are at greater risk than their peers of poverty, family breakdown and isolation. Further, they are at risk of being unable to make the transition to adulthood and a full and independent life. While the nature of these risks is well known, their source is explained differently by the two main ways of thinking about disability. The first, which has until recently prevailed within policy and practice discourse and public understanding, sees these risks as arising from the impairment itself. Conversely, the social model of disability emphasises the potential risks of societies' attitudes and behaviour towards those with impairments.

The way in which disability is defined and understood therefore has serious implications for the human rights of individuals with impairments. The United Nations Convention on the Rights of the Child (UN, 1989) suggests the ambiguity surrounding disabled children. It makes it clear that disabled children are 'children first', and should be accorded the same rights as any other child (Articles 2 and 23). However, inclusion of a specific section on the rights of disabled children (Article 23) testifies to the risk that these rights might otherwise go unrecognised or be considered a low priority for resources.

A sizeable minority of children in Britain are disabled. According to the General Household Survey, approximately 4% of children aged under five and 8% of children aged 5 to 15 in Great Britain have a limiting long-standing illness, disability or infirmity (ONS, 2004). A report from the Prime Minister's Strategy Unit estimated that around 800,000 children under age 16 in the UK have a limiting long-standing illness or disability, of whom at least 320,000 are defined under the

1995 Disability Discrimination Act (DDA) as disabled and about 110,000 are described as severely disabled (PMSU, 2004, pp 54-5).

The nature and impact of impairment and disability vary across many dimensions, and '[p]roblems and solutions for disabled children and their families are complex, multi-faceted and highly interdependent' (Audit Commission, 2003, p 11). Impairments can affect any aspect of bodily function, and public and professional awareness and understanding of different impairments vary. An increasing proportion of disabled children have multiple impairments and complex needs (PMSU, 2004, p 55). Living with impairment from birth is different from becoming disabled during childhood, while severity and stability over time also vary. Features such as gender, social class and ethnicity mediate the impact of impairment and disability. Nevertheless, disabled children share certain risks and are more likely, for example, to experience social exclusion, disadvantage and stigma. Understanding of risk must take into account both the diversity and the shared features of childhood and disability.

This chapter explores notions of risk associated with different models of disability and considers contemporary policy and practice in relation to childhood disability in this context. Risks emerging during adolescence are beyond this chapter's scope. It uses a range of secondary sources, including official policy documents and material produced by voluntary and campaigning organisations. Many of these offer critiques of government policy, utilising their members' experiences to provide evidence of the impact of particular policies and services on disabled children and their families.

Disability, impairment and risk

The predominant understanding of disability in our society is an individualised, 'medical', model that assumes a direct causal relationship between impairment and problems experienced. For example, section 1 of the 1995 DDA defines a disabled person as someone with 'a physical or mental impairment which has a substantial and long-term adverse effect on ... ability to carry out normal day-to-day activities'. Lay usage of the term 'disability' also commonly equates it with impairment. Embedded in the medical model is a notion of 'normality' and, by implication, 'abnormality'. These concepts also underlie theories of child development, until recently the predominant paradigm for understanding childhood in Britain. Priestley (2003, pp 64-7) argues that the practice of assessing children against developmental milestones fostered the construction of children with impairments as inferior and 'backward'. This feeds a societal assumption that disabled children as adults will be economically inactive, unable to 'pay their way' and in need of continuing protection and supervision.

Disabled people have challenged this conventional view of disability by developing the 'social model' of disability. This distinguishes between impairment and disability. Disability is defined as disadvantage to individuals with impairments caused by environmental barriers and social oppression. Impairment is thus extended from its medical definition of 'problems in body function or structure such as a significant deviation or loss' (WHO, 2001, p 8) to encompass any directly consequential loss of activity, sometimes termed 'impairment effects' (Thomas, 1999, pp 42-4).

The medical model has been criticised for its view of disability as 'personal tragedy', which can lead to disabled people being stereotyped as different or 'other', pitied for having 'lives not worth living', patronised, protected, sometimes feared and simultaneously canonised for 'bravery in their suffering' and for achieving 'against all the odds' (Oliver, 1990). Critics maintain that underlying even these laudatory images are negative perceptions of disabled people as having impairments and inabilities that disqualify them from full social acceptance (Goffman, 1968; Hunt, 1966). 'Normality' thus becomes a tyrannical construct (Priestley, 2003).

The social model reconstructs disability as a political issue concerning equal opportunities and civil rights, rather than a medical issue best left to health and other professionals. It views disabled people as valuable human beings with, like everyone, a range of abilities and inabilities. Impairment and its effects are 'facts of life' for the individual and many problems disabled people encounter are due to society's failure to accommodate the needs of all its citizens. Thus, it de-emphasises disabled people's difference. Disabled children have the same basic needs and aspirations as their peers (Shakespeare and Watson, 1998, p 16). Research evidence suggests that what matters to them is 'being respected and listened to, being able to play and have friends, feeling safe and comfortable' (Audit Commission, 2003, p 2). This indicates the importance to disabled children of psycho-emotional factors (Thomas, 1999).

Risk has not featured explicitly in these debates, but these two views of disability imply radically different understandings of the risks associated with disability. In the medical model, the risks faced by children arise directly from their impairment. Protection against risk involves both medical interventions to reduce 'abnormality' and separation from potentially risky situations. Segregated services may be seen as the most efficient way to provide for disabled children's 'special' needs, distancing them from their peers and communities both physically and in terms of life experiences and activities.

Disabled children have also been constructed as presenting risks to society. The most important of these is the risk to societal resources. While state provision for children is justified partially as investment in human capital (Gough, 1979), the implicit rationale for services for disabled children has been more on moral grounds. This fosters paternalism, while making such spending precarious and dependent on goodwill rather than on enforceable rights.

Disabled children have also been portrayed as a threat to the quality of the 'national stock', and therefore to be prevented from reproducing (Priestley, 2003). A related threat is to perceived aesthetic sensibilities. This has encouraged the hiding away of disabled children to prevent 'contamination'. In sharp contrast to other infanticides, killing your disabled child is treated leniently by society and the criminal justice system (Kotecha, 2006). Disabled children's 'deviance' from 'normality' is thus constructed as risky for themselves, their families and for society; they 'embody' risk.

The social model, on the other hand, construes the risks faced by disabled people as arising from society: from inaccessible environments and oppressive attitudes. Disabled people risk being defined predominantly by their impairment, and thus their childhood contributions to community and society go unrecognised. This leads to inadequate preparation for adult roles as sexual partners, parents, householders, workers and, more generally, people with control over their lives. Other people's low expectations affect the opportunities offered to disabled children (Lonsdale, 1990, pp 92-7) and reduce their 'aspirations, self-confidence and [their own] expectations' (Singh, 2005, p 5). Such 'internalised oppression' (NWGCPD, 2003a, p 58) is by no means inevitable, however. The following 16-year-old girl's account demonstrates resistance against these constructions of disabled young people's lives:

> I know my disability does not stop me from living.... Just because we have a difficulty does not mean we have to be different.... I know my limitations and there are certain things I cannot take part in or go to, but what is worse is being prevented from things I can go to or join in with just because of unsuitable access.... We have just as much right to enjoy life as anybody else and people should be

able to see the person and not the disability. (Wyllie, 2004, p 18)

The policy framework

The 1989 Children Act obliged local authorities to treat disabled children primarily as children. Middleton (1999) argues, however, that although the Act covers all children, the designation of disabled children as 'children in need' can be experienced as stigmatising, and that the distinction between disabled and other children 'served only to reinforce difference' (Middleton, 1999, p 132).

Under New Labour, social model ideas have been incorporated into disability policy discourse.[1] The government envisages that by 2025, 'disabled people in Britain should have full opportunities and choices to improve their quality of life and will be respected and included as equal members of society' (PMSU, 2005, p 4). There is a commitment to listen to disabled people, including children. Although welcomed by disability rights campaigners (for example, Pridmore, 2005; RADAR, 2005), this policy promises neither additional rights nor any firm assurance of extra funding. Moreover, today's disabled children will be adults before the promised equality is achieved.

Government policy for disabled children has been developed in a fragmented and piecemeal fashion, often within departments operating independently, and using different definitions of disabled children and their 'needs'. Responsibility for disability issues cuts across many departmental boundaries (PMSU, 2005, p 184), while services for disabled children are delivered through a range of national and local agencies and increasingly provided through voluntary organisations and private care agencies, often with different application procedures and eligibility rules. Although providing examples of good practice, the Audit Commission identified many shortcomings in services. These include 'postcode lotteries', with a lack of comprehensive provision in many areas; delays in accessing benefits, home adaptations and essential equipment and services; inappropriate services; and overly bureaucratic systems (Audit Commission, 2003). Separate organisation, criteria and funding streams can lead to perverse results, for example funding by local authorities of expensive residential placements when coordinated support of local education, housing adaptations, equipment and care could enable children to live at home.

Families seeking services or financial help must negotiate a maze of systems and personnel, about which inadequate information is available (Leonard, 1994; PMSU, 2004). Significant numbers of children qualify for services on account of impairment in one arena but not in another, due to different criteria and thresholds.[2] Minority ethnic parents of disabled children believe they receive poorer services due to providers' assumptions about cultural norms and preferences as well as language barriers and some families' unfamiliarity with British welfare systems (Chamba and Ahmad, 2000; Jones et al, 2001; Broomfield, 2004). Parents may become worn down, frustrated and angered by the operation and attitudes of service providers (Duncan, 2003; Holmes and Logue, c. 2004), as the following comment illustrates:

> It's a nightmare…. It's such hard work. Looking after Sarala is no problem whatsoever. Taking on social services, social security, taking on community care is a nightmare … you can do all the good things with Sarala, but why should you have to argue with somebody that she needs this, she needs that, and it's a privilege that we get it. (Audit Commission, 2003, p 8)

Attempts to achieve 'joined-up' provision for disabled children through national policies and local partnerships include the alignment of children's services with education under the Department for Education and Skills (DfES) following the Green Paper *Every Child Matters* (DfES, 2003). In some areas, new Children's Centres and Children's Trusts are responsible for a wide range of services. A number of recent initiatives aim to address the support needs of parents of young disabled children, for example 'Together from the Start', launched in 2002 by the DfES and the Department of Health. A new Office for Disability Issues (ODI) was set up within the Department for Work and Pensions (DWP) in 2005 as 'a discrete cross-government unit' (PMSU, 2005, p 184) to drive forward strategy on disability. The ODI, however, has 'few executive functions' (PMSU, 2005, p 210) and it remains to be seen whether it will achieve sufficient priority for disability issues.

Another problem is neglect of disabled children's interests within mainstream policies, sometimes leading to incompatibility between provision for disabled children and other policy goals. Departments are increasingly driven by financial and performance targets, which may lead them to ignore the needs of disabled children.

Since the 1980s, there has been a trend towards the privatisation of responsibility for care, with increasing pressures on parents to look after even severely impaired children at home. Long-term hospitalisation has greatly decreased and many local authorities have closed children's homes. Large charities such as Barnardo's and NCH

(National Children's Homes) have redirected resources from long-term residential care into supporting families. These trends are consistent with children's preferences (Abbott et al, 2001) and right to family life (UN, 1989, Article 9). Parental responsibility for care is not, however, matched by rights to domiciliary and community services. Only 29,000 disabled children, less than a third of all those classed as severely disabled in Britain, receive help from local authority social services (PMSU, 2004, p 61).

In a policy environment increasingly driven by risk avoidance, disabled children are in particular danger of losing out. Part III of the 1995 DDA, fully implemented only in 2004, prohibits discrimination on the grounds of disability by providers of goods and services except where 'reasonable adjustments' prove impracticable. Health and safety law, however, takes precedence over this legislation. Although risk assessments are expected to contribute to identification and implementation of 'reasonable adjustments' by anticipating and preventing likely difficulties and dangers (DfES, c. 2002), they might equally justify exclusion of disabled children, for example from some school or leisure activities, depending to some extent on the definition of 'reasonable adjustments'. In a qualitative study in six Yorkshire primary schools, Woolley et al (2006) noted that training for mainstream staff with responsibilities for disabled children concentrated mainly on issues such as health and safety. Increased regulation to prevent accidents and injuries during school and organised leisure activities, in playgrounds (see Ball, this volume, Chapter Four) and on the roads (Williams et al, 2002; Lupton and Bayley, this volume, Chapter Five) is likely to impact on disabled young people by reducing the threshold of 'acceptable' risk.

Growing up with risk

Growing up disabled involves a number of risks. While some may be directly due to a particular impairment, many could be avoided, reduced or managed through social policy based on the right of the disabled child to full inclusion. Below we discuss a number of these risks.

Negotiating health services

Many disabled children undergo prolonged medical treatment, frequent outpatient appointments and periods in hospital or other healthcare settings. Medical treatment saves many children's lives. Improved neonatal care enables more very-premature babies, at high risk of impairment, to survive. Medical and paramedical services can also improve disabled children's quality of life through, for instance, operations to lessen pain and drugs to control it, remedial treatments including physiotherapy and speech and language therapy, and wheelchairs and prostheses to enhance mobility.

Notwithstanding the undoubted benefits of medical intervention, the social model also sees health services as a major source of social oppression. Medical services are based on notions rooted in the medical model of disability with its focus on bodily and mental 'deficiencies'. Despite changes in health services over recent decades that have promoted 'partnership' between health professionals and patients, such interactions do not take place on an equal basis. The power of health professionals derives from many sources, including their technical expertise and control over referral, diagnostic testing, treatment (all, for NHS patients, under imposed financial and organisational constraints) and information. Diagnosis is a complex, socially constructed enterprise, which gives professionals power to decide whether to take seriously the concerns of children and their parents.[3]

Operations, medical procedures and medication inevitably involve an element of risk. While some treatments have been developed specifically for children ('orthopaedics' means literally 'child correction'), most medicines have not.[4] The medical model, based on assumptions about 'normality', may produce unwarranted negative assumptions about patients' quality of life. This can lead to unnecessary or risky procedures, for example to 'normalise' disabled children's appearance or behaviour. These implicitly assume children's unacceptability, and thus generate insidious risks to their self-identity (Priestley, 2003, p 71). Clinical and judicial opinions based on questionable 'quality of life' prognoses may also deny a disabled child life-saving treatment (*Disability Now*, 2001; Campbell, 2002, p 474).

An aspect of medical intervention that has perhaps been downplayed in the recent literature is the cost to the child of long periods in hospital for treatment and recovery at home. This segregates disabled children, reduces their opportunities to participate in a whole range of childhood activities and has longer-term implications for their life chances. One woman with cerebral palsy in Lonsdale's sample commented that, in retrospect, occupational therapy and a good education would have been better than the physiotherapy and exercises prescribed for her as a child (Lonsdale, 1990, p 54).

Family life

Families with disabled children are at greater risk of poverty (Woolley, 2004) and debt (Harrison and Woolley, 2004) than families with non-disabled children owing both to higher expenditure to cater for the needs of the disabled child and to lower income. Parental costs are estimated as three times higher for disabled children than for non-disabled children (Dobson and Middleton, 1998) and benefit levels do not match these additional expenses. The Family Fund recommended a tripling of Child Benefit for severely disabled children (Harrison and Woolley, 2004).

The current government's pledge to halve child poverty by the year 2010 and to end it by 2020 has so far offered little to families with disabled children because increasing parental employment, its major policy thrust, is problematic for them. The employment rate for mothers of disabled children is low (HM Treasury, 2004) as a result of higher levels of lone parenthood (Sharma, 2002), non-availability of suitable and affordable childcare (Sharma, 2002)[5] and frequent hospital appointments (Dowling and Dolan, 2001, pp 27-8, 31). Dearth of wage income is compounded over time by the lack of access to work-related benefits, and by other forms of exclusion such as unsuitable housing (PMSU, 2005, p 99), poor access to transport and difficulties in accessing services (Gough et al, 2006). Poverty can rule out spending on 'non-essentials' such as school trips, leisure activities and holidays away from home, particularly as accessible facilities cost more (Sharma and Dowling, 2004; Woolley, 2004).

Material disadvantages compound other pressures on families with disabled children. Spontaneous family outings to unfamiliar territory may be impractical due to the absence of an accommodating environment, for example where children have mobility impairments or incontinence. Other people's reactions to disabled children and intolerance of 'challenging' behaviour discourage people from making family outings at all (Dowling and Dolan, 2001, p 31). All these factors contribute to social isolation for disabled children and their families.

The process of accessing services can be stressful. Subjection to close scrutiny questions parents' veracity and motives, emphasising their supplicant position. The time and energy required add to the strains of family life, sometimes threatening mothers' mental health (Dowling and Dolan, 2001, pp 30-1; Duncan, 2003, p 350) or the parents' relationship, both known risk factors for children (Duncan and Reder, 2000; Fellow-Smith, 2000; PMSU, 2004, p 68).

'Respite' care can provide temporary relief for parents, but many parents find services inflexible and too limited (Dowling and Dolan, 2001, pp 30-31). Respite services can also give disabled children wider perspectives and opportunities (Dowling and Dolan, 2001, pp 29-30). Historically, however, this form of care has paid little attention to disabled children's own preferences or needs (Cocks, 2000). It can involve segregation in respite centres and separation from parents at an age at which it is otherwise accepted that children should be with their families. Further, respite care could be interpreted as 'propping up' families rather than providing the resources they need 'to provide optimum care, lifestyle and enablement' (Cocks, 2000, p 514).[6]

Segregation and social isolation

Despite the trend towards living at home, disabled children are more liable to be away (Morris, 2003) in education, care or health settings.[7] The pressures on families with disabled children mean that disabled children have a high risk of being in care, but only 40% are fostered compared to 66% of all children 'looked after' by local authorities (Stuart and Baines, 2004b, p 19). Residential schools can offer advantages, such as a signing community for deaf children. Some children away from home have more opportunity to develop peer friendships (Cook et al, 2001), but may find them impossible to maintain after leaving. For minority ethnic children, loss of home-neighbourhood contacts can lead to estrangement from culture and religion (Ahmad et al, 2000).

Those in mainstream schooling may face isolation from teachers and peers. Ofsted (2004, p 17) encountered disabled children who were taught separately by teaching assistants for most of the day. Disabled children may experience exclusion from aspects of the school curriculum, such as physical education, although the recent Schools White Paper attributes this to disabled children's reluctance to participate (DfES, 2005, p 80). Disabled children are also disadvantaged in less formal aspects of school life, for example if their individual routines encroach on playtimes, although some schools are able to avoid this through careful management (Woolley et al, 2006). Other children's behaviour, for example staring at or studiously avoiding disabled peers (Katbamna et al, 2000), can compound isolation and cause distress. Caryer (2004, p 38) contrasts the 'yucky and awful' behaviour of her school contemporaries with the 'wonderful' attitudes of secondary schoolchildren she encountered later at a theatre project. She speculates about adults' power to 'set the tone' of children's interactions:

> I began to rethink of the times when I was their age and struggling as a disabled child in a school with no understanding of disability.... I was probably not the only one with problems, and the kids who were not brilliant around me at my school might have shone in a different atmosphere where the adults seemed very fond of young people. (Caryer, 2004, p 38)

Seemingly impairment-related restrictions are not necessarily inevitable. For example, the charity Whizz-kidz argues that, with appropriate adult supervision, powered wheelchairs are not unacceptably risky for young disabled children (Rankin, 2005). However, public bodies consider them unsuitable, thus preventing independent mobility and inhibiting children's ability to forge and maintain peer friendships.

Abuse

Abuse includes bullying and physical, sexual and emotional mistreatment, and encompasses such behaviour by other children (including other disabled children) as well as adults. Although disabled children's vulnerability to abuse has been acknowledged only comparatively recently in Britain (Westcott, 1993), they are now recognised as at far higher risk than other children of all types of abuse (NWGCPD, 2003a).

Some of the risks discussed above increase the likelihood of abuse. Children who lack social contacts are particularly vulnerable, especially if their abuser is a carer on whom they rely for protection. They may fear losing essential services if they reveal abuse (DfES, 2004b, p 6, citing DH, 2001), or have no one to tell. Impairments can restrict children's ability to avoid, resist or report abuse, while assumptions about incapacity make it less likely that they will be listened to (McDowall, 2002). Since the publication of *People Like Us* (Utting, 1997) some systems have been changed to protect children living away from home (Stuart and Baines, 2004a, 2004b). Nevertheless, wherever parents are unable to take day-to-day responsibility, provide or oversee care and champion their disabled children, these children are put at risk (NWGCPD, 2003a). Sparse provision leads to many 'out of area' education and social care placements, which can leave children effectively cut off from the authority responsible for their well-being. The responsibilities of education and social services departments for children in residential special schools are unclear (NWGCPD, 2003a). The duties imposed on health, education and social care authorities to share information about disabled children in their care are frequently neglected (Abbott et al, 2000; Stuart and Baines, 2004a, p 7).

Negative stereotypes of disabled children make them both more vulnerable and less likely to be taken seriously. Bernard (1999) describes cases where social workers attributed a sudden change of behaviour to impairment, failing to consider the possibility of abuse. She argues that racism compounds the risk for disabled minority ethnic children.

The boundary between acceptable and abusive behaviour may be defined differently for disabled children, with less regard for their bodily integrity. This mother of a 12-year-old daughter attributes her daughter's abuse to such attitudes:

> He thought that because she was handicapped, he could get away with it and that it didn't matter.... They think that because the person's handicapped, that overrides their feelings, their rights as a person and everything else. (Read, 2000, p 39)

Davis and Watson (2001) observed that physical force, while unacceptable in mainstream schools, was an aspect of special school practice. There is clearly a need for development and dissemination of techniques for managing disabled children without resorting to force. Boundary setting is a particular issue in relation to disabled children who receive personal care, since the usual limits may not be maintainable. This increases children's exposure to risk, especially where there are a number of carers (Westcott, 1993, p 17).

Despite their high risk, disabled children are scarcely mentioned in mainstream policy documents concerned with abuse, including *Every Child Matters* (DfES, 2003). The National Working Group on Child Protection and Disability (NWGCPD, 2003b) called for independent advocates for all children at residential special schools, clarification of their status as 'looked-after' children and specific duties to help protect disabled children from abuse. None of these recommendations was incorporated into the 2004 Children Act. NWGCPD member Jenny Morris, a leading researcher with disabled children, commented: 'It is not enough to say that a good child protection system for all children will be a good child protection system for disabled children. It won't' (*Disability Now*, 2004, p 3).

Several studies have found that disabled children are more likely than other children to experience bullying at school (Gray, 2002, pp 12-13). Protection from bullying is one reason why parents choose segregated education, although bullying is also widespread in special schools (Davis and Watson, 2001). One young man turned an adult's negativity into a personal challenge, developing resilience to resist it, and becoming an Enterprising Young Brits award winner:

> My headmaster always told me: 'You're going to be bullied all your life, so you'd better get used to it'. I think that's what gave me the determination to get where I am now. (Calvi, 2004, p 18)

Protection, autonomy and control

Disabled children may find it particularly difficult to develop independence and some control over their lives. They are likely to have much more, and much closer, contact with adults than do other children. While this may give them greater confidence in adults' company (Woolley et al, 2006), some disabled children name an adult support worker or carer as their closest friend (Morris, 2001, citing Morris, 1998). Close surveillance by adults makes it more difficult for disabled children and young people to develop their own decision-making skills, restricting their ability to engage in the risk taking necessary to learning and development (see Ball, this volume, Chapter Four).

Social isolation, restricted play and leisure opportunities and the continuous presence of adults can all limit disabled young people's opportunities to cultivate and maintain peer friendships (Woolley et al, 2006). Segregated education restricts the peers they encounter and their opportunities for peer learning. This in itself is an important limitation to their autonomy. Further, lack of friends their own age in childhood is likely to be a disadvantage during adolescence and young adulthood.

Disabled children living at home may continue to depend on their parents for essential self-care tasks long after other children have achieved autonomy in this respect. Parents, usually mothers, may become fully employed in mediating their disabled children's relationship with the outside world, placing extra demands on the mother–child relationship (Read, 2000, p 109). This increases difficulties in judging how and when to allow children to develop independence.

Disabled children frequently have little choice in relation to residential placements and schooling. Decisions are often made according to adults' concerns and current vacancies at a time of dispute or crisis, without children's views or feelings being ascertained

(NWGCPD, 2003a, pp 46-7). This violates children's right to be involved in decisions affecting them (UN, 1989, Article 12) and may leave children feeling confused, guilty and rejected. Children who spend periods away from home include many with complex needs. Often they must rely on previously unknown adults, sometimes for the most intimate care. Ironically, children seen as requiring extra protection due to their impairments are then exposed to other serious risks, as described in the previous section, through institutions such as health services, social care and education (NWGCPD, 2003a, pp 58-9).

Disabled children's reliance on services can also impact on the development of autonomy. While appropriate and good-quality support can help young people to fulfil their potential and to live full and independent lives, their dependence on 'care' inevitably puts others in positions of power. Young people have little access to independent resources and therefore lack control over the amount and nature of their care. Children's gradual assumption of responsibility for themselves is vital in building confidence, developing independence and extending the range of choices they can make over their lives. Disabled children may be denied these opportunities. Without such decision-making experience accumulated during childhood, disabled young people cannot be expected to be well equipped to make lifetime choices.

Conclusion

This chapter has shown that, while impairments commonly involve specific health risks, social processes account for many of the risks disabled children are perceived to 'embody'. Policies and practices rooted in the medical model of disability tend to deny disabled young people opportunities to develop independence. Their impairments are seen as inherently risky and limiting, so their experiences are controlled. At the same time, failure to provide adequate support can expose disabled children to other risks. The social model of disability emphasises the socially constructed and created nature of disability and the importance of support in promoting autonomy and the ability to live full lives. However, while these ideas have become part of the new policy discourse, resource constraints and conflicts with other policy aims mean that they have often remained no more than paper commitments. This is particularly true in relation to childhood and adolescence, where these problems are intensified by financial, physical and emotional dependence. Much work remains to be done before the vision of equality (PMSU, 2005) can become a reality for disabled children and their families.

From a social model perspective, this chapter shows that the idea of risk offers a fruitful way of exploring understandings of disabled young people's lives. Perceptions of risk differ widely according to different conceptual approaches to disability, between disabled and non-disabled people and between adults' and children's views (see Ward and Bayley, this volume, Chapter Three). There has as yet been little research on disabled children's own perceptions of the risks they encounter and their attitudes to risk taking. Such research could make a significant contribution to the development of policy and practice that promotes well-being and fulfilment throughout childhood and beyond.

Notes

[1] Examples of particular relevance to childhood impairment include Disability Rights Task Force (1999); Audit Commission (2003); DfES (2004a); and PMSU (2005).

[2] Some children who qualify as disabled under the 1995 DDA do not have Special Educational Needs (SEN), while others with SEN are not disabled under the DDA. For example, children whose impairments do not affect activities of daily living, such as dyslexia and other specific learning difficulties, have SEN but are not disabled under the DDA.

[3] These points were well illustrated in 'Loving Lucy', *Home Truths*, BBC Radio 4, 2 April 2005.

[4] 'Over 50% of all medicines given to children (and some 90% of those given to the newly-born) have never been tested or authorised for use on them' (House of Lords European Union Committee, 2006, p 6).

[5] Local authorities' duty under Section 6 of the 2006 Childcare Act to secure childcare for disabled children under the age of 18 in England whose parents wish to enter employment 'so far as is reasonably practicable' will not guarantee adequate provision.

[6] The pejorative term 'respite' implies negativity; the alternative 'short break' at least allows for comparable benefits for disabled children.

[7] An estimated 13,300 disabled children, mostly boys over the age of 11, are in long-term residential placements in England (Pinney, 2005). The majority are in education placements.

References

Abbott, D., Morris, J. and Ward, L. (2000) 'Disabled children at residential school', *Findings* 420, York: Joseph Rowntree Foundation.

Abbott, D., Morris, J. and Ward, L. (2001) 'Residential schools and disabled children: decision-making and experiences', *Findings* 031, York: Joseph Rowntree Foundation.

Ahmad, W.I.U., Darr, A. and Jones, L. (2000) "I send my child away to school and he comes back an Englishman': minority ethnic deaf people, identity politics and services', in W.I.U. Ahmad (ed) *Ethnicity, Disability and Chronic Illness*, Buckingham: Open University Press, pp 67-84.

Audit Commission (2003) *Services for Disabled Children and their Families*, London: Audit Commission.

Bernard, C. (1999) 'Child sexual abuse and the black disabled child', *Disability & Society*, vol 14, no 3, pp 325-39.

Broomfield, A. (ed) (2004) *All our Children Belong*, London: Parents for Inclusion.

Calvi, N. (2004) 'Look who's laughing now', *Disability Now*, January, p 18.

Campbell, J. (2002) 'Valuing diversity: the disability agenda – we've only just begun', *Disability & Society*, vol 17, no 4, pp 471-8.

Caryer, K. (2004) 'Candid Kate', *Disability Now*, October, p 38.

Chamba, R. and Ahmad, W. I. U. (2000) 'Language, communication and information: the needs of parents caring for a severely disabled child', in W. I. U. Ahmad (ed) *Ethnicity, Disability and Chronic Illness*, Buckingham: Open University Press, pp 85-102.

Cocks, A. (2000) 'Respite care for disabled children: micro and macro reflections', *Disability & Society*, vol 15, no 3, pp 507-19.

Cook, T., Swain, J. and French, S. (2001) 'Voices from segregated schooling: towards an inclusive education system', *Disability & Society*, vol 16, no 2, pp 293-310.

Davis, J. M. and Watson, N. (2001) 'Where are the children's experiences? Analysing social and cultural exclusion in 'special' and 'mainstream' schools', *Disability & Society*, vol 16, no 5, pp 671-87.

DfES (Department for Education and Skills) (c. 2002) *Disability Discrimination Act 1995 Part 4: Code of Practice for Schools*, London: The Stationery Office, www.drc.org.uk/thelaw/practice.asp

DfES (2003) *Every Child Matters*, Cm 5860, London: The Stationery Office.

DfES (2004a) *Removing Barriers to Achievement: The Government's Strategy for SEN*, (0118/2004), London: DfES.

DfES (2004b) *Disabled Children in Residential Placements*, London: DfES, www.dfes.gov.uk

DfES (2005) *Higher Standards, Better Schools for All: More choice for Parents and Pupils*, Cm 6677, London: The Stationery Office.

Disability Now (2001) 'Down's discrimination', May, p 8.

Disability Now (2004) 'Residential schools need monitoring', June, p 3.

Disability Rights Task Force (1999) *From Exclusion to Inclusion*, London: Department of Education and Science.

Dobson, B. and Middleton, S. (1998) *Paying to Care: The Cost of Childhood Disability*, York: Joseph Rowntree Foundation.

Dowling, M. and Dolan, L. (2001) 'Families with children with disabilities – inequalities and the social model', *Disability & Society*, vol 16, no 1, pp 21-35.

Duncan, N. (2003) 'Awkward customers? Parents and provision for special educational needs', *Disability & Society*, vol 18, no 3, pp 341-56.

Duncan, S. and Reder, P. (2000) 'Children's experience of major psychiatric disorder in their parents: an overview', in P. Reder, M. McClure and A. Jolley (eds) *Family Matters: Interfaces between Child and Adult Mental Health*, London: Routledge, pp 83-95.

Fellow-Smith, L. (2000) 'Impact of parental anxiety disorder on children', in P. Reder, M. McClure and A. Jolley (eds) *Family Matters: Interfaces between Child and Adult Mental Health*, London: Routledge, pp 96-106.

Goffman, E. (1968) *Stigma*, Harmondsworth: Penguin.

Gough, I. (1979) *The Political Economy of the Welfare State*, London: Macmillan.

Gough, J. and Eisenschitz, A. with McCulloch, A. (2006) *Spaces of Social Exclusion*, London: Routledge.

Gray, P. (2002) *Disability Discrimination in Education: A Review of the Literature on Discrimination across the 0-19 Age Range*, London: Disability Rights Commission.

Harrison, J. and Woolley, M. (2004) *Debt and Disability: The Impact of Debt on Families with Disabled Children*, York: Contact a Family & Family Fund.

HM Treasury (2004) *Child Poverty Review*, London: HMSO.

Holmes, E. and Logue, J. (c. 2004) *Fighting Hard: Parents' Experience of Accessing Communication Support for their Child*, London: Scope.

House of Lords European Union Committee (2006) *Paediatric Medicines: Proposed EU Regulations*, 20th Report of Session 2005-06, HL Paper 101, London: The Stationery Office.

Hunt, P. (1966) 'A critical condition', in P. Hunt (ed) *Stigma: The experience of disability*, London: Geoffrey Chapman, pp 143-59.

Jones, L., Atkin, K. and Ahmad, W. I. U. (2001) 'Supporting Asian deaf young people and their families: the role of professionals and services', *Disability & Society*, vol 16, no 1, pp 51-70.

Katbamna, S., Bhakta, P. and Parker, G. (2000) 'Perceptions of disability and care-giving relationships in South Asian communities', in W. I. U. Ahmad (ed) *Ethnicity, Disability and Chronic Illness*, Buckingham: Open University Press, pp 12-27.

Kotecha, P. (2006) 'The parents who kill and are spared jail', *Disability Now*, February, pp 14-15.

Leonard, A. (1994) *Right from the Start*, London: Scope.

Lonsdale, S. (1990) *Women and Disability*, London: Macmillan.

McDowall, A. (2002) 'Mistreatment of disabled children is routinely ignored', *The Guardian*, 2 December, www.guardian.co.uk

Middleton, L. (1999) 'The social exclusion of disabled children: the role of the voluntary sector in the contract culture', *Disability & Society*, vol 14, no 1, pp 129-39.

Morris, J. (2001) 'Social exclusion and young disabled people with high levels of support needs', *Critical Social Policy*, vol 21, no 2, pp 161-83.

Morris, J. (2003) 'Children on the edge of care', available at: www.leeds.ac.uk/disability-studies/archiveuk

NWGCPD (National Working Group on Child Protection and Disability) (2003a) *'It Doesn't Happen to Disabled Children': Child Protection and Disability*, London: NSPCC.

NWGCPD (2003b) *Every Child Matters: Response from NWGCPD*, London: NSPCC, www.nspcc.org.uk

Ofsted (2004) *Special Educational Needs and Disability: Towards Inclusive Schools*, London: Ofsted, www.ofsted.gov.uk

Oliver, M. (1990) *The Politics of Disablement*, Basingstoke: Macmillan.

ONS (Office for National Statistics) (2004) *Living in Britain: Results from the 2002 General Household Survey*, London: HMSO.

Pinney, A. (2005) *Disabled Children in Residential Placements*, London: DfES, www.dfes.gov.uk

PMSU (Prime Minister's Strategy Unit) (2004) *Improving the Life Chances of Disabled People: Analytical Report*, London: PMSU.

PMSU (2005) *Improving the Life Chances of Disabled People*, London: PMSU.

Pridmore, A. (2005) *'Improving the Life Chances of Disabled People': A Response from the British Council of Disabled People*, available at: www.bcodp.org.uk

Priestley, M. (2003) *Disability: A Life Course Approach*, Oxford: Polity.

RADAR (2005) 'Prime Minister's Strategy Unit Report: *Improving the Life Chances of Disabled People*', Press Release, 3 February.

Rankin, A. (2005) 'Whizz-kidz response to: *Improving the Life Chances of Disabled People*', www.strategy.gov.uk/work_areas/disability/interim_responses.asp

Read, J. (2000) *Disability, the Family and Society*, Buckingham: Open University Press.

Shakespeare, T. and Watson, N. (1998) 'Theoretical perspectives on research with disabled children', in C. Robinson and K. Stalker (eds) *Growing up with Disability*, London: Jessica Kingsley, pp 13–27.

Sharma, N. (2002) *Still Missing Out? Ending Poverty and Social Exclusion: Messages to Government from Families with Disabled Children*, Barkingside: Barnardo's.

Sharma, N. and Dowling, R. (2004) *Postcards from Home: The Experience of Disabled Children in the School Holidays*, Barkingside: Barnardo's.

Singh, B. (2005) *Improving Support for Black Disabled People: Lessons from Community Organisations on Making Change Happen*, York: Joseph Rowntree Foundation.

Stuart, M. and Baines, C. (2004a) *Progress on Safeguards for Children Living Away from Home*, York: Joseph Rowntree Foundation.

Stuart, M. and Baines, C. (2004b) *Safeguards for Vulnerable Children: Three Studies on Abusers, Disabled Children and Children in Prison*, York: Joseph Rowntree Foundation.

Thomas, C. (1999) *Female Forms: Experiencing and Understanding Disability*, Buckingham: Open University Press.

UN (United Nations) (1989) *Convention on the Rights of the Child*, Geneva: UNICEF.

Utting, W. (1997) *People Like Us: Report of the Review of the Safeguards for Children Living Away from Home*, London: Department of Health.

Westcott, H. L. (1993) *Abuse of Children and Adults with Disabilities*, London: NSPCC.

WHO (World Health Organization) (2001) *International Classification of Functioning, Disability and Health*, Geneva: WHO.

Williams, K., Savill, T. and Wheeler, A. (2002) *Review of the Road Safety of Disabled Children and Adults*, Report TRL559, Wokingham: Transport Research Laboratory.

Woolley, H. with Armitage, M., Bishop, J., Curtis, M. and Ginsborg, J. (2006) 'Inclusion of disabled children in primary school playgrounds', *Findings* 0016, York: Joseph Rowntree Foundation.

Woolley, M. (2004) *Income and Expenditure of Families with a Severely Disabled Child*, York: Family Fund.

Wyllie, K. (2004) 'Teen spirit', *Disability Now*, April, p 18.

ELEVEN

Young women, sexual behaviour and sexual decision making

Lesley Hoggart

Introduction

> Let me make one point perfectly clear. I don't believe young
> people should have sex before they are 16. I have strong
> views on this. But I also know that no matter how much
> we might disapprove, some do. We shouldn't condone their
> actions. But we should be ready to help them avoid the
> very real risks that under-age sex brings. (Tony Blair, preface
> to *Teenage Pregnancy* report, SEU, 1999, p 4)

The concept of risk has become central to policy debate on young
people and sexual behaviour in at least two ways. First, one prominent
view, drawn upon in recent policy developments and by Tony Blair in
the extract quoted above, sees sex as potentially risky and young people
as sexual risk takers. The main risks associated with sexual intercourse
are sexually transmitted infections (STIs) and unintended pregnancy.
For teenage mothers, a further consequential risk is social exclusion
for themselves and their children (SEU, 1999). Second, a currently
less influential meaning characterises sex itself as a risk that young
people should be taught to avoid (Family Education Trust, 2002).
These two approaches are evident in debate around sexual health
services for young people in the UK. Indeed, they represent opposing
views on the development of such services and have different
implications for policy development. They are at different stages in a
continuum, which ranges from approaches based upon 'anything goes'
to advocating abstinence.

As sexual health policy was developed in the 1980s, in response to
concern about HIV/AIDS, it drew heavily on the concept of risk.
There was a new urgency to analyse the extent to which sexual
behaviour could be described as safe or unsafe, and formulate policy

to promote the practice of safe sex (Wellings et al, 1994). Towards the end of the 1990s, as New Labour began to prioritise reducing the rate of teenage pregnancy, the focus on the risks of sex to young people was strengthened. The aim was to promote 'health-seeking behaviour' and develop policies that would curtail 'risk behaviour' (SEU, 1999; DH, 2001). It was not sex as such that was deemed 'risky' but rather sex in particular circumstances. Those circumstances include the age of the participants. Such considerations invariably connect sexual health policy and practice to public and political debate on sexual morality and what constitutes acceptable sexual activity. One area in which the debate is now played out is in relation to protection: are young people best protected from the risk of unsafe sex by encouraging them to 'say no', or by sex education that helps them gain the knowledge and confidence to practise safe sex on the basis of informed choice? This issue is particularly pertinent for those under the age of 16, the legal age of consent in the UK.

This chapter considers the meanings currently attached to risk in the area of sexual health and young people. It begins by introducing the policy context for the current debate on young people and sexual behaviour, placing this within a comparative European framework. It then draws upon two recent empirical research projects on 'young women, sex and choices' (Hek and Hoggart, 2005; Hoggart, 2006). These projects, commissioned by local teenage pregnancy coordinators, sought to gain insights into the sexual decision-making processes of young mothers in relation to their pregnancies, and to assess their views on sexual behaviour and morality.

Debate around young people and sexual risk taking in the UK is struggling to move beyond the conflicting approaches to sex and sexuality that go back at least a century. Many of those who argue for abstinence campaigns, for example, draw upon particular religious traditions that sought to contain sexual activity within defined parameters, such as marriage (Hoggart, 2003). The research suggests that elements of this thinking do find their way into young women's moral frameworks in relation to sexuality. However, the young women demonstrated particular attitudes to morality and notions of risk and responsibility that were also sensitive to social and cultural contexts.

The policy context

The New Labour government, elected in 1997, first prioritised teenage sexual health in *Our Healthier Nation* (DH, 1999). The Social Exclusion Unit then published the *Teenage Pregnancy* report (SEU, 1999). This connected teenage pregnancy to the risk of social exclusion, highlighting what it suggested were negative consequences of the consistently high rates in the UK. These included suggesting that the children of teenage parents were at higher risk of living in poverty, in substandard housing and having a poor diet than other children (SEU, 1999). In 1999, the government's 10-year national Teenage Pregnancy Strategy was launched. The main aims of the strategy are to:

- halve the rate of conception among the under-18s, and set a downward trend in the conception rate for the under-16s by 2010;
- increase the participation of teenage parents in education, training and employment to 60% by 2010, and reduce their risk of long-term social exclusion.

An important reason for the government's determination to reduce teenage pregnancy was the high rate of conception relative to the rest of the developed world. More teenagers were becoming pregnant in the UK than anywhere else in Europe (UNICEF, 2001). This is still the case even though the rate has fallen recently. The most recent confirmed figures show that between 1998 and 2003 the under-18 conception rate in England fell from 46.6 to 42.1 per thousand population aged 13-17, a decline of 8.66% (ONS, 2005). This downward trend needs to accelerate if the government's targets are to be achieved.

A number of factors contribute to the UK's relatively high teenage conception rate. The Acheson Report concentrated on social, economic and cultural inequalities affecting health, claiming that disadvantaged young people are more likely to become unintentionally pregnant (Acheson, 1998). This assessment was supported in the *Teenage Pregnancy* report (SEU, 1999), but this also highlighted other factors. It developed explanations based upon young people's poor knowledge of contraception; an accompanying lack of understanding about forming relationships and parenting; mixed messages about sexuality from the media and society in general; and low expectations among a significant number of young people (SEU, 1999).

Placing this within a comparative perspective may shed light on the reasons for different conception rates. The UK teenage birth rate is twice as high as Germany's, seven times that of France, and six times as high as in the Netherlands. The average age at first sexual encounter is, however, not markedly out of line with these and other European countries (SEU, 1999, p 29). What is different is the low use of contraception by sexually active teenagers in the UK. One reason suggested for this is that families and society in many European countries, such as the Netherlands, are more open in talking to children about sex from an early age and there is a greater acceptance of teenage sexual activity (Knijn and Lewis, 2002). Such acceptance is associated with improved use of contraception among young people (Chambers et al, 2001). In Sweden, practical steps taken to prevent teenage childbearing were judged to be effective only when implemented in the full acceptance that teenagers will be sexually active regardless of the views of others (Santow and Bracher, 1999).

UK research on decision making in relation to 'risky' sexual activity has shown that, lacking adequate knowledge or self-confidence, young people struggle to negotiate 'safe' sexual encounters (Thomson and Scott, 1991; Holland et al, 1992; Holland et al, 2004; West, 1999; Counterpoint, 2001). The most recent National Survey of Sexual Attitudes and Lifestyles (NATSAL) found that non-use of contraception at first sexual intercourse was reported by 18% of men and 22% of women aged 13-14 years. The likelihood of using contraception increased with the age of first sexual intercourse (Wellings et al, 2001).

Effective use of contraception among young people is associated with good-quality information and education about sexual matters including school-based sex education and community sexual health services (Chambers et al, 2001; Swann et al, 2003). These are two important areas that the Teenage Pregnancy strategy targeted for improvements (SEU, 1999). These aims are clearly more amenable to local intervention than attempts to change patterns of deprivation and social inequalities described in the report. An important explanation of the decline in the teenage birth rate internationally is the increased motivation of young women, with personal goals other than motherhood, to achieve higher levels of education (Singh and Darroch, 2000). The *Teenage Pregnancy* report refers to young people with low expectations who 'see no reason not to get pregnant' (SEU, 1999, p 7). The subsequent policy, however, focuses on the sexual behaviour of young people and the development of appropriate services (Arai, 2003), and the strategy has been criticised for not prioritising a consideration of social deprivation and poor job prospects for many young people (FPSC, 1999). The UK became one of the most unequal societies in Europe during the Thatcher years, with a significant rise in poverty, especially child poverty (Stewart and Hills, 2005). Although under New Labour poverty has been substantially reduced, inequalities remain high relative to the rest of Europe. These are compelling criticisms that suggest that New Labour may well struggle to meet its teenage conception targets.

With respect to sexual behaviour and unplanned pregnancy, what seems to be peculiar to the UK within a European context is the clash between changing family structures and patterns of sexual encounters and a strong conservative resistance to such changes. The resistance continues to influence mainstream policy makers and hamper efforts to provide effective sex education. There is a long history of conflict around sexual morality. Before contraceptive developments and legislative reform, including abortion liberalisation, in the 1960s and 1970s, women were not able to engage in sex without a high risk of pregnancy and this was often seen as a punishment for sexual activity (Cook, 2004). Although the possibility of pregnancy then shifted from a necessary risk to one possible outcome of sexual intercourse, women's (especially young women's) access to contraception and abortion continued to be contested. While feminists pressed for such reforms to go further, opposing pressure groups resisted reform, promoting a view of sex as dangerous and undesirable and reasserting pregnancy as the potential punishment for sex outside marriage. Such resistance was most evident in the 1980s, and most vociferous around the issue of abortion (Sheldon, 1997; Hoggart, 2003).

The 1980s' 'backlash' against the 'permissive' politics of the 1960s involved a number of extra-parliamentary campaigns that sought to restore traditional views of the family and reverse many of the reforms of the 1960s and early 1970s (Durham, 1991; Faludi, 1991). What became known as the New Right in Britain and the US contained within it a number of 'morality' campaigns that sought to influence the sexual politics agenda. Their influence was particularly prominent in debates on sex education. Portrayed as a vehicle for an anti-family amoralism that encouraged intercourse and corrupted the young, some organisations, such as Family and Youth Concern, argued for the end of sex education altogether (Durham, 1991, p 110). In response to pressure from these groups, parents were given the right to withdraw their children from school-based sex education and teachers were required to promote 'family values', a policy that has been continued under New Labour.

Another campaign with significant implications for young people was the challenge by Victoria Gillick to Department of Health and Social Security guidelines (DHSS, 1974) that stated that contraception should be available to all regardless of age. The debate revealed widespread anxieties about teenage sexuality (Hawkes, 1995), and particularly the view that easily available contraception encourages sexual promiscuity in young people by removing the controlling factor of risk from sexual encounters. Although the House of Lords decided in favour of the DHSS in October 1985, these concerns continue to influence the policy debate.

These were always minority campaigns, largely disappointed by the failure of successive Conservative governments to adopt their policies, which declined significantly with the election of New Labour in 1997. Nevertheless, those working in the sexual health field today, for example in designing sex education, remain apprehensive about reactions from conservative campaigners and this influences the context in which they work. This was evident in both the research projects discussed below. The widespread acceptance within government of the view that sex education should promote the family is possibly the most enduring outcome of previous policy conflict. This was evident in the consultation for revised guidelines on sex and relationships education. The government developed an ambiguous framework in which 'pupils should be taught about the nature and importance of marriage for family life and bringing up children' alongside recognition that there are 'mutually supportive relationships outside marriage' (DfEE, 2000, p 4). The press release from the Department of Education on the launch of the *Teenage Pregnancy* report talked about the importance of marriage and the role of sex education to 'enhance pupil confidence to say no to peer pressure and delay sexual activity' (*The Guardian*, 16 June 1999).

This historical legacy has contributed towards a situation in which young people may be poorly informed about sex and contraception while the potentially controlling factor of the risk of pregnancy has greatly diminished. In the UK, changing family structures, with nearly 50% of marriages ending in divorce and a diversity of family forms (Williams, 2004), have clearly contributed to reducing the social stigma attached to unmarried motherhood. Live births outside marriage have risen dramatically from 8.2% in 1971 to 38.7% in 1999 (ONS, 2001). Recent research has shown a significant social acceptance of teenage motherhood among British working-class communities (Tabberer et al, 2000; Lee et al, 2004). As a comparative report points out, 'those countries with the highest teenage birth rates tend to be those that have marched far along the road from traditional values whilst doing little to prepare their young people for the new and different world in which they find themselves' (UNICEF, 2001, p 13).

The development of policies and services to implement the Teenage Pregnancy strategy thus remains fraught with controversy. Abortion, in particular, remains controversial, as evidenced by recent calls for lowering the time limit.[1] While some, such as the Sex Education Forum, focus upon learning about the possible risks of sexual activity, others seek to uphold traditional values, arguing that more knowledge will simply result in more 'undesirable' sexual activity (Family Education Trust, 2002). The former approach is now driving policy, and much of the work of the Teenage Pregnancy Unit has been concerned with improving young people's knowledge of, and access to, contraception, thus explicitly seeking to reduce the risk of teenage pregnancy and STIs.

'Young women, sex and choices' projects

The two qualitative research projects discussed below sought to examine how young mothers had experienced and negotiated sexual relationships, and their feelings about the possible risks of unsafe sex. One project took place in an inner London borough (Hoggart, 2006); the other was in a Midlands new town (Hek and Hoggart, 2005). Both areas included wards with high levels of deprivation and both had teenage pregnancy rates significantly above the national average. The ethnic composition of the two areas was very different, with a diverse population in the London borough and a majority of white UK in the Midlands town.

The research included focus groups in local schools and interviews with key informants, as well as individual interviews with young women who were, or were about to become, teenage mothers. The youngest age at time of giving birth was 14 and the eldest 18. The discussion below focuses only on these interviews, 13 of which took place in London and 12 in the Midlands. Most participants came from the more deprived segments of the areas, and their ethnic composition reflected that in their wider communities. The two areas are discussed together. Quotations are selected to indicate broader opinion rather than the opinion of only one participant. Names are therefore not used, a practice that also protects the anonymity of the informants.

The debates outlined above were echoed in complex ways in the young mothers' understandings, and rationales, of the decisions that they had made. This was particularly the case with discussion around 'safe sex' and with the possible consequences of 'risky sex'. To varying degrees, participants drew upon notions of risk and blame, and talked about the need for individuals to take responsibility for their own actions. The following section discusses the two areas in which the concepts of risk and responsibility were most evident: negotiating sexual encounters and deciding between abortion and motherhood.

Negotiating sexual encounters

Becoming pregnant can be seen as a consequence of unsafe, risky sex. However, such an understanding is highly dependent on notions of intent. When motherhood is the desired outcome of sexual activity, for instance, risk is irrelevant for the individual involved. Many young mothers drew upon notions of responsibility and the need to accept the consequences (pregnancy) of their own 'risky' behaviour. For others it was clear that becoming pregnant was not a risk but something to be welcomed. A threefold typology, related to risk and intent, was developed in order to give some indication of the different pathways that can be identified. Participants were fairly evenly spread between the three groups. However, exact numbers could not be given for each group since, as with most analytical categories, there is considerable blurring and it is not always possible to place each individual firmly within one category. The typology is as follows:

- *unintended* pregnancy (contraceptive failure, presumed ignorance and/or inability to negotiate safe sex);
- *indifference* or fatalism (lack of caution in practising 'safe sex');
- possible *intention* to become pregnant.

In the first two (often overlapping) categories, notions of risk, blame and innocence were often drawn upon as part of a moral justification for the mothers' decision-making processes. The mothers saw themselves as taking responsibility for their own actions after knowing they were pregnant. This theme was common across both districts.

Unintended pregnancy

The mothers in this group spoke of their pregnancies as accidents, although it was clear that in many cases their sexual practice was far from 'safe'. Many claimed that sex education had not prepared them for sexual decision-making; indeed they were vague about what they had been taught. Several told us that they became pregnant because the contraceptive they had been using had not worked:

> Well I was on the Pill and then what happened, I got an infection and I took antibiotics and didn't use any other protection. So that was that really, the Pill didn't work and I was pregnant.

A significant number seem to have become pregnant during the gap between contraceptive injections. Others told us they had been on the Pill and could not understand how they became pregnant: 'Well they say that I didn't take it properly but I know I did so I just see it as one of them things'. This comment also illustrates fatalism regarding sexual activity and the possibility of accidental pregnancy evident in many of the accounts.

The young mothers had found negotiating sexual encounters on their own terms difficult and had not necessarily made a conscious decision about the best time to start having sex. In addition, although some said that their sexual partners had been willing to use contraception, most complained that young men could pressurise them into not using contraception. There was not much confidence about their ability to practise 'safe sex', or indication that they felt able to control their sexual encounters:

> When I first got pregnant I asked him what had happened,
> he goes 'the condom burst'. I was like 'condoms don't burst'
> ... when I had the baby I was 'so what happened?' He was
> like, 'oh I didn't use a condom'. I said 'why' and he goes
> 'because I wanted to have a baby'.

Accounts like this indicate the absence of a sense of ownership of their own bodies or independence of their own sexuality, both of which are important for effective negotiation of safe sex (Holland et al, 2004).

A common theme was the role of drugs and alcohol in making it difficult for young people to maintain control of their sexual encounters and to practise safe sex. Previous research has shown that alcohol and drugs often contribute towards young women 'getting out of it' and engaging in unprotected sex (Counterpoint, 2001, p 10). One mother indicated that alcohol played a part in whether she used contraceptives or not. She acknowledged random contraceptive use but then appeared to imply that she became more careless as she drank more:

> The first time I did use a condom, and after that it was just
> when I had them with me, or he had them with him. After
> that I often didn't, I drank a lot, started drinking a lot.

Taken together, the explanations of their sexual behaviour indicate a lack of control and/or a lack of concern about possible negative consequences of sexual risk taking. This may represent post hoc rationalisation of their behaviour, and for some it is possible that their pregnancies were intentional. Despite often describing their pregnancies as accidents, young mothers who could be placed in this group spoke about taking responsibility for their own 'mistakes' and this meant continuing with the pregnancy rather than having an abortion. This decision was presented as the 'right' thing to do; it involved a measure of self-blame and often coincided with a fatalistic approach. Such an approach was even more apparent in the second category.

Indifference or fatalism: neither planned nor totally unplanned

Many participants described random, often careless, contraceptive use despite understanding the risks of pregnancy and STIs. This attitude spanned all groups but was most evident in this category. Most were more worried about STIs than pregnancy, and, in London, some had had themselves and their partners tested for HIV/AIDS and saw no need to use condoms afterwards.

As already mentioned, contraceptive use for this group was random. Some said that they had been using condoms but that their partners had not wanted this every time and so they took a chance. Many said that they generally used condoms, but had not done so on a few occasions. Others knew that they were not using the contraception properly but decided to go ahead with sex anyway. Some said that they would not do this again. One was on the Pill but was not taking it properly – she described herself as careless but also said that she did want a baby sometime. Others told us that they were using contraception around the time they fell pregnant, but were unable to specify what contraception they were using and why it failed.

The messages were often ambiguous and difficult to interpret. This seems to indicate confusion about (or an unwillingness to discuss fully) their own intentions and the possible consequences of their action, as well as an absence of anxiety about the possibility of pregnancy. Within the space of about five minutes, one mother told us that she had been on a contraceptive injection at the time but then explained that they had not been using condoms because she was taking the Pill every day. Another had become pregnant three times within the space of approximately four years, the first time at 13. She had not been using contraception:

> To tell you truthfully, even after I got pregnant the first time I didn't think I would get pregnant again. I didn't think of contraception. I was just a normal teenager and I

> didn't really think of pregnancy and having a baby or going
> to the clinic or anything like that.

What is noticeable about the mothers who were placed in this group
is their ambivalence about their intentions and their unwillingness to
say with any degree of certainty that the pregnancy was planned or
unplanned. They acknowledged that they were careless regarding
contraceptive use and often engaged in unsafe sex, but this does not
seem to be because they lacked knowledge about contraception: rather
they were not overly concerned to avoid pregnancy. They do not
seem to have seen the possibility of becoming pregnant as a risk to be
avoided. Although they may not have made a conscious decision to
become a mother, they talked about becoming pregnant in a fatalistic
manner, as 'one of those things'. They tended to talk about their sexual
decision making that had resulted in pregnancy as a passive process
rather than something over which they had control.

This changed when they were faced with the decision of whether
or not to continue the pregnancy: at this stage they asserted agency
and claimed this decision for themselves. They had all decided that
abortion was not for them personally. An important part of their
explanations for this decision revolved around taking responsibility
for the consequences of the risk they had taken. Underpinning much
of this dialogue, therefore, was a moral framework superficially similar
to that employed by those who seek to curtail teenage sexual activity
that connected notions of risk to blame and responsibility. Although
many stated that they had not wanted to have a child as a teenager, the
decision to proceed with the pregnancy was presented as a positive
choice. They faced up to the consequences of their 'risky' behaviour
but this is not seen as punishment. This was even more evident in the
third category where pregnancies appeared to be intended.

'Intentional' pregnancy

> I was on the Pill but I missed my Pill because it was on
> purpose, it wasn't because it was a mistake. No, it wasn't a
> mistake.

Between a quarter and a third of the young women appeared to have
made a positive choice to start a family. They gave a variety of reasons,
although it is interesting that most of those who planned the baby
told us that they had been unsettled or unhappy in their lives in some
way before becoming pregnant. Most had been disillusioned with

school and many had stopped attending before they became pregnant. They often talked about 'hating school'. For the majority of these girls, becoming a mother was seen as a positive achievement. This confirms other research. Elphis Christopher (1987) drew upon work in Haringey in London to argue that some young mothers seem to have an emotional 'need for a baby'. More recently, it has been established that school excludees, persistent truants and young people in families with high levels of conflict are more likely to become teenage parents (Swann et al, 2003). The most recent national study of teenage abortion decision making found that teenagers who saw their lives as insecure were more likely to decide in favour of motherhood, whereas those who had a personal focus on education were more likely to choose termination (Lee et al, 2004).

These young mothers had either not used contraception in full knowledge that this might result in a pregnancy, or had made an active decision to become pregnant:

> I don't know I just, I know it sounds stupid but I just kept seeing programmes with people's babies and that and I just said I wanted a baby and all that. He just agreed to it really, just agreed to stop using any contraception and we went from there.

Since pregnancy was the desired outcome of sexual activity, notions of risk were irrelevant.

Abortion or motherhood: risk and responsibility

Most of the young mothers had been involved in some discussion about whether to terminate their pregnancies. They stressed the importance of making this decision themselves:

> I think if you get pregnant and things it's up to you. Don't listen to anyone. It's entirely up to you. It's your baby, it's your body. If you want to have an abortion you have it, if you want the baby you have it. It's entirely up to you. Don't let anybody, anybody at all, tell you what to do. Don't let anybody tell you, it's up to you.

A strong theme across all the groups was the need to take responsibility for their actions. This was most marked in those who described their pregnancy as an accident. Fatalism regarding their negotiation of the 'risks' of sexual encounters contrasted with a strong sense of individual agency in decisions to continue with their pregnancies.

The young mothers drew on moral frameworks to discuss their decision, sometimes using the language of innocence, blame, rights and responsibilities. They had all made the decision that termination was not right in this case, but nevertheless expressed very different views about the morality of abortion, from outright opposition to views based on individual choice.

Some were not against abortion in principle but had felt that it was 'not right' to terminate this particular pregnancy. This was often presented as an individual moral choice for them, in that they had made the decision to accept the consequences of engaging in unsafe sex. Others were more ambivalent but had decided that on this occasion they were ready to embrace motherhood. Many had terminated earlier pregnancies and were quite comfortable in talking about this. Although some had been pressurised into this earlier decision by their parents, they did not say that they disagreed with abortion. Most of those who did not express moral opposition to abortion, but had nevertheless opted for motherhood, could be placed in the indifference/fatalism category. Although they stated that they had not intended to become pregnant, it was clear that it was not an outcome that they were particularly concerned to avoid. They took a very matter of fact view about becoming pregnant and described how quickly they accepted their new status. Because they were either indifferent or intended to have a baby, the decision against abortion was relatively straightforward.

A significant number of mothers were morally opposed to abortion. Their initial response was to state a categorical opposition, using such terms as 'killing babies'. They were highly moralistic and talked about 'innocence' (of the baby) and 'blame' (of the pregnant woman):

> I'd heard about stories from people about having an abortion and that it's like young women that go out like on the piss, basically they have an abortion after a one night stand, it's their own fault, not the baby's. All these people who do it are taking the risk so why can't they take the consequences? You just shouldn't just throw away something because it's not convenient.

Even for this group, however, there were circumstances in which they saw abortion as acceptable. This is when the pregnant woman can, in some way, be viewed as 'innocent' herself. Her innocence matches the innocence of the foetus and the exercise of personal choice is thus based upon firm moral foundations. However, they expressed disapproval of the exercise of this choice by someone who had been careless or rash, maybe under the influence of alcohol or drugs:

> I don't agree with that unless you've been attacked or like if they did use contraception and they did get pregnant well maybe it is acceptable then but other than, if they didn't use contraception and they did get pregnant then I think it's their fault, they shouldn't have an abortion, it's their responsibility. It's their own fault. Like I say, not unless I was attacked or anything.

> In some circumstances, in some situations it's necessary to have it done because if someone like got raped and got pregnant it's a permanent reminder of what happened to them isn't it? In some situations it's all right.

Although none took an absolute moral position centred on the right to life of the baby, regardless of the circumstances of the pregnancy, the young women drew upon a discourse long associated with the wider debate about abortion: one of guilt and innocence. As Radcliffe-Richards (1994) argued, underlying such views is the notion of pregnancy as a punishment for sexual activity. However, these young women also articulated a distinctive moral agenda, in which they stressed the importance for them of taking responsibility for their actions, through continuing the pregnancy.

Conclusion

It has been argued that the 20th century has witnessed 'the transformation of conception and pregnancy from an uncontrollable risk to a freely chosen outcome of sexual intercourse' (Cook, 2004, p 339). It is clear, however, that the concept of risk is still evident when considering sex and young people. It is, however, a contested concept. The connection between one's view of the world and perceptions of risk (Douglas, 1992) is apparent in the field of sexual health. There is continuing conflict between those who seek to limit sexual risk without necessarily limiting sexual activity, and those for whom risk management involves the prohibition of sex among young people. Current policy and practice reflects the tensions between these two positions and this has inhibited the development of strategies to expand substantially young people's opportunities to learn about minimising risk in their sexual relationships.

This research, however, suggests that better access to sex and relationships education, and contraceptive provision, may help reduce the incidence of unintentional pregnancies but that it is not the whole answer. For these young women, inefficient contraceptive use was not always a result of ignorance or poor access to these services. Often it occurred when they were unable to assert their own wishes in a sexual relationship, or were indifferent to the risk involved.

The policy discourse in which underage sex is connected to risk does not reflect the complexity of these young women's representations of their own sexual decision making. For many, pregnancy was the chosen outcome, so the subjective meaning of risk for this group is in direct conflict with those seeking to drive down the teenage pregnancy rate. This group was the most dissatisfied with their lives, and pregnancy represented a positive choice in the face of limited options. Others were not consciously seeking to avoid the risk of pregnancy, and expressed unconcern about whether they became pregnant.

The policy implications of this risk behaviour suggest that the aims of current policy deserve more scrutiny. Strategies should move beyond a narrow concern with teenage pregnancy or sexual health towards thinking about young people and risk more broadly. Policy needs to take account of the social circumstances, including deprivation and inequality, which breed low expectations among some young people, as well as the importance of belief systems and attitudes towards sexual behaviour, teenage pregnancy and motherhood. One of the most significant findings to emerge from this research was the strong sense of individual agency and responsibility shown by young mothers in their decision to continue with their pregnancies, which was in marked contrast to the fatalism that many displayed in their negotiation of sexual encounters. Policy in this area needs to recognise and build on this in working with young women.

Note

[1] The issue was debated in the House of Commons, 19 July 2005; see Hansard Debates, 9 July 2005, cols 385-409.

References

Acheson, D. (Chair) (1998) *Independent Inquiry into Inequalities in Health Report*, London: The Stationery Office.

Arai, L. (2003) 'British policy on teenage pregnancy: the limitations of comparisons with other European countries', *Critical Social Policy*, vol 74, pp 89–102.

Chambers, R., Wakley, G. and Chambers, S. (2001) *Tackling Teenage Pregnancy: Sex, Culture and Needs*, Abingdon: Radcliffe Medical Press.

Christopher, E. (1987) *Sexuality and Birth Control in Community Work* (2nd edition), London: Tavistock Publications.

Cook, H. (2004) *The Long Sexual Revolution: English Women, Sex, and Contraception 1800-1975*, Oxford: Oxford University Press.

Counterpoint (2001) *Young People's Perception of Contraception and Seeking Contraceptive Advice*, London: Counterpoint (UK).

DfEE (Department for Education and Employment) (2000) *Sex and Relationship Education Guidance*, London: DfEE.

DH (Department of Health) (1999) *Saving Lives: Our Healthier Nation*, Cm 4386, London: The Stationery Office.

DH (2001) *The National Strategy for Sexual Health and HIV*, London: DH.

DHSS (Department of Health and Social Security) (1974) *Family PlanningService Memorandum of Guidance*, issued with Circular HSC(IS)32, London: DHSS.

Douglas, M. (1992) *Risk and Blame: Essays in Cultural Theory*, London: Routledge.

Durham, M. (1991) *Sex and Politics: The Family and Morality in the Thatcher Years*, Basingstoke: Macmillan Press.

Faludi, S. (1991) *Backlash: The Undeclared War Against American Women*, New York: Crown Publishers.

Family Education Trust (2002) *Why the Government's Teenage Pregnancy Strategy is Destined to Fail*, London: Family Education Trust.

FPSC (Family Policy Studies Centre) (1999) *Teenage Pregnancy and the Family*, Family Briefing Paper 9, London: FPSC.

Hawkes, G. (1995) 'Responsibility and irresponsibility: young women and family planning', *Sociology*, vol 29, no 2, pp 257–73.

Hek, R. and Hoggart, L. (2005) *Young Women, Sex and Choices: A Study of Young Motherhood in Shropshire*, Middlesex: Telford and Wrekin NHS Primary Care Trust and Middlesex University.

Hills, J. and Stewart, K. (2005) *A More Equal Society: New Labour, Poverty, Inequality and Exclusion*, Bristol: The Policy Press.

Hoggart, L. (2003) *Feminist Campaigns for Birth Control and Abortion Rights in Britain*, Lampeter: The Edwin Mellen Press.

Hoggart, L. (2006) *Young Women, Sex and Choices: A Study of Young Motherhood in Haringey*, London: Haringey and Enfield NHS Primary Care Trust.

Holland, J., Ramazanoglu, C., Sharpe, S. and Thomson, R. (1992) 'Pleasure, pressure and power: some contradictions of gendered sexuality', *Sociological Review*, vol 40, no 4, pp 645-74.

Holland, J., Ramazanoglu, C., Sharpe, S. and Thomson, R. (2004) *The Male in the Head: Young People, Heterosexuality and Power*, 2nd edn, London: The Tufnell Press.

Knijn, T. and Lewis, J. (2002) 'The politics of sex education policy in England and Wales and the Netherlands since the 1980s', *Journal of Social Policy*, vol 11, no 4, pp 669-94.

Lee, E., Clements, S., Ingham, R. and Stone, N. (2004) *A Matter of Choice? Explaining National Variation in Teenage Abortion and Motherhood*, York: Joseph Rowntree Foundation.

ONS (Office for National Statistics) (2001) *Population Trends*, 103, London: ONS.

ONS (2005) www.statistics.gov.uk

Radcliffe-Richards, J. (1994) *The Sceptical Feminist: A Philosophical Enquiry* (2nd edition), London: Penguin.

Santow, G. and Bracher, M. (1999) 'Explaining trends in teenage childbearing in Sweden', *Studies in Family Planning*, vol 30, no 3, pp 169-82.

SEU (Social Exclusion Unit) (1999) *Teenage Pregnancy*, Cmd 4342, London: The Stationery Office.

Sheldon, S. (1997) *Beyond Control: Medical Power and Abortion Law*, London: Pluto Press.

Singh, S. and Darroch, J. (2000) 'Adolescent pregnancy and childbearing: levels and trends in developed countries', *Family Planning Perspectives*, vol 32, no 1, pp 14-23.

Swann, C., Bopwe, K., McCormick, G. and Kosmin, M. (2003) *Teenage Pregnancy and Parenthood: A Review of Reviews*, London: Health Development Agency.

Tabberer, S., Hall, C., Prendergast, S. and Webster, A. (2000) *Teenage Pregnancy and Choice*, York: York Publishing Services/Joseph Rowntree Foundation.

Thomson, R. and Scott, S. (1991) *Learning about Sex: Young Women and the Social Construction of Sexual Identity*, London: The Tufnell Press.

UNICEF (United Nations Children's Fund) (2001) 'A league table of teenage births in rich nations', *Innocenti Report Card No 3*, July, Florence: Innocenti Research Centre.

Wellings, K., Field, J., Johnson, A. M. and Wadsworth, J. (1994) *Sexual Behaviour in Britain*, London: Penguin.

Wellings, K., Nanchahal, K., Macdowall, W., McManus, S., Erens, B., Mercer, C., Johnson, A. M., Copas, A. J., Korovessis, C., Fenton, K. A. and Field, J. (2001) 'Sexual behaviour in Britain: early heterosexual experience', *The Lancet*, vol 358, pp 1843-50.

West, J. (1999) '(Not) talking about sex: youth, identity and sexuality', *Sociological Review*, vol 47, no 3, pp 525-47.

Williams, F. (2004) *Rethinking Families*, London: Calouste Gulbenkian Foundation, UK Branch.

TWELVE

Risk and resilience: a focus on sexually exploited young people

Jenny J. Pearce

Introduction

This chapter looks at the relationship between risk, resilience and sexual exploitation as experienced by young people. First it defines sexual exploitation. It then looks at the different types of risk factors that have been identified to make a young person vulnerable to exploitation. It looks at the risks that young people might face while being involved in a sexually exploitative relationship and the interventions that might support vulnerable young people. It explores these in relation to the young person's resilience: their capacity to manage different forms of risk. It looks at the interplay between risk and resilience by referring to case study work with 55 sexually exploited young women (Pearce, 2002). The chapter then identifies a specific case study to look at resilience factors that contribute to the young person feeling stronger, more capable of recovering from abuse and of preventing it from reoccurring.

Sexual exploitation

Sexual exploitation is the process through which a young person under the age of 18 is enticed or coerced into a sexual relationship against their will. It has been asked: can a young person under the age of 18 choose to sell sex (Chasc and Stratham, 2005; Harper and Scott, 2005)? Hidden within this question is the issue of the young person's agency. Are they a victim of sexual exploitation – a victim of abuse exercising no choice in the matter – or are they a young prostitute – someone who is exercising some choice, being capable of deciding to earn money through the sale of sex (Phoenix, 2002; Melrose and Barrett, 2004)?

Local government protocols for safeguarding sexually exploited children and young people ask services to respond first and foremost to the young person as a victim of abuse, employing child protection procedures where appropriate (DH, 2000). Consultation papers are currently looking at enhancing ways of safeguarding children, mentioning the need to address sexual exploitation as one of the key objectives in keeping children safe (DfES, 2004). The government is also addressing law enforcement issues within prostitution and trafficking, looking at some of the related policy and practice interventions that emerge (DH, 2005). Despite these developments, government policy is contradictory. Although the 2003 Sexual Offences Act makes it an offence for someone to entice a young person under the age of 18 into prostitution, the 2006 Prostitution Strategy allows for young people themselves to be arrested for offences relating to prostitution. The Prostitution Strategy (HO, 2006) provided an ideal opportunity for a consistent message to be given positioning sexually exploited young people as victims of abuse. Instead, it upholds the caveat in the original guidance from the Department of Health (DH, 2000) that allows those who persistently and voluntarily return to selling sex to be arrested for offences relating to prostitution. The message, therefore, is mixed. The young person who responds to social service intervention can be deemed to be a victim of abuse, while the resistant and persistent returner is an active perpetrator of criminal offences. This is relevant as it is informed by a distinction between a compliant young person at risk from the harm others can do to them (the child as 'at risk') and a challenging young person who creates risks for themselves or others (the child as 'a risk'). The interest in this chapter is in exploring how young people can be supported to make the shift from being 'at risk' of sexual exploitation to being free from risk without necessarily becoming 'a risk' to themselves or others. Central to this is how young people build their own resilience against the harm and abuse that can be inflicted upon them by others.

'Routes into sexual exploitation'

Young people who sell or swap sex for money or other returns may find themselves in this situation for a number of reasons, and through a range of different 'routes in'. They may have decided themselves that they would sell or swap sex for reward, knowing of no other immediate way to access money, drugs or accommodation. If they are running away from home, they might choose to take a bed for the night in exchange for some sexual activity. If they stay in that home for a while, they may fall 'in love' with the host. They may think that they can manage what is happening to them, or they may think that the exploitation is something that they will tolerate so that the relationship can continue and they can receive gifts, drugs, accommodation or other repayments that appear to be essential to their survival. The young person may resent interference from professionals in their lives, rejecting any offers of support, saying that they want to be left alone. Indeed, they may have built a resilience that enables them to tolerate their situation and, through weighing it up, decide that it is better than being on the run, homeless or without any money.

Alternatively, they may have been manipulated into a dependent relationship with an adult who then encourages (or forces) them to sell or swap sex as a means of gaining, at best, a joint income for them both, and, at worst, an income for the abuser with no return to the young person concerned. The typical scenario with this 'grooming' results in the young person being isolated from any friends or family and, in many cases, becoming a victim of extreme intimidation and violence. Some young people may have been trafficked into the country specifically for the purpose of prostitution, although stories of such happenings are as yet anecdotal and are not supported by credible research data.

Risk factors

The impact of poverty has been identified as a key risk factor for many young people entering sexually exploitative situations. Their need for money, accommodation, drugs or rewards may, in their eyes, be unobtainable in any other way. Also, poor school attendance, long-term truancy and the resulting social exclusion from being outside of mainstream provision can compound the impact of poverty, making the young person feel that they will never be able to access legitimate education or training. They may then decide to engage with an informal economy selling sex for money or other returns. They may believe that they are exercising choice, albeit constrained choice, over how to earn their money when few other alternatives are available (Harper and Scott, 2005). These risk factors are seen as resulting from structural and environmental problems that could be remedied through improved targeted outreach educational and recreational services for young people who have drifted out of mainstream schooling (particularly 16- to 18-year-olds) and through improved supported teenage foster care placements or supported housing schemes for young people who cannot remain at home (Pearce, 2002).

Other research has argued that the risk factors are more individual than environmental. The grooming model of sexual exploitation mentioned above, where an adult isolates a young person and makes them dependent upon them, focuses attention on the individual vulnerability of the young person to abuse. In so doing it has encouraged recognition of the impact of risk factors such as low self-esteem and previous experiences of physical or sexual violence within the home. These risk factors are seen to make the young people vulnerable to abusive adults who are skilled in flattery and manipulation. The grooming model has also been applied to the way that particular young people who are looking for friendship are enticed into sexual relationships by paedophiles over the internet (Palmer and Stacey, 2004). Although the medium is different, the process of enticement is seen to be similar and the 2003 Sexual Offences Act provides legislation aimed at prohibiting the process.

Interventions responding to risk factors

The grooming model clearly positions sexual exploitation as a form of child abuse, a concern for child protection agencies (Barrett, 1997). It leads to interventions that focus on individual risk factors rather than on environmental risk factors such as poverty and disadvantage. A dual approach has been called for that addresses both individual and social problems (Pearce, 2002), arguing that the child protection agencies cannot address individual risk factors in isolation from interventions that support education and employment opportunities. Research findings suggest that taking a young person into local authority care cannot, on its own, be a solution (Dodsworth, 2000). It is known that a disproportionately high number of sexually exploited young people have been 'looked after' by the local authority. Evidence suggests that most adults working in the sex industry began their work when under the age of 25 (McKeganey and Barnard, 1996; Sanders, 2005) and that many had histories of being in local authority care, particularly residential care (Pitts, 1997). Cusick et al (2003) conducted a retrospective study of women and men involved in prostitution. Forty-two per cent of the total 125 participants had experience of being 'looked after'. Of the 18 'most vulnerable' young people involved in prostitution before the age of 18, 14 had been 'looked after'. Of those, 10 had been living in, or running from, local authority care when they first 'prostituted'. Such histories are prevalent across all racial and cultural barriers. Lee (2002) highlights particular vulnerabilities facing black and minority ethnic young people in care that need to be addressed. In current circumstances, therefore, 'care' does not necessarily safeguard individual young people from harm but can become a risk factor in its own right.

While it is important to focus on the impact of inadequate and disrupted parenting, poor self-esteem, problems with addiction and personal health, this should not be done at the expense of policy interventions that challenge risks created by economic and environmental disadvantage. However, 'individual responsibility' is a key concept within much current policy directed towards young people. As noted, the sexually exploited young person may change from being a young person 'at risk', to being 'a risk': a young offender who persistently and voluntarily returns to selling sex. So too will a young person receive 'opportunity cards' as rewards from proposals outlined in the Green Paper *Youth Matters* (DfES, 2005) only as long as they respond to certain expectations. They will be penalised if they do not. The Green Paper laudably claims that 'we will ensure that young people with more serious problems receive an integrative package of support from someone they know and trust' (DfES, 2005, p 2). However, it also advocates withholding the 'opportunity card' from those young people who demonstrate antisocial behaviour. The meaning behind the language is clear: only those who behave will receive support and encouragement. New opportunities (through the use of opportunity cards) will be available to all young people:

> except where they become involved in unacceptable or anti-social behaviour. In this case opportunity cards would be suspended or withdrawn ... poor behaviour is not acceptable. ... Sanctions should be used in response to any breaches ... [And] increased opportunities do not come for free ... we therefore expect young people to respect the opportunities made available to them ... we will therefore not top up the opportunity cards of young people engaging in unacceptable behaviour.... In these circumstances, we believe that local authorities should withdraw or suspend use of the card. (DfES, 2005, paras 94, 80, 89 and 116)

Similarly, while the 'respect agenda' advocates provision of opportunities for all, it also supports zero tolerance for behaviour that is deemed to be antisocial. What is overlooked and ignored here is the fact that the young people who are the most impoverished, the most 'in need' or 'at risk' are often those who are the most badly behaved and the most challenging to work with. Previous experiences of abuse or relationship breakdowns may mean that the young person finds it extremely difficult to build a trusting and respecting relationship with an adult. If they also have experienced extreme poverty and deprivation in their local area, they may well be cynical about the value of an opportunity card. Disruptive behaviour is often a demonstration of frustration and anger experienced by young people who are growing into adulthood with limited resources and support. They may have learnt to feel resentful or suspicious of offers of support, continuing to reject help as a means of exerting some control over a life that might feel chaotic (Howe, 1998).

Without condoning behaviour from young people that puts themselves or others in danger or at risk, it is important to look at how behaviour that may be seen to be 'abusing the opportunities and services provided', can be worked with (DfES, 2005, para 116). In terms of sexual exploitation, it is important that the behaviour that causes persistent and voluntary return to selling or swapping sex is understood and addressed, rather than temporarily silenced through punitive interventions. This does not mean rewarding bad behaviour, but it does mean understanding the behaviour in context. It means looking at how the young person is attempting to gain some control over their circumstances, how they are building resilience against future abuse by trying to manage their current situation. It means supporting the young person through contact with a responsible adult while also enabling them to access structural advantage through adequate housing, education and employment. Rather than having a cut-off point beyond which welfare interventions stop and criminal proceedings ensue, practitioners need to be supported to develop trusting relationships with the most difficult and challenging adolescents, aiming to build the young person's resilience so that they can protect themselves from future abuse. Accepting that the welfare professions have a duty to protect young people from the risk of abuse, there needs to be a related acceptance that work with those who have been abused will present challenging behaviour that is resource intensive to work with. A punitive response may provide a temporary quick fix for a short period, but will not tackle the longer-term problems that put the young person at risk in the first place. In summary, this means addressing the individual and structural risks that can lead young people into sexual exploitation while supporting the development of resilience to cope with them.

Drawing on case study research with young women who have been sexually exploited, it is possible to address how the young people concerned can be supported in ways that build their resilience. First, however, it is helpful to explore what is meant by resilience.

Resilience

Resilience can be defined as the capacity to transcend adversity. The more resilient the young person, the more they are able to draw on their own resources to overcome difficult conditions (Gilligan, 1999).

Resilient children are better equipped to resist stress and adversity, cope with change and uncertainty, and to recover faster and more completely from traumatic events or episodes (Newman, 2002, p 2).

The notion of resilience is not founded on protecting young people from all risks or adversities, but rather on helping them to learn to judge what is possible to manage. Risk and resilience work together, resiliencies being built up through successful management of risk. There is, as Rutter (1985) explains, a balancing act in helping young people to develop resilience to adversity. It means helping them to alter their exposure to risk, to interrupt a chain reaction of negative events (one bad thing leading to another), to establish and maintain self-efficacy and self-esteem and to create opportunities for change. Newman (2002) argues that interventions with young people need to be focused on how they can be helped to cope with adversities during periods of transition. He argues that more attention needs to be focused on how to support young people to build their resiliencies. Recent trends in health and social care have focused on factors that pose risks to children rather than on protective factors that can build resilience and opportunities for growth and adaptation. The more resilient the young person, the more they can access their own protective factors to help them to overcome adversity. 'The successful management of risk is a powerful resilience-promoting factor in itself' (Newman, 2002, p 3).

Newman suggests that protective factors emerge within the individual, the family and the environment. Individual attributes such as a developed awareness of self and of others, a sense of humour and a feeling of some self-worth all help the individual to overcome adversity. The individual is also supported by the family; the relationship between the young person, their parent or parent substitute being recognised as important. This means that the parent or parent substitute needs to value the importance of good care, and be consistent in its provision. Finally, environmental factors such as support of an extended family, a local community, care networks and educational resources can enhance resilience. Evidence from longitudinal studies shows that where these protective factors are in place, children and young people tend to recover from short-lived childhood adversities better than when they are not in place (Newman, 2002, 2004). Where adversities are continuous and severe and where protective factors are absent, young people are less resilient and less able to recover on their own from trauma or distress. However, even in these circumstances, there are still opportunities to build resilience. Resilience is understood as being dynamic, having the capacity to emerge later in life after earlier periods of coping problems. Research from the US and UK shows that if the individual young person can be encouraged to be active and independent, and can be supported by a parent or a parent substitute (a key worker for example), resilience can be enhanced. In other words, it is not too late to provide protective factors for adolescents whose earlier childhoods might have been disrupted.

A key method of enabling this is through giving the young person some control in dealing with their problems. Protective factors are enhanced by 'the promotion of self efficacy and self esteem through enabling children to exert agency over their environment' (Newman, 2002, p 5). Young people need to be encouraged to identify and draw on some of the benefits of their actions and to take control over their environment themselves:

> A key protective factor for children who have experienced severe adversities is the capacity to recognise any *benefits* that may have accrued, rather than focusing solely on negative effects, and using these insights as a platform for affirmation and growth. (Newman, 2002, p 5, emphasis in original)

Risk and resilience: sexually exploited young people

To explore this in relation to sexually exploited young people, reference is made to a case example drawn from a qualitative research project with 55 young women who were at risk of, or who experienced, sexual exploitation (Pearce, 2002). Developed in partnership with the National Society for the Prevention of Cruelty to Children (NSPCC), this work was conducted over a two-year period to create child-centred case studies with young women. This particular project worked only with young women, but referred any young men contacted through outreach to a local young men's project. The research partnership with the NSPCC was developed to provide follow-up casework for the young women who were contacted through the course of the research project. It also gave professional consultation to the research staff on questions of confidentiality and child protection. The young women were contacted for the research through street-based outreach, through referral from voluntary and statutory agencies and through 'snowballing' whereby young women brought their friends to drop-in sessions run by the research staff in partnership with the NSPCC. The aim of the research was to give child-centred accounts of their experiences of sexual exploitation, making recommendations for service delivery to meet their needs. It was achieved by undertaking casework with the young women over an 18-month period. A variety of 'youth work' activities, such as photography, art and drama, were employed to enable the young women to tell their stories.

The resulting case studies were analysed and three different categories of young women at risk were identified:

- The first was of young women who were at risk of being sexually exploited. Their behaviour and circumstances meant that they were putting themselves in situations where exploitative relationships could develop. They were spending time with older men in local parks and near taxi ranks, they were accepting rides in cars, sometimes in exchange for sexual favours, and they were running away from home, finding accommodation in local flats known to be used by those who dealt in drugs and who had reputations locally for pimping. There were 19 young people in this category.
- The second category consisted of 15 young women who spoke of swapping sex for accommodation, drugs, alcohol and transport. These young women did not define themselves as sex workers or as prostitutes, but as swapping sex in attempts to survive.
- Finally, there were a further 21 young women who did self-define as prostitutes, all aged between 16 and 18 inclusive, all selling sex from the street in attempts to manage poverty and problem drug and alcohol use. These young women had a range of other problems including homelessness, sexual health problems, criminal convictions, depression and self-harming behaviour.

The case studies are used here to identify the development of resilience. The 21 young women in the third category would all have been defined as persistently and voluntarily returning to sell sex on the street and for whom, under the Department of Health (DH, 2000) guidance and Home Office (HO, 2006) Prostitution Strategy, criminal proceedings could be applied. They are referred to as they needed the greatest resilience to withstand the problems they faced. Nineteen of the 21 were contacted through street-based outreach work, 11 having no other contact with any support services other than with street-based outreach workers. They had given up on contacting support services, saying that 'if services wanted to help, they should have helped in the past' (Sue, aged 16) and 'social services can't do nothing for people on the run' (Fiona, aged 18). However, service providers themselves felt that they had very little that they could offer. They spoke of the young women having rejected previous offers of support, of the many previous placement breakdowns and disrupted relationships and of the young women being difficult, if not impossible, to manage. The young women were described as lying, uncooperative, difficult to engage with, aggressive and unmanageable. Indeed, rather than being 'at risk', these young women were considered 'a risk' to themselves and to others.

These are the very young people who, according to current policy initiatives, should be penalised through Anti-Social Behaviour Orders (ASBOs) or through withdrawal of rewards, such as the opportunity card. However, review of their cases showed that, of the three categories of young women, they were the ones who had the most problems at any one time. Nineteen were regular heroin users, 16 had 'boyfriends' who were violent, 15 were homeless, 12 were regularly self-harming, eight had been raped, seven had attempted suicide, five had been abducted and held against their will for more than two nights, and three had had a baby. Thirteen of the young women had police records, three of whom had been in prison within the last year of the research. The only services that these young women were in contact with were outreach services that met them on the street. The majority were too depressed, ill or disillusioned to manage to make appointments with project-based services. A stalemate had developed where service providers felt rejected and unable to help while the young people felt cynical, abandoned and unable to access mainstream support.

Rather than focusing on the risks these young women posed to themselves and others, it is helpful here to look at the resiliencies that they demonstrate, as illustrated in the following case study.

Case study

To maintain confidentiality and anonymity, the details given about 'Karen' below draw on a number of similar cases.

Karen had been 'looked after' by the local authority since she was 14. She had been taken into care because she had been physically and sexually abused within her family home. She was placed in foster care, a placement that soon broke down. She was then placed in a residential unit. She repeatedly ran away from the unit and met a drug dealer who abducted her for three nights in his flat and raped her. He encouraged her to sell sex to his friends, saying that he needed the money for their own heroin use. She spent a lot of time in his flat and talked of being in love with him, calling him her boyfriend. She did not want to press charges against him for rape, abduction or for enticing her into prostitution. When she was out working on the street she met up with outreach workers. She lied to them about her age and circumstances, but accepted refreshments and support regarding sexual health.

She then became pregnant and had her first termination. Following the termination she developed a better relationship with her social worker and was offered a new foster placement. This went well for a short period. Her heroin use decreased dramatically and she began to talk about trying to pick up her work at school to see if she could study for some of her GCSEs. She saw less of her boyfriend and stopped selling sex on the street. However, she became pregnant again with a new, different boyfriend. While this new boyfriend wanted to be supportive, he felt unable to help her care for the child and wanted her to have a termination. Following this second termination she started using heroin again and returned to selling sex on the street. The foster placement broke down and she became homeless.

Karen then went missing for three months and was not seen until she telephoned the local detached outreach project premises, very depressed because she was pregnant for a third time. It took the project workers three attempts to meet with her at an arranged time and place so that they could take her to the sexual health clinic. In the first attempt to meet up, Karen did not turn up to the agreed meeting place. The second time she was very drunk, aggressive and depressed, saying that she did not want to go and that she was going to run away again. The third time she was ready to go to the clinic where she began to discuss how to deal with the pregnancy. The fact that the outreach workers continued to make determined efforts to contact her despite her rejecting behaviour was a turning point for Karen. She started to drop into the local youth work project more often, underwent the third termination and began to talk to a project drug worker about ways of beginning to manage her heroin use. She also talked to project workers about her abduction, the rape and the impact that her three terminations had had upon her. Eventually Karen worked with police to bring a case against her first boyfriend who had abducted her and introduced her to heroin. She said:

> You know when you get such emotion, you just feel like exploding and you can't take no more regardless of what

anyone is telling you to do.... That day when I finally phoned the police I was so relieved. I would say that was definitely the happiest day of my life. I've actually done something. (Karen, aged 17)

Analysis: risk and resilience

Karen's past had presented her with many of the risk factors that are known to make a young person vulnerable to sexual exploitation. She had experience of physical and sexual abuse within her family home, had been in care (both foster and residential care), had experienced a disrupted care history and had truanted from school. These problems from her past had undermined her self-esteem and confidence. Her own individual and family problems were compounded by the fact that her early years of growing up were in an overcrowded, run-down social housing estate with few financial resources available. Her individual, family and community resources were limited, undermining opportunities for her to build resilience against future risks and adversity.

This was demonstrated through her difficulty in challenging inappropriate and exploitative advances from her first boyfriend, the development of her problem heroin use and her difficulty in sustaining any constructive, long-term relationship with carers. Instead of being wary of the risks involved, she was persistently and voluntarily returning to selling sex on the street and would have been demonstrating behaviours, such as soliciting, that were arrestable offences and could be deemed antisocial. The risks that she faced were extensive and it could be argued that her behaviour may be best challenged through use of the criminal justice system. This is the argument that can be put into practice with current policy initiatives that advocate zero tolerance of antisocial behaviour and use of criminal proceedings for young people who persistently and voluntarily return to selling sex. However, a criminal conviction would do little other than add to Karen's problems and to her feeling of low self-worth and guilt. An alternative perspective could understand her return to face risks on the street and to run away from home as an effort to take some control over her life. Indeed, her attempts to 'do something' showed a strength and self-determination; a resilience that could become the central focus of interventions aiming to support her. This need not romanticise dangerous behaviour but could, instead, aim to focus on her own attempts to take some control over her circumstances.

Following Karen's third termination, the outreach workers' contact with her was maintained despite her rejecting behaviour. In turn, they received supervision and support that enabled them to understand her rejection of them as an expression of her distress, rather than as a personal attack on them. Karen was encouraged to see how she had managed some very difficult experiences. She did life-story work with the outreach workers to see how she had coped with violent and abusive relationships with men. She was enabled to see how a negative chain of events had developed and how, by maintaining contact with outreach workers, she was able to interrupt this chain of events. She was encouraged by workers to think of to periods of stability, particularly the period following her first termination where she had decided herself to focus on her schoolwork and to try to develop constructive relationships with her carers. In essence, workers tried to identify times that Karen had made decisions for herself, demonstrating her capacity to 'do something'.

The workload that was needed to maintain this positive contact with Karen was intensive. The ongoing supervision was essential to maintain the workers' energy and commitment and to help hold onto a sense of purpose despite failed appointments and challenging and rejecting behaviour (Melrose, 2002). Rather than focusing on the risks that faced Karen, this work concentrated on looking at how she had overcome adversities in the past. The project workers recognised that Karen, as other young women they met during outreach, may take a long time to reach a position where she would be able to make significant changes to her behaviour. However, they saw the achievements that had been made as ones that built resilience against further risk of abuse. Alongside this the outreach workers were able to negotiate with sexual health services and social services on Karen's behalf. This focus on individual and community work meant that Karen was supported to realise her own strengths and access the local support services that could assist her.

Conclusion

With support from her outreach workers, who needed support themselves through good supervision, Karen felt increasing control over her circumstances. She was eventually able to work with police and challenge her abductor and rapist. To allow this work to take place, specialist local outreach projects are needed. Investment in local, accessible resources that can provide targeted provision for young people who are most at risk are needed. This aims to look at where young people's strengths lie and to develop policies that will support these strengths. Enhancing young people's resiliencies need not undermine the fact that they have been victims of abuse. Instead, in helping them to make choices, albeit choices from a limited arena, young people can gain some confidence in managing their situation, however dire and dysfunctional it might appear.

Safeguarding young people from abuse through sexual exploitation cannot only be done through efforts to protect them from risk. Neither can it be achieved with punitive responses delivered through criminal proceedings that do little than add to the problems these young people experience. Rather, approaches are needed that offer local resources to help young people build their confidence and make changes they own and understand. Policy and practice need to support workers to enable them to sustain commitment with their clients, despite experiencing rejection. This way they can help young people build their own protective factors. Young people living in deprived and impoverished communities with disrupted and/or abusive care histories will face added challenges in their transition to adulthood. As noted, protective factors operate at both individual, family and community levels. The broader social, political and economic context within which sexual exploitation occurs must therefore be addressed with as high a profile as are the individual circumstances of the young people concerned. Specialist detached outreach projects that can access young people need to be supported to work alongside efforts to enhance education and employment opportunities within deprived communities.

These services are badly needed to support recommendations made by multi-agency panels that might not have the time or resources to work with the young people themselves. For specialist projects to be properly supported the punitive rhetoric of punishing young people's challenging behaviour needs to be confronted. Young people's strengths and resiliencies need to be identified and channelled constructively through support rather than through retribution. This way they can start to identify and build their resilience against the inevitability of risk during their transition to adulthood.

References

Barrett, D. (ed) (1997) *Child Prostitution in Britain: Dilemma and Practical Response*, London: The Children's Society.

Chase, E. and Stratham, J. (2005) 'Commercial sexual exploitation of children and young people in the UK – a review', *Child Abuse Review*, vol 14, pp 4-25.

Cusick, L., Martin, A. and May, T. (2003) *Vulnerability and Involvement in Drug Use and Sex Work*, HOR 268, London: Home Office.

DfES (Department for Education and Skills) (2004) *Every Child Matters: Change for Children*, London: HMSO www.dfes.gov.uk

DfES (2005) *Youth Matters*, Green Paper, London: DfES.

DH (Department of Health) (2000) *Safeguarding Children in Prostitution*, London: HMSO.

DH (2005) *Victims of Violence and Abuse Prevention Programme: Prostitution, Pornography and Trafficking Group*, London: DH.

Dodsworth, J. (2000) *Child Sexual Exploitation/Child Prostitution*, Social Work Monographs, 178, Norwich: University of East Anglia.

Gilligan, R. (1999) 'Enhancing the resilience of children in public care by mentoring their talent and interests', in *Child and Family Social Work*, vol 4, no 3, pp 187-96.

Harper, Z. and Scott, S. (2005) *Meeting the Needs of Sexually Exploited Young People in London*, Barkingside: Barnardo's.

HO (Home Office) (2006) *A Coordinated Prostitution Strategy and a Summary of Responses to Paying the Price*, London: Home Office.

Howe, D. (1998) 'Relationship-based thinking and practice in social work', *Journal of Social Work Practice*, vol 12, no 1, pp 45-56.

Lee, S. (2002) 'Gender, ethnicity and vulnerability in young women in local authority care', *British Journal of Social Work*, vol 32, no 7, pp 907-22.

McKeganey, N. and Barnard, M. (1996) *Sex Work on the Streets*, Milton Keynes: Open University Press.

Melrose, M. (2002) 'Labour pains: some considerations of the difficulties in researching juvenile prostitution', *International Journal of Social Research Theory, Methodology and Practice*, vol 5, no 4, pp 333-51.

Melrose, M. and Barrett, D. (eds) (2004) *Anchors in Floating Lives: Interventions with Young People Sexually Abused through Prostitution*, Lyme Regis: Russell House Publishing.

Newman, T. (2002) *Promoting Resilience in Children and Young People during Periods of Transition*, Edinburgh: Scottish Executive, available: www.scotland.gov.uk/library5/education/ic78-00.asp

Newman, T. (2004) *What Works in Building Resilience*, Ilford: Barnardo's.

Palmer, T. and Stacey, L. (2004) *Just One Click*, London: Barnardo's.

Pearce, J., with Williams, M. and Galvin, C. (2002) *It's Someone Taking a Part of You: A Study of Young Women and Sexual Exploitation*, London: National Children's Bureau.

Phoenix, J. (2002) 'In the name of prostitution: youth prostitution policy reforms in England and Wales', *Critical Social Policy*, vol 22, no 2, pp 353-75.

Pitts, J. (1997) 'Causes of youth prostitution, new forms of practice and political responses', in D. Barrett (ed) *Child Prostitution in Britain: Dilemmas and Practical Responses*, London: The Children's Society, pp 139-58.

Rutter, M. (1985) 'Resilience in the face of adversity: protective factors and resistance to psychiatric disorders', *British Journal of Psychiatry*, vol 147, pp 589-611.

Sanders, T. (2005) *Sex Work: A Risky Business*, Cullompton: Willan.

THIRTEEN

In need of protection? Young refugees and risk

Rosemary Sales

Introduction

Public discourse and policy in Britain towards young refugees has been deeply ambivalent. On the one hand young refugees are seen as 'at risk' both as refugees who have endured difficult and sometimes traumatic circumstances and as vulnerable children who may also be separated from families and others who are able to care for them. On the other hand, as asylum seekers, they are presented as posing a risk to society. During the debate on the Green Paper *Every Child Matters* (DfES, 2003), the government pledged that this title applied to all children without exception. The imperatives of an increasingly restrictive immigration policy, however, have taken precedence over other considerations in government policy in this area, often to the detriment of the rights of these children. Immigration policy poses particularly sharply the dichotomy between care and control or risk and protection in policy and practice. Since the early 1990s there has been an unprecedented number of measures concerning asylum and immigration, with six major Acts since 1993. These have increased controls on the entry of asylum seekers and on their social rights while awaiting a decision on their application. The implications of these measures for children's rights have been among the most strongly opposed during the passage of this legislation.

Asylum seekers are increasingly represented, in both official and popular discourse, as a threat to society. This supposed threat has several dimensions. They are seen as a burden on social services and housing, an argument used to justify the system of compulsory dispersal and the deterrent effect of benefit restrictions. They are presented as endangering the social order and the 'British way of life'. Asylum seekers, whose numbers are unpredictable, are also presented as hampering official attempts to manage migration on the basis of

Britain's economic interests (Flynn, 2005). After 11 September, they have been seen, in even more threatening terms, as potential terrorists. The 2001 Anti-terrorism, Crime and Security Act, passed in the wake of these attacks, introduced new measures to restrict the rights of asylum seekers who might be suspected of involvement in terrorism. This association of asylum seekers with risk was intensified in London in July 2005, as it was revealed that two of the failed London bombers had been granted asylum in Britain. Young refugees were singled out as a specific risk during the debate on the 2002 Nationality, Immigration and Asylum Bill, when Home Secretary, David Blunkett, claimed that in some schools there were too many asylum seekers and that this harmed the education of other children.

Asylum seekers under the age of 18, however, also come within the scope of national and international measures designed to protect the rights of children. The conflict between punitive immigration legislation and the duty of care imposed by these measures have been the subject of several legal battles and campaigns and create day-to-day tensions for professionals working with asylum seekers (Duvell and Jordan, 2001; Sales and Hek, 2004).

Asylum-seeking children who enter with their families may not be specific targets of policy but are affected, often disproportionately, by general asylum legislation. Those entering as 'unaccompanied minors' are the responsibility of social services departments and have been the focus of specific policy initiatives, as have 'trafficked children'. The protection afforded to these latter two groups is, however, conditional. The 'temporary protection' granted to unaccompanied minors expires when they reach the age of 18, leaving them facing possible deportation. The government is now piloting the forcible repatriation of children, beginning with 500 Vietnamese children (Lewis, 2006). Trafficked children are generally offered only temporary stay and may themselves be criminalised if they do not have the correct documentation (Mayor of London, 2004a, p 61).

This chapter focuses on young people involved in claiming asylum on their own behalf or as members of asylum-seeking families. These groups face uncertainty in relation to their status and future residence in Britain in addition to the risks related to their refugee experience. There has been a substantial body of research, including work commissioned by voluntary agencies and service providers, on the experiences and needs of young refugees. The chapter draws on these as well as data from research projects with refugees since 1996. These projects addressed a variety of issues relating to refugees' experiences in Britain, and included two sets of interviews with refugee children and teachers in London secondary schools.[1] This material is referred to below through the publications or reports arising from them or as quotations from individual interviews.

Who are refugees?

The late 1980s saw a dramatic increase in numbers of refugees worldwide, as economic and political crises forced many people to leave their homes. Most went to neighbouring countries, but a minority sought asylum in Europe or other developed countries. Applications in Britain reached a peak of 84,130 in 2002 (Home Office, 2004) but have fallen significantly since then with only 25,710 in 2005 (Home Office, 2006). Fluctuations in numbers reflect conditions in the countries of origin as well as policies designed to discourage applications. Official figures for adult asylum applications do not include dependants and no reliable figures exist for the numbers of refugee children (Dennis, 2002, p 4). The Home Office provides separate figures for applications by unaccompanied minors. There were 655 applications in the second quarter of 2006 (Home Office, 2006, p 22). These figures should be treated with caution, since there are considerable difficulties in defining this group and often uncertainty about the age of applicants (UNHCR, 2004). Some young people who are apparently accompanied may have been trafficked and are therefore at risk of abuse.

The 1951 Geneva Convention is the basis for international refugee law and has been ratified by all major states. It provides the right to make an individual asylum claim and protection from being returned to face danger (non-refoulement). Those seeking protection go through a formal process to determine whether they fit the Convention definition of a refugee as someone who:

> Owing to a well-founded fear of being persecuted for reasons of race, religion, nationality, membership of a particular social group or political opinion , is outside the country of his nationality and is unable or, owing to such fear, is unwilling to avail himself of the protection of that country of his nationality.... (UNHCR, 1951, Art 1(2))

This definition has been widely criticised as too restrictive. It requires both objective (well-founded) and subjective (fear) grounds for the claim and the persecution must be shown to be based on membership of a particular group. A significant omission is persecution on grounds of gender and sexuality. Unaccompanied minors must make their claim within the same process as adults but their particular needs and situations are not properly addressed and 'children are increasingly being subjected to accelerated immigration procedures which offer insufficient protection' (Barnardo's et al, undated, p 7). Traumatised people, especially victims of torture or rape, are generally reluctant to discuss their experiences (Refugee Council, 2005a, p 4), particularly in the stressful conditions of an interview with immigration officers, an issue that is magnified for children.

With the rise in asylum applications in the 1980s, the proportion of applicants granted Convention status fell dramatically, from 59% in 1982 to less than 10% in 1991 (Duke et al, 1999, p 106). In 2003, only 5% of applications resulted in full asylum, although 28% of applicants received some form of long-term status (Home Office, 2004, p 1). Research by the Refugee Council found that 'decision making is based on the assumption that asylum seekers are 'bogus' until proved otherwise' (Refugee Council, 2004a, p 7). An audit by the United Nations Children's Fund (UNHCR) in 2005 of Home Office practice was highly critical of the decision-making process.[2]

Young refugees

Most young asylum seekers entering Britain come with their families. A minority come alone or with other adults, for a variety of reasons. Parents may be dead, missing, imprisoned or too sick to travel, or may have fled leaving the children with relatives or other carers. Some children have witnessed the violent death of a parent or a relative (Ayotte and Williamson, 2001, p 16). Others may have been abused or abandoned by parents (Ayotte, 2000, p 9). In some cases parents send children abroad to safety, as was the case with Jewish refugees in the *Kindertransport* during the Nazi period. Sometimes relatives pool money to send a child. A Somali boy, aged 14, described being sent to London from a refugee camp in Kenya:

> My brother took me to the airport. I was 'chosen' by my family to go. I was the middle one, I was old enough to be sent, but not too old to get education. I thought I would have a better life in England, I would be able to help. (Interview with unaccompanied Somali refugee, 18 July 1996)

Some children have faced detention and torture as a result of their own involvement in political activity or that of family members. They are especially vulnerable to certain forms of exploitation and oppression, for example forcible recruitment into the armed forces, while in some conflicts child civilians become targets for murder and torture. For girls, sexual violence and rape are particular risks (Ayotte, 2000, p 9). Children may be trafficked 'for the purposes of ... prostitution, child pornography, sweatshop work, forced begging, pick pocketing and drug trafficking' (Mayor of London, 2004a, p 59).

Young refugees thus bring with them experiences of dislocation and loss. They are torn, often violently, from their past life and thrust into a new environment where they do not understand the rules of social life or of the legislation that they must negotiate. In the current climate of hostility to asylum seekers, they face suspicion and mistrust. They experience 'a rupture in the narrative threads running through their lives' (Summerfield, 1998, p 16, cited in Kohli and Mather, 2003, p 16), which can be experienced as 'cultural bereavement' (Ahern et al, 1999, p 228). Disruption in schooling and family life may impact on social skills and the ability to form relationships (BMA, 2002, p 8). This experience of loss is magnified for unaccompanied minors who are vulnerable as children, as refugees and through separation from people who provide care and protection. This separation makes them 'vulnerable to a number of risks and likely to be disadvantaged in emotional, social, educational and economic terms' (Ayotte and Williamson, 2001, p 15).

Asylum seekers are prone to particular health problems, for example malnutrition, disease and disability as a result of the general or immediate circumstances that forced them to flee, including the effects of war and torture (BMA, 2004). The traumatic events that they may have undergone or witnessed can bring mental health problems, including depression and anxiety (BMA, 2004, p 1). Western psychiatric categories have often been ascribed to refugees in ways which ignore the social, political and economic factors of their experience (Watters, 2001). As Ahern et al (1999, p 231) put it, '(t)he refugee family, including the children, are generally ordinary people who have experienced extraordinary events'. Furthermore, these problems may result from experiences in Britain. The punitive asylum system means that asylum seekers often face a repetition of the trauma from which they fled, with damaging effects on mental health (see, for example, Silove et al, 2000). Refugees who survive dangerous situations, to negotiate the difficult journey and the immigration process, have often displayed considerable resilience. Rather than portraying refugees as 'passive victims', Watters (2001) argues that attention should be given to their resistance and the ways in which they interpret and respond to experiences.

Asylum policy in Britain

The driving force of recent asylum policy has been the perceived 'risk' posed by asylum seekers. Increasingly restrictive legislation (see Box 13.1) has made it more difficult to enter Britain, forcing people to enter illegally often in dangerous conditions and forcing reliance on people who may themselves exploit or abuse them. A survey by the Refugee Council (2004a, p 4) found that 69.4% had used agents to enter the country. A young Kurdish boy described his journey to London:

> There was this big storm…. The boat was a small lifeboat, and everyone was squashed in and it was terrible. I remember lots of small kids, one was crying for his dad. His hands were tied to his dad as they were trying to get in, so the dad he let go of the rope so his son could get in, and the boy was crying because [his father] died…. We had no food or water and people were starving and thirsty…. We were washed up on an island. There were four boats of us and so many died because they were so hungry. (Hek et al, 2001, p 11)

Box 13.1: UK asylum legislation: key points

1993 Asylum and Immigration Appeals Act
- Created processes for dealing with asylum applications.
- Withdrew right to secure tenancy in social housing for asylum seekers.
- Benefits for asylum seekers set at 70% of Income Support.

1996 Asylum and Immigration Act
- Withdrew cash benefits for asylum seekers.
- Introduced vouchers following court judgement that local authorities should provide basic subsistence for 'destitute' asylum seekers.

1999 Asylum and Immigration Act
- Introduced vouchers for all asylum seekers.
- Established National Asylum Support System (NASS).
- Introduced compulsory dispersal for families and single people.

2002 Nationality, Immigration and Asylum Act
- Introduced new controls on entry.

- Proposed induction/accommodation/removal centres for asylum seekers.
- Vouchers phased out.
- Section 55 – support refused for individuals if asylum claim not made 'as soon as reasonably practicable'.
- Removed 'concession' allowing asylum seekers to apply to work after six months.

2004 Asylum and Immigration (Treatment of Claimants, etc.) Act
- Limited rights of appeal on asylum.
- Electronic monitoring of asylum seekers who 'appear' over 18.
- Support can be refused for failed asylum-seeking families with dependent children *deemed to be in a position to leave the UK* if they do not cooperate with removal.

2006 Asylum and Immigration Act
- Targets for removals of 'failed' asylum seekers – detention to become 'the norm' for this group.
- Refugees granted temporary leave to remain, to be reviewed after five years.
- New processes for considering asylum claims introduced to enable greater control over asylum seekers.
- Pilot project set up for returning unaccompanied asylum-seeking children.

Each new policy measure has created an additional system of support alongside previous arrangements, 'leaving a complex tangle of law, provision and regulation' (Mayor of London, 2004b, p 8). A social category of 'asylum seeker', increasingly segregated from mainstream society, has been created (Sales, 2002). The National Asylum Support System (NASS) was introduced in 1999 to provide social support to asylum seekers outside mainstream benefit structures. Compulsory dispersal to areas outside London, often without previous significant minority ethnic populations, was introduced in 2000 for those in need of accommodation. Racist attacks have been common, with several murders reported.[3]

Detention centres were renamed 'removal centres' in 2002 as part of 'normalising' the process of deportation of failed asylum seekers. There have been attempts to exclude some asylum seekers from all forms of support (Cunningham and Tomlinson, 2005). The 1996 Asylum and Immigration Act removed benefits from people claiming asylum within the country rather than at the port of entry. A subsequent court ruling that destitute asylum seekers were entitled to support under the 1948

National Assistance Act led to the introduction of vouchers for subsistence. In 2004, support was removed from 'failed asylum seekers' who did not cooperate with removal, including those with dependants. It envisaged that children of those made destitute would be accommodated in local authority care, a policy described by the Bishop of Southwark as the 'social policy of the workhouse' (Cunningham and Tomlinson, 2005, p 256).

The rights of asylum-seeking children

The UN Convention on the Rights of the Child (UNCRC), ratified by the British government in 1991, gives widespread protection to children and their families (Henricson and Bainham, 2005). Article 3.1 states that '[I]n all actions concerning children, whether undertaken by public or private social welfare institutions, courts of law, administrative authorities or legislative bodies, the *best interests of the child shall be paramount*' (emphasis added). The Convention includes a number of general rights relevant to refugee children and some specific to refugees, including Article 22, which requires states to ensure that they 'receive appropriate protection and humanitarian assistance'. The 1989 Children Act was the key mechanism for fulfilling the UK's responsibilities under the UNCRC. The Convention has not, however, been incorporated into domestic law, which would make these rights enforceable in UK courts. In formally ratifying the Convention, the British government was one of only two countries to enter a derogation in relation to immigration law, which reserved the right to:

> apply such legislation, in so far as it relates to the entry into, stay in and departure from the United Kingdom of those who do not have the right ... to enter and remain in the United Kingdom ... as it may deem necessary from time to time. (cited in Williamson, 1999, p 162)

The UN Committee on the Rights of the Child suggested that this reservation is incompatible with the principles and provisions of the UNCRC (Lumley, 2003, p 4) but it has remained in place through successive administrations. Much immigration legislation has been criticised as inconsistent with human rights obligations, particularly in relation to children. An area of particular concern is detention that the Refugee Children's Consortium claims breaches 15 Articles of the UNCRC (Lumley, 2003, p 4). Anne Owers, HM Inspector of Prisons, in a report on Yarl's Wood Detention Centre, suggested that 'there was no evidence that children's welfare was taken into account when making decisions about initial and continued detention' (Owers, 2006, p 5). Owers interviewed 13 children detained at the centre and 'their comments and fears illustrate potently the distress of detained children and their anxieties about their current and future situation' (Owers, 2006, pp 14-15). Some spoke about the intimidating nature of the process by which they were brought into detention, like this 13-year-old boy:

> When they came to the house like an earthquake the way they knock. I think there were ten of them spread all around our house.... The way they look at you is like you are a criminal.... My two hands were cuffed in front. (Owers, 2006, p 5)

British immigration policy makes a sharp distinction between 'accompanied' and 'unaccompanied' young refugees. Those arriving with a parent or an adult deemed by the authorities as responsible for them are dealt with as part of the family in relation to their asylum application and are supported through NASS and subject to dispersal. Those entering alone are classed as 'unaccompanied minors' and local authority social services are responsible for providing care. Unaccompanied minors have the same formal rights as citizens until the age of 18, while those living with families have lesser rights.

Asylum-seeking children living in families

The policy changes outlined above affect young refugees through their impact on the family and in specific ways. The low level of income provided perpetuates poverty in which some live for months or years. This is intensified by the ban on employment, which forces many into informal work, often in highly exploitative conditions.[4] A survey of asylum-seeking families housed in London found serious problems with damp, disrepair, infestation, security, safety and overcrowding (Mayor of London, 2004b, p 16). These conditions impact on health, which may deteriorate after entry to the UK (BMA, 2002). Asylum seekers are entitled to healthcare and schooling, but access to appropriate services sometimes proves difficult. Dennis (2002, p 7) reports that nearly half of the children participating in a survey had not yet been offered a school place. They are not entitled to the range of social work provision and thus 'the full protection of the

Children Act in terms of either meeting their needs or protecting them from harm' (Morris, 2003, p 1).

Dispersal has particularly serious impacts for children. Dunkerley et al (2006, p 84) found that children were particularly vulnerable within the NASS system as the continual uprooting from friends and familiar places creates stress. They quote a local authority officer in a dispersal area as saying: 'These children are in limbo and have been in limbo all along' (Dunkerley et al, 2006, p 85). In the 2002 Nationality, Immigration and Asylum Act the government proposed to house most asylum seekers in 'accommodation centres' and to educate children in these centres rather than mainstream schools. This was justified by Home Secretary David Blunkett, in language reminiscent of Thatcher's notorious anti-immigrant speech of 1978,[5] by the claim that asylum seekers were 'swamping' local schools. During the parliamentary debate, 103 Members of Parliament declared this proposal contrary to the UNCRC. Jill Rutter, an expert on refugee children's education, argues that 'for refugee children, inclusion within mainstream education has special significance. Attending school may be a therapeutic and normalising experience' (Rutter, 2003, p 9). The Home Office argued that separate education would improve the quality of provision since 'children will not be out of education for weeks or months whilst a suitable placement is found'.[6] This statement acknowledges the problems in accessing services but does not address concerns about segregation. No accommodation centres have yet been built, largely due to opposition from local people, which has fed on notions of the threat posed by asylum seekers.

In proposing dispersal and the NASS system, the government claimed that those 'genuinely fleeing persecution' would 'not be overly concerned about whether that support is provided in cash or in kind, nor about the location in which they are supported' (Home Office, 1998, p 5). The system, however, undermines the rights of asylum seekers – including those subsequently deemed 'genuine refugees' – delaying the process of integration that should begin on arrival (Refugee Council, 2004b). For children, integration cannot wait until a decision has been made on their asylum claim. What may be a relatively short time for an adult can seem like a lifetime for a child and constitutes a significant part of their childhood (Refugee Children's Consortium, 2002, p 1).

Unaccompanied minors

Unaccompanied minors have remained the responsibility of social services through successive legislation. In spite of examples of good practice, breaches of human rights legislation routinely occur in the treatment particularly of older teenagers, placing them at risk of abuse (Cemlyn and Briskman, 2003). Social work practice with refugees is affected by the punitive thrust of immigration policy and the negative discourses surrounding it and 'assumptions about the needs and circumstances of these children, together with pressure on local authority resources, have encouraged practice that is at variance with both the specific terms of the Children Act and its wider intentions' (Morris, 2003, pp 3-4). A Department of Health Good Practice Guide issued in 1995 (DH/SSI, 1995) stated that asylum seekers should be treated as 'children first', but, 'in many cases, they do not receive the same standard of care routinely afforded to indigenous children in need, even though their legal rights are identical' (Audit Commission, 2000, p 66, cited in Morris, 2003, p 7).

Age is crucial in determining the treatment of young asylum seekers, but establishing age is not straightforward. Many do not have correct documentation and there is no reliable medical test. The burden of proof is with the applicant (Mitchell, 2003) and children may be held in detention when their age is disputed (Barnardo's et al, undated). Even for those judged to be minors, age determines their treatment by social services. A court judgment in 2003 (the 'Hillingdon Judgment') reiterated local authorities' duty to support all unaccompanied children under Section 20 of the 1989 Children Act. Many social services departments, however, remain reluctant to treat 16- and 17-year-olds as 'children in need' (Morris, 2003, p 12) often treating them with suspicion and at best assuming them 'to be too "street wise" to need "looking after"' (Morris, 2003, p 40). Despite their 'resilience and apparent maturity' (Stanley, 2001, p 6), the experiences that young separated refugees have undergone place them at high risk and in need of specialist care and protection. Most are supported under Section 17 of the Act, often in unsuitable and poor-quality bed and breakfast accommodation (Mayor of London, 2004a, p 15). The organisation Save the Children, in research across England, reported concerns about children living with adults not known to them. Some were placed in hostels with adults who take drugs or have mental health problems (Mayor of London, 2004a, p 16). Many were placed outside the borough, often away from community members, and experienced problems in accessing legal advice, interpreters and support networks (Mayor of London, 2004a, p 25). Many faced hostility from local populations.

Although unaccompanied minors must claim asylum in their own right, Home Office decision making often does not take into account the child-specific forms of persecution that occurs in some source countries, leading to a 'protection deficit' (Bhabha and Finch, 2006). There is no statutory right to advocacy. The Refugee Council has a panel of advisers, but it is not statutory and there is no obligation on social services to work with it (NSPCC, 2004). Of 6,404 referrals to the panel, only 1,500 were allocated a named adviser in 2004 (Mayor of London, 2004a, p 19). Lack of proper advice and support can jeopardise their claim. Miri,[7] an orphan now aged 15 from Vietnam, was brought to England by an agent. On arrival, he advised her to tell immigration officers that she was 19. She was taken into the care of social services in London as an unaccompanied minor, and attended classes in a voluntary project where she was a 'brilliant student'. Five months later she was detained in Yarl's Wood Detention Centre. Although she had a birth certificate confirming her age as 15, she was deported to Belgium where she had stopped briefly on her way to England. Her teacher, who visited her at the Centre, described her as 'utterly distraught' and Centre staff as 'embarrassed' because they knew she was too young to be held there.

British law recognises as 'unaccompanied' only those who enter alone. Immigration officials assume that children accompanied by an adult are safe (Bostock, 2003, p 17), which can leave children vulnerable to abuse. Children's rights campaigners argue that the important question in relation to the risks faced by children is whether they are separated from parents or their legal/customary primary caregiver.[8] An unknown number enter with family members or others who are 'unwilling, unsuitable or unable to provide the children with appropriate care in their destination country' (Ayotte and Williamson, 2001, p 15). The relationship may be caring, but the adult (for example a 19-year-old sibling new to Britain) may have difficulty in fulfilling the parenting role (NSPCC, 2004) and be struggling themselves to adjust to life in Britain. Other children may be 'accompanied' by traffickers who abuse them sexually or economically. The Victoria Climbié case brought this issue to public attention, but her abuse by relatives entrusted with her care was not an isolated incident. Children from Central Africa are frequently brought to Britan to be exploited in domestic work and prostitution, while Chinese and Vietnamese boys are brought in for restaurant work (Somerset, 2004, p 10). Social services departments are unlikely to be aware of these children. A senior social services manager warned that '[T]he management of risk in relation to those young people who are placed with 'family' members, often with quite tenuous links, is ... of major concern' (quoted in Mayor of London, 2004b, p 36). The government's response to trafficking has focused on combating crime rather than supporting victims (UNICEF UK, 2004). The penalties for not having documentation give an incentive to hide the method by which they entered, deterring them from cooperating with the prosecution of abusers, and may jeopardise their asylum claim.

Growing up in Britain

Refugee children, particularly separated children, have multiple needs but often bring resilience and 'a willingness to succeed and overcome the challenges of settlement' (Kohli and Mather, 2003, p 204). Their development may be accelerated in some areas and arrested in others (Morris, 2003, p 5). They have had to cope with traumatic experiences, often alone, sometimes looking after younger siblings, taking responsibility for their journey and for finding a place for themselves in their new environment. Settlement is a multifaceted and multi-staged process. Refugees tend to be preoccupied initially with basic needs for shelter, subsistence and safety and it may only be when practical issues are resolved that they are able to face deeper concerns. As Kohli and Mather (2003, p 208) put it 'young people want to face the present first, the future next and the past last'.

Aspirations for the future

For refugee families, children may be the route to settlement, their hope for a future they feel they have lost themselves. Many parents have high aspirations for their children, and refugees often have a 'hunger for education' (Kohli and Mather, 2003, p 205). An Ofsted report in 2003 found that '[M]any asylum seeker pupils make good progress in relatively short periods of time and almost all made at least satisfactory progress. The combination of their determination to succeed and the strong support of their parents provided a potent recipe for success' (cited in Mayor of London, 2004a, p 44). But although academic achievement can help them to 'find some justification for coming so far away from home', for some 'commitment can outrun capability when they are emotionally drained, or intellectually unable to manage the goals that their desire for success has set for them' (Kohli and Mather, 2003, p 209). Research in two

London schools found that refugee children had high ambitions but did not always have a realistic idea of the requirements for the work they aimed for (Hek et al, 2001).

Refugee children may carry a heavy burden of expectations, which can be particularly difficult for unaccompanied asylum seekers who see themselves as 'the carrier of hope' for the family and may experience this 'simultaneously as an honour and a punishment' (Kohli and Mather, 2003, p 204). Fahroud, sent alone from Somalia, talked of the pressure to 'give something back' through succeeding academically and financially (interview with Somali asylum seeker, London school, 18 July 1996). They may also feel guilt and anxiety about people left behind. Mehmet, who left Turkey because of his political activity, said:

> I feel I ran away from my friends in Turkey. I was opportunist, I shouldn't have left my friends – we were five boys, we were always together. Three of them were imprisoned and one died there. I feel guilty. Now I want to study so that I can help. I want to be a lawyer and work in human rights. (Interview with Kurdish asylum seeker, London school, 5 June 1996)

Refugee children face huge obstacles to realising these ambitions. The problem of interrupted schooling may be exacerbated by language difficulties, which can make them feel they are failing on a daily basis. This can cause children to misbehave, often leading to suspension or exclusion from school. As one boy put it: 'Sometimes I do push past those teachers but I can't take it. They make me small but I can't see what they're going on about. I don't know English enough and they don't take no time' (Hek et al, 2001, p 15). School policy and practice can make a real difference to the ability of refugee students to settle and achieve in the new environment. One of the schools in Hek et al's (2001) study had developed whole-school procedures for supporting refugee students and this positive valuing of their experiences appeared to be reflected in the feelings of belonging that the children expressed. A teacher described a project he had initiated in 1996:

> I planned a whole-class project on refugees. There were several refugee children in the class, and I wanted them all to be happy about it so I asked each individually. They all said that we should go ahead, but 'don't talk about me'. So I invited someone in to talk about his experience as a

refugee. As he was talking, one girl started crying and I felt I had made a terrible mistake. But when I apologised to her she said: 'No, he was telling my story. Now I want to talk about it myself'. (Interview with a teacher, London school, 5 June 1996)

Changing family relationships

Refugee families experience changing roles, as children learn English and adapt faster than their parents and may take the role of 'managing and mediating the new culture for parents' (Ahern et al, 1999, p 230). This can rob parents of authority, making them feel infantilised, while children may take on too much responsibility. As interpreters for their parents, children may become involved in issues that increase anxiety, such as parents' medical problems or immigration issues (interviews with Kurdish refugees, London, June 2000). Young people have frequently taken the lead in fighting deportation, showing 'a degree of resilience and independence which makes them effective leaders and activists within peer groups and local communities' (Mayor of London, 2004a, p 2). Muyeke Lemba, who led a successful campaign with the support of her school and local organisations in London, described her experience:

> The government had sent a letter to my Dad saying we have to leave the country … I took it very seriously and was very upset, we all suddenly became closer to each other.... People who knew our case were so supportive, they wrote petitions, letters to the Home Office, we had meetings, and people from different coalitions helped.... I was able to take care of the campaign and school work. (NCADC, www.ncadc.org.uk, accessed June 2005)

Becoming 18

Uncertainty over their asylum application dominates the lives of young asylum seekers, making it difficult to settle. For unaccompanied minors, the formal transition to adulthood at 18 is particularly difficult. As well as the usual problems associated with growing up, they lose their entitlement to care and often their right to remain in Britain. Instead of gradually taking on responsibility, these changes take place overnight, often with little preparation. As their discretionary leave to remain expires, they face dispersal as an adult asylum seeker, or, if their claim has failed, deportation. Rather than looking forward to their 18th birthday, they may dread its approach. Although the 2000 Leaving Care Act recognised that young vulnerable people need continuing support beyond the age of 18, refugees are expected to find their way in an adult system, often with minimum information about how it works. This often leads to crisis, destitution and homelessness (Mayor of London, 2004a, p 21) and the loss of friends and support networks (Stanley, 2001, p 5). Some choose to 'disappear' rather than face dispersal (Mayor of London, 2004a, pp 18-19).

Roy Ekundayo Ajala's story graphically illustrates these problems. Roy came to Britain from Nigeria when he was 11 following abuse by an uncle. He joined his parents who were already in Britain. He came on a false passport but had no idea that he was brought in illegally. Roy's father also physically and sexually abused him and he and his brother were taken into care. Roy was treated for depression but his asylum application was refused on the grounds that his case did not fit the Geneva Convention definition. At 18, he was homeless, unable to work or claim benefits and faced deportation. Although he waged a successful campaign to remain, Roy described his feelings:

> I want somebody to take some of the load.... I've got the feeling I've got to grow up too fast. I'm already 18 and all I want is to be a child, just for someone to come and look after me, but that's not possible. (http://tv.oneworld.net/article/view/104576/1/)

Conclusion

The Green Paper *Every Child Matters* (DfES, 2003), which paved the way for the 2004 Children Act identified unaccompanied asylum-seeking children as a group in 'greatest need'. Although children's charities proposed specific measures to protect them (see, for example, NSPCC, 2004), the legislation included no such measures. Subsequent asylum legislation, on the contrary, has further undermined their rights, most notoriously in the return of unaccompanied minors. The Act places a new duty on public agencies to have regard to the need to safeguard and promote the welfare of children (Section 11) but, in the spirit of the derogation from the UNCRC, immigration authorities are excluded from this duty. The Refugee Council expressed itself as 'mystified at the continued resistance to place the same duty on the NASS, centre managers of immigration removal centres and immigration officers at the port of entry' (Refugee Council,

2004b, p 3). As it noted in its briefing on the *Five-Year Strategy on Immigration*, 'it is clear that the best interests of the child will be a secondary consideration to the determination to demonstrate tough enforcement measures' (Refugee Council, 2005b, p 3).

A basic contradiction remains between the rights of refugee children and punitive immigration legislation. Recent policy has given priority to protecting society against the risk that, the government claims, asylum seekers pose. This has undermined the protection of vulnerable children, placing them at ever greater risk.

Notes

[1] The first was a pilot study on the experiences of refugee children, carried out in 1996. It involved semi-structured interviews with 12 asylum-seeking children aged between 13 and 17. All names have been changed. The second, in 2000, involved two schools, including the same one as in the first project, and focused on policies and practices to promote settlement. The methodology and findings are presented in Hek et al (2001).

[2] Reported in *File on Four*, BBC Radio 4, 21 June 2005.

[3] For example, the *Manchester Evening News* (25 April 2005) reported an attack by nine people on a Kurdish asylum seeker in Salford, in which his leg was broken.

[4] The 2002 Nationality, Immigration and Asylum Act withdrew the concession under which asylum seekers could apply to take up employment after six months. A European Union directive, which came into force in 2005, allowed this after one year.

[5] In an interview for Granada Television's *World in Action* programme on 30 January 1978, Mrs Thatcher, then Leader of the Opposition, claimed that British culture was being 'swamped' by immigrants.

[6] Personal communication from Home Office staff member, 27 May 2005.

[7] Information supplied by a teacher, 7 June 2005.

[8] www.separated-children-europe-programme.org

References

Ahern, F., Loughry, M. and Ager, A. (1999) 'The experiences of refugee children', in A. Ager (ed) *Refugees: Perspectives on the Experience of Forced Migration*, London: Continuum, pp 1-23.

Ayotte, W. (2000) *Separated Children Coming to Western Europe: Why they Travel and How they Arrive*, London: Save the Children.

Ayotte, W. and Williamson, L. (2001) *Separated Children in the UK: An Overview of the Current Situation*, London: Refugee Council/Save the Children.

Barnardo's, The Children's Society, NCH, NSPCC and Save the Children (undated) *Room for Improvement: A Manifesto for Children*, London: NSPCC Publications.

Bhabha, J. and Finch, N. (2006) *Seeking Asylum Alone: Unaccompanied Children and Refugee Protection in the UK*, Report funded by John D. and Catherine Macarthur Foundation, Cambridge MA: President and Fellows of Harvard College, available from www.humanrights.harvard.edu/conference/SAA_UK.pdf

BMA (British Medical Association) (2002) *Asylum Seekers: Meeting their Health Care Needs*, London: BMA.

BMA (2004) *Asylum Seekers and their Health*, London: BMA.

Bostock, L. (2003) *Effectiveness of Childminding Registration and its Implications for Private Fostering*, London: Social Care Institute for Excellence.

Cemlyn, S. and Briskman, L. (2003) 'Asylum, children's rights and social work', *Child and Family Social Work*, vol 8, no 3, pp 163-78.

Cunningham, S. and Tomlinson, J. (2005) '"Starve them out": does every child really matter? A commentary on Section 9 of the Asylum and Immigration (Treatment of Claimants, etc.) Act, 2004', *Critical Social Policy*, vol 25, no 2, pp 253-75.

Dennis, J. (2002) *A Case for Change: How Refugee Children in England are Missing Out*, First findings from the monitoring project of the Refugee Children's Consortium, London: Refugee Council, Save the Children and The Children's Society.

DH (Department of Health)/SSI (Social Services Inspectorate) (1995) *Unaccompanied Asylum-seeking Children: A Training Pack (with Practical Guide)*, London: HMSO.

DfES (Department for Education and Skills) (2003) *Every Child Matters*, Green Paper, Cm 5860, Norwich: HMSO.

Duke, K., Sales, R. and Gregory, J. (1999) 'Refugee resettlement in Europe', in A. Bloch and C. Levy (eds) *Refugees, Citizenship and Social Policy in Britain and Europe*, Basingstoke: Macmillan, pp 105-31.

Dunkerley, D., Scourfield, J., Maegusuku-Hewett, T. and Smalley, N. (2006) 'The experiences of frontline staff working with children seeking asylum', in C. Jones Finer (ed) *Migration, Immigration and Social Policy*, Oxford: Blackwell.

Duvell, F. and Jordan, B. (2001) "How low can you go?' Dilemmas of social work with asylum seekers in London', *Journal of Social Work Research and Evaluation*, vol 2, no 2, pp 189-205.

Flynn, D. (2005) 'New borders, new management: the dilemmas of modern immigration policies', *Ethnic and Racial Studies*, vol 28, no 3, pp 463-90.

Hek, R., Sales, R. and Hoggart, L. (2001) 'Supporting refugee and asylum seeking children: an examination of refugees' experience and the support structures that facilitate settlement in school', Unpublished report, Middlesex University.

Henricson, C. and Bainham, A. (2005) *The Child and Family Policy Divide: Tensions, Convergence and Rights*, York: Joseph Rowntree Foundation.

Home Office (1998) *Faster, Fairer and Firmer: A Modern Approach to Immigration and Asylum*, White Paper, Cm. 4018, London: Home Office.

Home Office (2004) *Asylum Statistics United Kingdom 2003*, Home Office Statistical Bulletin (2nd edition 11/04), London: Home Office.

Home Office (2006) *Asylum Statistics United Kingdom: 2nd Quarter 2006*, London: Home Office.

Kohli, R. and Mather, R. (2003) 'Promoting psychosocial well-being in unaccompanied asylum seeking people in the United Kingdom', *Child and Family Social Work*, vol 8, no 3, pp 201-12.

Lewis, P. (2006) '500 children face forcible repatriation', *The Guardian*, 18 August.

Lumley, R. (2003) *Children in Detention: A Refugee Council Policy Paper*, London: Refugee Council.

Mayor of London (2004a) *Offering More than they Borrow: Refugee Children in London*, London: Greater London Authority.

Mayor of London (2004b) *Safe and Sound: Asylum Seekers in Temporary Accommodation*, London: Greater London Authority.

Mitchell, F. (2003) 'The social services response to unaccompanied children in England', *Child and Family Social Work*, vol 8, no 3, pp 179-90.

Morris, J. (2003) 'Children on the edge of care', Paper commissioned by the Joseph Rowntree Foundation, Unpublished.

NSPCC (National Society for the Prevention of Cruelty to Children) (2004) *NSPCC Response to the Government Green Paper 'Every Child Matters'*, NSPCC: London, available at nspcc.org.uk

Owers, A. (2006) *Report on an Unannounced Follow-up Inspection of Yarl's Wood Immigration Removal Centre*, London: Home Office.

Refugee Children's Consortium (2002) *The Nationality, Immigration and Asylum Bill, Second Reading Briefing*, London: Refugee Council.

Refugee Council (2004a) *The Impact of Section 55 on the Inter-Agency Partnership and the Asylum Seekers it Supports*, London: Refugee Council.

Refugee Council (2004b) *The Refugee Council's Submission to the Education and Skills Committee Inquiry into* Every Child Matters, London: Refugee Council.

Refugee Council (2005a) *Asylum and Immigration Act 2004: An Update*, London: Refugee Council.

Refugee Council (2005b) 'The Government's five-year asylum and immigration strategy', Refugee Council Briefing, London: Refugee Council, February, available at www.refugeecouncil.org.uk

Rutter, J. (2003) *Working with Refugee Children*, York: Joseph Rowntree Foundation.

Sales, R. (2002) 'The deserving and the undeserving: refugees, asylum seekers and welfare in Britain', *Critical Social Policy*, vol 22, no 3, pp 456-78.

Sales, R. and Hek, R. (2004) 'Dilemmas of care and control: the work of an asylum team in a London borough', in D. Hayes and D. Humphries (eds) *Immigration Control and Social Work*, London: Jessica Kingsley, pp 59-76.

Silove, D., Steel, Z. and Watters, C. (2000) 'Policies of deterrence and the mental health of asylum seekers', *Journal of the American Medical Association*, vol 284, no 5, pp 604-11.

Somerset, C. (2004) *Cause for Concern? London Social Services and Child Trafficking*, London: EPAT UK.

Stanley, K. (2001) *Cold Comfort: Young Separated Refugees in England*, London: Save the Children.

UNHCR (United Nations High Commissioner for Refugees) (1951) *Convention relating to the Status of Refugees* (the Geneva Convention), Geneva: UNHCR, available at www.unhcr.org

UNHCR (2004) *Trends in Unaccompanied and Separated Children Seeking Asylum in Industrialized Countries, 2001-2003*, Geneva: UNHCR.

UNICEF UK (United Nations Children's Fund UK) (2004) "Child trafficking' – position statement', 3 June, www.unicef.org

Watters, C. (2001) 'Emerging paradigms in the mental health care of refugees', *Social Science and Medicine*, vol 52, no 11, pp 1709-18.

Williamson, L. (1999) 'Unaccompanied refugee children: legal framework and local applications in Britain', in A. Bloch and C. Levy (eds) *Refugees, Citizenship and Social Policy*, Basingstoke: Macmillan.

FOURTEEN

Alcohol: protecting the young, protecting society

Betsy Thom

Introduction

The physical, psychological, social and economic risks of alcohol misuse have received much attention in recent years and the dangers of excessive drinking, especially by young people, have been prominent in policy debate (PMSU, 2004). However, it is recognised that, in a society where most people drink, young people need to learn how to drink without incurring risks to themselves or others. The process includes both cognitive learning about alcohol and its effects and experiential learning about what is appropriate and acceptable in different social contexts.

Awareness of the risks involved in alcohol use and the development of strategies to manage risks mark the transition from childhood to adulthood; risk taking, like alcohol use, is a feature of growing up, which entails experimentation and boundary testing, trial and error. As Honess et al (2000, p vii) have commented, drinking is as much 'young people' behaviour as 'adult' behaviour and interventions to address risk need to operate within that context.

Thus, alcohol policy faces the challenge of protecting the young from the risks of alcohol misuse without hindering the process of learning to manage alcohol and avoid alcohol-related harm. At the same time, alcohol policy is a complex arena where diverse social groups and stakeholders hold different – and often conflicting – views on alcohol and its uses (Thom, 2005). Policy statements emerge from a sea of contested facts and the interests of the economy or the safety of communities may take precedence over the needs of young people. Indeed, as is the case in recent years, young people's use of alcohol is frequently portrayed as a matter of concern and a threat to society.

This chapter discusses how the protection of children from risk and the control of 'risky' youth behaviour have influenced the formation of alcohol policy in two historical periods, at the turn of the 20th century and again at the turn of the 21st century. Although both issues, protection and control, were important at both times (Humphries, 1995), 'protection' has been chosen to illustrate policy approaches in the earlier period and 'control' for the later period. During the late 19th and early 20th centuries, there was a strong emphasis on the protection of children from adult behaviour, including parental use of alcohol and the exposure of children to drink and drinking environments. By contrast, from the late 20th century till the present time, public concern has focused on young people who are seen as 'out of control' and policy responses aim to address the threat posed by young people's drinking to public health and social order. Clearly, there have been vast changes in the social and environmental contexts of young people's lives, in understanding of the concept of childhood and in the nature of 'risk'. There are, nevertheless, common strands of concern, which span the 19th to the 21st century. In both periods, the notion of 'failed parenting' and the relationship between the family and the state emerge as controversial undertones in policy debate; in both periods, the policy 'gaze' has singled out some social groups above others as cause for concern; and in both periods children and young people's perceptions and management of risk are subsumed to an adult view of the world, which frequently highlights problem or 'deviant' behaviour rather than providing a rounded picture of young people's lives.

Suffer little children – challenging the demon drink

> The foul and fetid breath of our slums is almost as poisonous as that of the African swamp. Fever is almost as chronic there as on the Equator. Every year thousands of children are killed off by what is called defects of our sanitary system. They are in reality starved and poisoned ... much of the misery of those whose lot we are considering arises from their own habits. Drunkenness and all manner of uncleanness, moral and physical, abound. Have you ever watched by the bedside of a man in delirium tremens? Multiply the sufferings of that one drunkard by the hundred thousand and you have some idea of what scenes are being witnessed in all our great cities at this moment. (Booth, 1890, p 14)

The quotation is indicative not only of the social conditions of the poor in Victorian England, but also of a shift towards concern for the welfare of children (Hendrick, 1994). The establishment of the National Society for the Prevention of Cruelty to Children (NSPCC) (in 1884) drew public attention to the plight of many children, especially those from poor and 'vulnerable' families. Throughout the 19th century, state intervention aimed to protect the young by securing their exclusion from harmful environments – such as factories and mines – and their inclusion in environments – such as schools – designed to mould the citizens of the future (Humphries, 1995). But state intervention was not without opposition, especially in the private sphere of the family, and the passing of the first Act of Parliament for the prevention of cruelty to children (1889), came only after heavy lobbying (NSPCC, undated). It is against this backdrop of change in the perceived needs for protection and control of children and young people that we turn to an examination of policy on alcohol.

Over the course of the 19th century, 'the demon drink' became inextricably linked in political debate with health and social problems, from insanity (McCandless, 1984), to family poverty (Rowntree and Sherwell, 1900), and the degeneration of the race (Bynum, 1984). The debates were fuelled by social reformers, professionals (especially doctors) and powerful lobbying groups such as the Temperance Movement and the Society for the Study of Inebriety. These groups amassed a vast body of 'evidence', which was used in public campaigns and in political lobbying for legislation to address the drink question. Subsequent critiques of the evidence have revealed its limitations, (McCandless, 1984). Nevertheless, the Temperance Movement, growing in strength and in medical and political alliances during the second half of the 19th century, seized on the evidence and disseminated it in numerous pamphlets, journal papers and public lectures, one of the many objectives being to influence national policy on alcohol.

Temperance ideals also underpinned the efforts of philanthropist factory owners and city planners to tackle the culture of drunkenness that permeated many of the trades and the habits of working-class life (King, 1979). For instance, in local areas such as Hornsey in London, new housing estates were built with regulations that forbade the establishment of public houses within a certain radius of the estate (*The Builder*, 1883). The belief that many physical, mental and social problems could be eradicated by appropriate intervention in public and family life, found its strongest expression in attempts to save children from the vice of inebriety. 'Bands of Hope' provided an environment within which young people could be engaged in educational and leisure activities and instructed in the temperance 'world view', which entailed taking a pledge of abstinence from alcohol (Shiman, 1988). Shiman notes, however, that the Bands of Hope were attended mainly by the respectable working class, failing to attract middle-class children and children from the poorest sectors of society.

The emotive picture of slum and working-class misery caused by drunkenness was supported by social research and 'political arithmetic'. Rowntree and Sherwell (1900) used statistical data, in particular a range of calculations showing the percentage of working-class income spent on alcohol categorised by different occupations and trades. Their research – applauded by contemporaries for its scientific rigour – was intended to demonstrate the dangers of alcohol to respectable working-class families living on the margins of poverty and, therefore, at risk of sliding towards degradation. Although concerned about the effects of alcohol on individuals and families, Rowntree and Sherwell shared, with others of their era, a belief that excessive alcohol use, especially among the working classes, posed a serious economic threat to society as a whole. In an age of international competition, they argued that the expenditure of one sixth of working-class income on alcohol indicated 'a grave national peril' since 'a nation must be seriously handicapped if two months' earnings of its working classes are spent every year upon drink' (Rowntree and Sherwell, 1904, p 2).

Concern for the well-being of children also fuelled critiques of women's behaviour. By the turn of the 19th century, women's drinking was a recurrent feature of debates on 'racial deterioration' (Gutzke, 1984). Statistical, observational and anecdotal evidence was used to build the case for alarm especially in poverty-stricken areas of Britain where, it was reported, women constituted up to a third of drinkers in public houses and, in some places, equalled men in number (Gutzke, 1984, pp 72-3). Rowntree and Sherwell (1900) estimated that, between 1877 and 1896, alcohol-related mortality had risen by 43% for men and by 104% for women and noted that approximately 28-30% of drunkenness offences were committed by women. Practices such as 'giving the young 'un a taste' by wetting a baby's lips with gin and water were observed in public houses (Sims, 1889, cited in Gutzke, 1984, p 77). Evidence to the Royal Commission on Liquor Licensing Hours (1897) provided similar examples, for instance the comment from Mr C. L. Rothera, a practising solicitor and coroner from the Borough of Nottingham, that, 'I have seen children in perambulators drinking beer' (p 10943). Robert Parr (1911), director of the NSPCC, in a lecture delivered to the Lancashire and Cheshire Band of Hope and Temperance Union, estimated that 90% of cases of neglect coming to their attention were the result of excessive drinking by one or both parents.

Infant mortality, in particular, became central to the campaigns against alcohol and more specifically against the lifestyles of women in the working classes. Led by eminent medical 'temperance' doctors, the effects of drink on pregnant women, infants and 'mothering' became the lever for securing policy change. The momentum for change was accelerated when the publicist George Sims mounted a campaign to draw attention to the environmental risks faced by babies and young children in public houses. In a series of six articles published in the *Tribune* in 1907, Sims blamed mothers and alcohol for children's exposure to a foul, smoky atmosphere, changes in temperature going to and from the public house, and disease such as tuberculosis contracted from crawling and playing in the dirty sawdust covering the floors (Gutzke, 1984).

Thus, by the turn of the 20th century, the rearing of physically and mentally robust children had become a key issue in concern to address the fear of progressive hereditary degeneration especially among the working class and the poor whose use of alcohol was seen as compounding the risks to their children (Bynum, 1984). By then, some legislative reforms had been achieved: from 1872, it was illegal to sell spirits in licensed premises to children under 16 years old and, from 1886, children under the age of 13 were not permitted to buy alcohol for consumption on licensed premises (Home Office, 2000); but these reforms were deemed inadequate by campaigners concerned with the protection of children and the health of the nation. Babies and young children were still allowed in public houses and children continued to act as 'messengers' buying alcohol to take home. After much debate, in 1902 the Child Messenger Bill forbade the practice of parents sending children to buy a jug of alcohol for home consumption and in 1908, partly as a result of Sims' efforts, children under the age of 14 were excluded from the bar (but could be elsewhere on the premises).

At the same time, the drive to link alcohol with issues such as child neglect and other social ills met opposition and had to be balanced against securing other policy reforms. Objections came not just from the alcohol trade but from people petitioned to support the cause of child protection. Some feared that they might be sent to prison for 'giving baby gin for wind!'; others were indignant at the thought of not being able 'to give my children a glass of wine on their birthdays' (*The Child's Guardian*, 1888, vol 2, no 23, p 109). The intention to include further restrictions on selling intoxicating drink to children in the 1889 Prevention of Cruelty to, and Protection of, Children Act, was 'greatly mutilated in its course through Parliament' so that, in the opinion of commentators at the time, it became a useless mockery. Indeed, it was recognised that clauses of the Act forbidding spirituous liquor to children had to be dropped to prevent the Bill being blocked on its way through Parliament (*The Child's Guardian*, 1887, vol 1, no 1, p 11).

Controversy also surrounded the parliamentary debates preceding the passing of the 1902 Licensing Act. Reports in the *Lancet* covering successive readings of the Bill, criticised the 'constant habit of Ministers of finding excuses for postponing its consideration', stressed the countrywide consensus that condemned serving alcohol to children and emphasised the importance of keeping children out of public houses (*Lancet*, 1900, vol 1, pp 788-9). While the *Lancet* disagreed strongly with those who regarded legislation as state interference with parental rights and responsibilities (*Lancet*, 1900, vol 1, p 1085), opponents argued that the proposed licensing reform was 'paternal', that it was instigated by the 'collared' portion of the community against the 'collarless' (*Lancet*, 1900, vol 1, pp 1454-5), arguments that were countered in turn by noting that, 'evidence was given proving that the proposed legislation is much desired by the working classes in the north' (*Lancet*, 1900, vol 1, p 1603). Similar splits in opinion, and in perceptions of the facts, were revealed in the statements given to the Royal Commission on Liquor Licensing Hours (1897). Superintendent Lucas of the West Clapham police division in London said that selling to underage children was not a prevalent offence (p 5078), an assessment supported by a London police magistrate who reported very few instances of offences by licence holders (p 3579). Temperance sources in Manchester seemed to disagree, noting that 1,764 out of 2,922 licensed houses were in the habit of serving children (*Lancet*, 1900, vol 2, p 1103). Lucas also expressed doubts about the apparent consensus on preventing children buying alcohol for parents. He was of the view that, 'It would be very hard on poor people, the mother having been out washing or at work all day, that she must not send a child to get her supper beer' (Royal Commission on Liquor Licensing Hours, 1897, p 5115).

In short, infant mortality and child welfare served as an emotive policy driver and the protection of children from the risks of parental drinking and from exposure to harmful drinking environments provided a platform on which anti-drink campaigners could attempt to build consensus across interest and pressure groups. The exposure of children to the risks of alcohol furnished a rationale for raising support to challenge the state, the alcohol trade and the lifestyles of the working classes. From the 1880s until the outbreak of the First World War in 1914, alcohol consumption was a highly political issue intertwined with broader national priorities (Greenaway, 2003). Concern for the protection of children as 'victims' has to be seen within this context where children are also viewed as both an 'investment' and a 'threat', due to their 'value' as future healthy, economically productive citizens (Hendrick, 1994).

Lager louts and binge drinkers: the risk to society

Alcohol's high policy profile waned after the outbreak of war in 1914 and the level of public concern and interest in alcohol remained low throughout subsequent decades (Baggott, 1990). Issues regarding the well-being of children and young people were never entirely absent from policy and professional literature; but aside from concerns expressed by the Temperance Movement – in rapid decline after the Second World War – little policy attention was paid to young people's access to alcohol, their exposure to public drinking environments or their drinking behaviour.

By the 1980s the situation had begun to change and when alcohol emerged again on the policy agenda, attention had become fixed on youth behaviour as 'threat'. Rising alcohol consumption, the greater availability of alcohol, more liberal approaches to drinking and changing youth cultures were some of the factors that resulted in new 'moral panics' around youthful drinking. At first, concerns were directed towards specific subgroups of young people. 'Lager louts', 'champagne Charlies', alcohol-fuelled football hooligans, 'ladettes' – girls who drank like boys – and underage drinking hit the media headlines from time to time but did not result in sustained interest in young people's alcohol consumption (Parker et al, 1998, p 51). In fact, changes in young people's leisure pursuits, including the expansion of a dance/rave culture, were accompanied by a decrease in young people's spending in public houses (Parker et al, 1998, pp 53-4). Illicit drug use became the new source of anxiety and, as Parker et al (1998, p 29) comment:

> this continuous focus on young people's drug taking makes this the single most talked about, written and broadcast about item in contemporary discourses about the state of the young in the UK.

Media coverage and policy responses to youthful substance use tended to adopt a 'risk' perspective, emphasising the dangers of drug use and the perceived links to other 'risky' behaviours, such as unprotected sex, unwanted pregnancy, crime and poor parenting. What seemed especially alarming was the apparent spread of drug use into 'mainstream' youth culture, although this claim was hotly disputed in the literature (for example, Shiner and Newburn, 1999). As with alcohol a century earlier, protection of the young from drug misuse and protection of society from the young became politically embroiled in a range of social problems from juvenile delinquency and school drop-out to dysfunctional families (especially single mothers), antisocial behaviour and community safety. Again, attention turned towards sectors of society deemed to be 'at risk' of falling through the net of social care and control. Changes in women's drinking, too, began to raise alarm but, this time around, 'moral panic' approaches were countered by strong opposition from feminist activists working in research and service provision (Thom, 1997a). As a result, arguments proposing an association between women's drinking and changes in women's social roles with the drinking behaviour of the young gained little headway even in a climate of increasing scrutiny on parenting and continuing policy intervention in family matters.

In contrast to the earlier period, when child protection was used as a dominant rationale for policy change, the latter part of the 20th century saw the emergence of a 'culture of blame' directed towards young people's alcohol and drug use. Children and young people were still the 'victims' of drug dealing and substance misuse but a more dominant public image was rapidly building up; the young now presented a threat to their families and communities and an economic burden on the state through their substance-using behaviour. This time the threat stemmed directly from the young themselves rather than from the accident of birth – into deprived circumstances or 'alcoholic' families – blamed in the earlier period for the moral and physical weakness of the working classes and unruly youth behaviour. The shifting response from protection to control is particularly clear if we look at youth from around 14 years of age.

By the 1990s, the regulations governing the drinking behaviour of children and young people had been altered in successive licensing Acts (see Box 14.1) and the extension of the period of 'childhood', through longer schooling, delay in entering the workplace and delay in assuming other adult roles, resulted in a new group of young adults still negotiating the boundaries between childhood and the adult world. It was the behaviour of this group that increasingly seemed to pose a challenge to society and which became associated with an ever-expanding range of social problems.

Box 14.1: Law regarding alcohol, children and young people

Persons under 18 cannot buy an alcoholic drink anywhere on licensed premises, whether in the bar or elsewhere, in an off-licence, supermarket or other outlet.

Exception: persons aged 16 and 17 can buy/drink beer, wine or cider for consumption with a meal in an area set aside for meals in a public house but not in the bar.

Persons aged 14 or 15 can go anywhere in a pub but not drink alcohol.

Persons under 14 are not allowed in the bar of licensed premises during permitted hours unless a Children's Certificate is in force; access restricted to certain areas.

Persons aged 5 or more can drink in a registered club, a public place (unless prohibited by bye-law) or at home.

It is an offence to give a **child under 5** an alcoholic drink.

Source: Home Office (2000, appendix 2)

Numerous interpretations of the reasons for problem substance use have emerged from the literature. Marketing to the young, in particular the marketing of alcopops, attracted attention for a time (Wright, 1999). Theories of a class-based clash between differing normative and moral frames of action, advanced in analyses of working-class childhood and youth between 1889-1939 (Humphries, 1995, pp 21-3), found an echo in historical accounts of alcohol consumption in other periods (for example, Warner, 2003) and in sociological 'underclass' and social structural explanations for problem substance use (for example, see summary in Neale, 2002). Other research has examined alcohol and drug use as a phenomenon within contemporary societies, which goes beyond class and subcultural differences. Writing about 'antisocial behaviour' in *The Guardian*, Robert Colls, Professor of English history at the University of Leicester, sees changes in youth behaviour as part of mass cultural shifts:

> The youth labour market has virtually disappeared. The link between apprenticeship, work, sexuality and marriage has been cut. Associational life has lost its civic, moral and religious significance. In Britain the use of drink and drugs is the highest in Europe.... Add to this the transformation of town centres into late-night drink marts, widespread drug use and the mass communication of hedonistic and transgressive lifestyles and one can begin to see the conditions for one of those shifts in cultural mass that mark our history. (*The Guardian*, 3 December 2003)

The feeling that young people are no longer linked to the social and moral fabric of community life is echoed in other analyses of contemporary society. Alexander (2004) considers alcohol misuse as one manifestation of an increasingly addicted society, a symptom of the mass-produced social dislocation attendant on free market economies in which marginalised, less integrated groups of young people are at greater risk of becoming dependent on alcohol and drugs. According to other accounts, the loss of external controls on behaviour has been countered to some extent by an increasing awareness and concern around 'risk' and risk management. For example, Tigerstedt (1999, cited in Bergmark, 2004, p 10) has suggested that the internalisation of risk information acts as a 'new form of remote control'. Casting doubt on this explanation, Bergmark contends that risk information on substances, embedded within a flood of generalised risk information, merely increases the degree of uncertainty that characterises modern society and may be especially pertinent when considering youth behaviour. However, within societies where cultural change may be eroding traditional forms of interaction and traditional controls on individual behaviour, the role of risk perception, risk factors and risk assessment has come to the fore in identifying individuals and groups likely to require intervention of one sort or another. Undoubtedly, this is a significant factor in directing the policy and professional gaze towards social groups already labelled as 'difficult' or problematic.

A key question running through the literature and in discourses on young people's substance use is the extent to which use is an individual choice or the result of social and contextual factors largely outside individual control. Some research studies explain drug and alcohol use as linked to the culture of consumption and postmodern society's preoccupation with individual choice and self-fulfilment (for example, Brain et al, 2000); substance use has become 'normalised' as an accepted part of youth recreation (Parker et al, 1998). Although recognising the importance of social and cultural contexts on behaviour, this body of research also highlights ways in which young people frame their drug use as 'consumption' decisions, a perception that stresses the user as an active agent pursuing rational means to facilitate social interaction, achieve a 'buzz' or purchase 'time out' from daily life. Although risk and harm are experienced, users make decisions about how, when and with whom they will drink or use other drugs. Brain et al (2000, pp 15-16) describe some young drinkers who might be considered as 'drinking delinquents' as engaging in a 'structured form of 'bounded' hedonistic consumption' within which their drinking was constrained by the demands of school or family. Comments made by the young people interviewed by Brain et al (2000) are illustrative of substance management strategies:

> Midweek you don't drink 'cos of school ... you can't get up in the morning. (Female, aged 15)

> Have to go somewhere where nobody sees us. If I go somewhere and they know me Mum I'm fucked aren't I? (Male, aged 14, indicating the importance of family supervision)

This picture emerges also from a study of young men's drinking in East London, which illustrated how young men between the ages of 16 and 24 moved through, and between, eight different drinking styles from 'childhood' to 'adolescent', 'experimental', 'recreational', 'safe', 'therapeutic' and 'structured' in the transition to adulthood. Even within the group of 'recreational' drinking styles, where excess drinking and intentionally getting drunk were a common feature of having fun, having 'a laugh' and taking risks, decisions regarding when and where to indulge in this sort of behaviour were tempered by considerations of cost, competing priorities with other significant activities and keeping safe (Harnett et al, 2000).

Research on a friendship group, undertaken in the late 1990s, also showed how young people moved through different drinking styles and drinking behaviours as they learned about alcohol and about how to manage the risk of negative effects. Jason, who started to drink when he was 15, described how:

> It wasn't long ago that I used to drink the super beers, the strong beers. I used to drink normal beer first of all then Steve started drinking super beers and he got me on – I didn't like the flavour, it tastes like treacle, but you get used to it after a while; but following that I used to drink them quite a few times and every morning I used to get up and it was normal for me before I go to work … just go in the toilet and puke, and sometimes it was blood, and I cut them down since then. If I had one now I'd be sick … it's disgusting. (Thom, 1997b)

Other young people changed their drinking as they began to discard more youthful images or take on adult responsibilities. Natalie, for instance, avoided one club because it was 'full of young, about 15, 16 year olds getting really drunk and acting really stupid. They are just screaming about'. Following the birth of her son, Sarah, Steve's partner, had restricted her preferred style – drinking to intoxication – to a few special occasions (Thom, 1997b).

The recognition that 'normal' young people participate in binge drinking is now reflected in media reports. In one newspaper review article, 'On the streets of binge Britain', the author highlights the fact that young binge drinkers can no longer be categorised as 'yobs'; they are conventional young people who work hard and play hard and see getting drunk as an aspect of personal choice. Mark is a typical example:

> I work my arse off from Monday to Friday as an engineer in the petrochemical business and during the week I don't want to go out … on Friday nights I'm going to have some beers. I'm going to have 10 or 11 beers….Yes I may be damaging myself but that's my right. (Rayner, *The Observer*, 5 September 2004, pp 1-2)

As indicated by the title of the newspaper item, such accounts from the perspective of young people themselves are, however, still embedded within reports that highlight the behaviours as problematic and threatening.

Protection and control: a policy dilemma?

Although insights from academic research and from accounts by young drinkers filter into the policy arena over time, policy and practice responses to alcohol-related risks and problems are more often informed by a very different base of empirical 'evidence' drawn predominantly from quantitative survey data on substance use and associated harms and from research studies on 'what works' by way of harm prevention, treatment and enforcement strategies (for example, Hibell et al, 1997a, 1997b; Plant et al, 1997; Babor et al, 2003).

The picture to emerge from survey evidence shows that:

- The proportion of young people under the age of 16 who drink has fluctuated between 20% and 27% since 1990; but those who do drink are consuming more.
- Compared to teenagers in other European countries, British youngsters are more likely to get drunk and to report problems associated with alcohol use.
- Young people aged 16-24 have the highest consumption compared to other age groups and are the most likely to binge drink; around 55% of men and 45% of women reported drinking more than the recommended guidelines on at least one day in the previous week.[1]
- Trend data since the 1970s show a rise in consumption by young women, an increase in the proportion exceeding recommended guidelines, a rise in 'binge' drinking and participation in a diversity of drinking 'cultures', which include patterns of consumption associated with risk (PMSU, 2003, pp 16-20).

There is no doubt that there are risks associated with underage consumption and heavy episodic (or binge) drinking. A study by Coleman and Cater (2005), for example, of underage 'risky' drinking among teenagers, aged 14-17 with experience of drinking in unsupervised environments, documented problems relating to health outcomes (sexual experiences, injuries, fighting, drug use, intoxication), safety outcomes (walking home alone, daring behaviour and pranks, dangerous driving) and legal outcomes (trouble with the police). At the same time, the authors note that most of the young people reported enjoying risky drinking and the study revealed that even among a group that might be considered 'high risk', safety strategies were adopted, in this case drinking in groups and eating adequately before drinking. Studies exploring self-reported motivations to drink and get drunk commonly find that 'pushing the boundaries' and feelings of invulnerability are as important as having fun, easing social interaction or unexpected loss of control in explaining alcohol-related risk behaviour (Harnett et al, 2000; Coleman and Cater, 2005). For a minority of young people, aggression and disorderly behaviour are expected as part of the drinking occasion and characterise a good night out (Honess et al, 2000).

Whatever the facts about alcohol-related antisocial behaviour, media coverage and political discourse have generated a public image of youth as engaging in risky drinking and leisure behaviour that pose a threat to the peace and security of communities. Current policy statements indicate the strength of these concerns. One of the objectives of the 1998 10-year strategy 'Tackling Drugs to Build a Better Britain' (HM Government, 1998) was to protect communities from drug-related anti-social and criminal behaviour, and considerable emphasis in criminal justice responses is directed towards young offenders. The government consultation paper *Drinking Responsibly* states that a fundamental change in attitude is required, 'so that binge and underage drinking are no longer regarded as socially acceptable' (Home Office, 2005, p 3). At the local level, alcohol licensing policies and guidance for applicants stress the duties of licensees to ensure order within and around their premises. Licensing policies are viewed as one aspect of measures to control antisocial behaviour and as linked to strategies such as Safer Communities, and Crime and Drugs, and Youth Partnership where the focus is often on the activities of young people. However, policy strategy rarely addresses key issues such as the differences between young people, the facilitation – or impeding – of the process of learning to drink without incurring undue risk, the possible adverse effects of the application of a rigid drinking age demarcation, or the need to consider youth drinking as an aspect of youth cultures.

Addressing youth behaviour has become as much a political ball game today as was protecting child welfare a century ago. In both cases, research has played a role in constructing a policy-relevant issue and in building a case around which to campaign for consensus between different interest groups and secure policy action. Just as the protection of children from alcohol-related harm was an emotive research and policy driver in the 19th century, fear of young people's antisocial behaviour is a key element in current responses to alcohol. After many years when alcohol issues had a low policy profile, it could be argued that perceptions of the use of alcohol by young people and associated social and public health risks has been a major factor in raising the importance of alcohol on policy agendas. The problem, as in former times, arises in trying to balance concerns for protection with concerns for controlling the problem aspects of drinking behaviour in a policy arena where economic, social and health interests are frequently in competition. Politics and expediency rather than 'evidence' or the needs of young people may be seen as determining the policy outcomes (for example, Room, 2004). In a society where the use of alcohol is culturally integrated into the lifestyles of most people, there is still a lack of understanding about the process of learning to use and manage alcohol and about the ways in which society, families and young people themselves learn about 'growing up with risk'. In particular, dominant stereotypes of youth and youth behaviour need to be challenged by closer examination of 'mainstream' youth and the differences between groups of young people in drinking cultures, patterns and behaviours.

Note
[1] Government recommended daily drinking guidelines: a maximum intake of two to three units for women and three to four units for men; alcohol free days are recommended. The measure of 'binge' drinking is six or more units for women and eight or more units for men on a single occasion. A unit is approximately 8g of pure alcohol (PMSU, 2003, 2004).

References

Alexander, B. K. (2004) 'A historical analysis of addiction', in P. Rosenqvist, J. Blomqvist, A. Koski-Jannes and L. Ojesjo (eds) *Addiction and Life Course*, Helsinki: Nordic Council for Alcohol and Drug Research, pp 11–28.

Babor, T., Caetano, R., Casswell, S., Edwards, G., Giesbrecht, N., Graham, K., Grube, J. W., Grunewald, P., Hill, L. and Holder, H. D. (2003) *Alcohol: No Ordinary Commodity*, Oxford: Oxford University Press.

Baggott, R. (1990) *Alcohol, Politics and Social Policy*, Aldershot: Avebury.

Bergmark, A. (2004) 'Risk, pleasure and information – notes concerning the discursive space of alcohol prevention', *Nordic Studies on Alcohol and Drugs*, English Supplement, vol 21, pp 7–16.

Booth, General (1890) *In Darkest England and The Way Out*, London: International Headquarters of the Salvation Army.

Brain, K., Parker, H. and Carnwath, T. (2000) 'Drinking with design: young drinkers as psychoactive consumers', *Drugs: Education, Prevention and Policy*, vol 7, no 1, pp 5–20.

Bynum, W. F. (1984) 'Alcoholism and degeneration in 19th century European medicine and psychiatry', *British Journal of Addiction*, vol 79, no 1, pp 59-70.

Coleman, L. and Cater, S. (2005) *Underage 'Risky' Drinking*, York: Joseph Rowntree Foundation.

Greenaway, J. (2003) *Drink and British Politics since 1830: A Study in Policy-making*, Basingstoke: Palgrave.

Gutzke, D.W. (1984) "The cry of the children': the Edwardian medical campaign against maternal drinking', *British Journal of Addiction*, vol 79, no 1, pp 71-84.

Harnett, R., Thom, B., Herring, R. and Kelly, M. (2000) 'Alcohol in transition: towards a model of young men's drinking styles', *Journal of Youth Studies*, vol 3, no 1, pp 61-77.

Hendrick, H. (1994) *Child Welfare: 1870-1989*, London: Routledge.

Hibell, B., Andersson, B., Ahlstrom, S., Balakireva, O., Kokkevi, A. and Morgan, M. (1997a) *The 1999 ESPAD Report: Alcohol and other Drug Use among Students in 30 European Countries*, Stockholm: The Swedish Council for Information on Alcohol and Other Drugs.

Hibell, B., Andersson, B., Bjarnason, T., Kokkevi, A., Morgan, M. and Narusk, A. (1997b) *The 1995 ESPAD Report: Alcohol and other Drug Use among Students in 26 European Countries*, Stockholm: The Swedish Council for Information on Alcohol and Other Drugs.

HM Government (1998) *Tackling Drugs to Build a Better Britain: The Government's Ten-year Strategy for Tackling Drugs Misuse*, Cm 3945, London: HMSO.

Home Office (2000) *Time for Reform: Proposals for the Modernisation of our Licensing Laws*, Cm 4696, London: Home Office.

Home Office (2005) *Drinking Responsibly: The Government's Proposals*, London: Department for Culture, Media and Sport, Home Office and Office of the Deputy Prime Minister, available at: www.homeoffice.gov.uk/documents/2005-cons-drinking/2205-cons-drinking-doc?view=Binary

Honess, T., Seymour, L. and Webster, R. (2000) *The Social Contexts of Underage Drinking*, London: Home Office.

Humphries, S. (1995) *Hooligans or Rebels? An Oral History of Working-class Childhood and Youth 1889-1939*, Oxford: Blackwell.

King, E. (1979) *Scotland Sober and Free: The Temperance Movement 1829-1979*, Glasgow: Glasgow Museums and Art Galleries.

Lancet (1900) 'Annotations: the sale of intoxicating liquors to children', vol 1, pp 788-9, 1085, 1454-5, 1603 and vol 2, p 1103.

McCandless, P. (1984) "Curses of civilisation': insanity and drunkenness in Victorian Britain', *British Journal of Addiction*, vol 79, no 1, pp 49-58.

Neale, J. (2002) *Drug Users in Society*, Basingstoke: Palgrave.

NSPCC (National Society for the Prevention of Cruelty to Children) (undated) *A History of the NSPCC Protecting Children from Cruelty Since 1884*, London: NSPCC.

Parker, H., Aldridge, J. and Measham, F. (1998) *Illegal Leisure: The Normalisation of Adolescent Recreational Drug Use*, London: Routledge.

Parr, R. J. (1911) *The Cruelty of the Drunken: How Children Suffer*, Lecture delivered at the 48th Autumnal Conference of the Lancashire and Cheshire Band of Hope and Temperance Union, 7 October, Published under the direction of the 'Hicks' Counties Lecture Fund Committee, Manchester: Onward Publishing Office.

Plant, M., Single, E. and Stockwell, T. (1997) *Alcohol: Minimising the Harm: What works?*, London: Free Association Books.

PMSU (Prime Minister's Strategy Unit) (2003) *Strategy Unit Alcohol Harm Reduction Project: Interim Analytical Report*, London: Cabinet Office, available at: www.strategy.gov.uk/downloads/files/SU%20interim_report2.pdf

PMSU (2004) *Alcohol Harm Reduction Strategy for England*, London: Cabinet Office, available at: www.strategy.gov.uk/downloads/su/alcohol/pdf/CabOffice%20AlcoholHar.pdf

Room, R. (2004) 'Disabling the public interest: alcohol strategies and policies for England', *Addiction*, vol 99, no 9, pp 1083-9.

Rowntree, J. and Sherwell, A. (1900) *The Temperance Problem and Social Reform* (7th edition), London: Hodder & Stoughton.

Rowntree, J. and Sherwell, A. (1904) *Public Interests or Trade Aggrandisement? An Examination of Some Important Issues Raised by the Licensing Bill 1904*, London: King & Son, Orchard House.

Royal Commission on Liquor Licensing Hours (1897) *Minutes of Evidence* (presented to Parliament), vol 1, London: HMSO.

Shiman, L.L. (1988) *Crusade against Drink in Victorian England*, Basingstoke: The Macmillan Press Ltd.

Shiner, M. and Newburn, T. (1999) 'Taking tea with Nocl: the place and meaning of drug use in everyday life', in N. South (ed) *Drugs: Cultures, Controls and Everyday Life*, London: Sage Publications, pp 139-59.

The Builder (1883) Artisans' Dwellings at Hornsey, 11 August, Bruce Castle local archives, Haringey, London

The Child's Guardian (1887–88), Series of letters/commentaries, London: London Society for the Prevention of Cruelty to Children (1887, vol 1, no 1, p 11; 1888, vol 2, no 23, p 109).

Thom, B. (1997a) 'Women and alcohol: a policy dilemma', *Policy Studies*, vol 18, no 1, pp 49-65.

Thom, B. (1997b) 'The role of alcohol in accidents among young people seen in A&E departments', Report to North Thames NHS Executive, London, Unpublished.

Thom, B. (2005) 'Who makes alcohol policy? Science and policy networks 1950-2000', in V. Berridge (ed) *Science and Health Policy: Historical Networks*, The Wellcome Series in the History of Medicine, London: Rudopi, pp 75-99.

Warner, J. (2003) *Craze: Gin and Debauchery in an Age of Reason*, London: Profile Books.

Wright, L. (1999) *Young People and Alcohol: What 11- to 24-year-olds Know, Think and Do*, chapter 4 'Marketing and advertising alcohol', London: Health Education Authority.

The prevention of youth crime: a risky business?

David Porteous

Introduction

With New Labour's ascent to power in 1997 came a 'new youth justice' (Goldson, 2000). In this reformed system, the assessment and management of risk has been given a pivotal role. All young people referred to Youth Offending Teams (YOTs) in England and Wales are now assessed using a common, structured risk assessment profile known as *Asset*. This is intended to guide practitioners' judgements as to the 'riskiness' of a young person and to enable them to identify the precise 'risk factors' contributing to their offending behaviour such that interventions can be tailored to individual needs. *Asset* is also expected to influence decisions about resource allocation both within YOTs and at regional and national levels under the auspices of the Youth Justice Board (YJB) (Baker, 2004). The accurate assessment of risk is therefore 'central to achieving the principal aim' (YJB, 2003, p 13) of the youth justice system – the prevention of offending by children and young people.

Prevention operates either side of risk and both inside and out of the youth justice system. In the aftermath of a legal transgression, once the risk factors precipitating a young person's offending behaviour have been identified using *Asset*, interventions to prevent further involvement in crime, based on knowledge of 'what works', can be set in place. But equally, because it is 'known' what the main risk factors are, pre-emptive action can also be taken. Thus, governmental schemes covering young people's transition from cradle to rave – Sure Start, the Children's Fund, Youth Inclusion Programmes, Connexions – all carry with them the promise that they will serve to prevent youth crime in the years to come.

This chapter attempts to tell the story of how the language of, and policies and practices associated with, risk in the new youth justice have come to hold such significance and to assess the consequences of these changes. It suggests that current policy constitutes a blend of particular academic, administrative and political discourses each of which define and mobilise the concept of risk in different ways. The chapter also attempts to evaluate the impact of recent reforms in the context of wider debates about risk assessment and management in the criminal justice system.

New Labour, new youth justice

In *No More Excuses* (Home Office, 1997), the White Paper outlining New Labour's plans for tackling youth crime, the language of risk was very much evident. The paper spoke of the general risk to society posed by 'today's young offenders who can too easily become tomorrow's hardened criminals' (p 2) and of the range of risk factors – being male, being brought up by a criminal parent, living in a family with multiple problems and so on – 'known' to be 'related to youth criminality'. Young offenders were both a risk and at risk. They disrupted their families and communities while at the same time 'wrecking their own lives' (p 2). They constituted a threat but were simultaneously vulnerable. 'As well as putting the public at risk, allowing young people to drift into a life of crime undermines their welfare and denies them the opportunity to develop into fully contributing members of society' (p 3). The new youth justice system would deal more swiftly and effectively with the 'serious and persistent' young offenders 'from whom the public needs most protection' (p 4) and increase early interventions with 'children under ten who are at risk of becoming involved in crime or who have already started to behave in an anti-social or criminal manner' (p 18). New Labour would be tough on risk and tough on the causes of risk.

In this and other governmental documents relating to youth crime, risk symbolises danger, threat, something to fear and be protected from. A key dimension of risk in this sense of the term is the uncertainty it generates. Unless we deal effectively with young people who commit crimes, our safety and our future well-being are placed in doubt. This connotation of risk was politically very useful to New Labour. Where Old Labour was concerned only about the needs of young offenders, New Labour looked to their deeds as well, and to the risks they posed to themselves and others. To talk of risk was to talk up the risk. In electoral terms, this proved highly successful:

If Worcester Woman was to change her voting habits, New Labour strategists reasoned, she must be made to feel that the government would contain the threat posed to her property, person, peace of mind, not to mention the educational opportunities of her children, by the roughly spoken, badly behaved, young people who haunted the streets of the inner city and the estates on its periphery. This strategy was designed to have a double pay-off for the Blair campaign, pulling in Tory votes whilst bridging political divisions in his own party by promising to be both 'tough' enough 'on crime' for the 'modernisers' and 'tough' enough on the 'causes of crime' for old Labour's remaining 'social engineers'. And it worked. (Pitts, 2003, p 31)

The term 'risk', therefore, lent itself towards New Labour rhetoric on crime and on youth crime in particular. However, the concept of risk informed New Labour's youth justice policy in other, perhaps more substantive ways. To look at these we need to step back a little in time.

The new penology

In a now famous article heralding the advent of what they termed the 'new penology', Feeley and Simon (1992) observed that in the latter part of the 20th century criminal justice systems in western societies had begun to talk in a language 'characterised by an emphasis on the systemic and on formal rationality'. The 'new penology' was:

> concerned with the rationality not of individual behaviour or even community organisation, but of *managerial processes*. Its goal is not to eliminate crime but to make it tolerable through *systemic coordination*. (Feeley and Simon, 1992, pp 454-5, emphasis added)

As well as a new discourse and new aims, there were new techniques: 'more cost-effective forms of custody and control and ... new technologies to identify and classify risk' (Feeley and Simon, 1992, p 457). Few documents illustrate this 'actuarial' turn in criminal justice policy better than the first report on the English and Welsh youth justice system by the Audit Commission – *Misspent Youth ... Young People and Crime*, published in 1996.

The Audit Commission was explicitly concerned with the formal rationality of the youth justice system, something it found wanting:

> The current system for dealing with youth crime is inefficient and expensive, while little is being done to deal effectively with juvenile nuisance. (Audit Commission, 1996, p 96)

The system was plagued with inconsistency. The various agencies dealing with young offenders were not always singing from the same hymn sheet. While the Conservative government had set out a strategy for tackling crime designed to ensure, among other things, that 'more criminals [were] brought to justice, targeting those who offend most frequently' and achieve 'greater success in preventing offending by convicted criminals', those with the most direct responsibility for working with young offenders – social services departments – were 'committed to diverting transient young offenders (other than serious offenders) from the criminal justice system' and only a 'few offered alternatives which tackled offending behaviour'. There was inconsistency too between areas, with the time taken for a young person to move from arrest to sentence, for example, varying from 70 to 170 days across the sites studied. There was inconsistency in court decisions. For example, the authors note that young offenders interviewed for their research had 'commented on the apparently arbitrary nature of the system' for deciding whether or not to proceed with a prosecution. And there was inconsistency in the treatment of different ethnic groups with African Caribbean young people in particular being more likely than white young people to be stopped by the police, prosecuted rather than cautioned, committed to a crown court, remanded in custody and receiving a custodial sentence (Audit Commission, 1996, pp 16-45).

Although the Commission was damning about current arrangements for dealing with young offenders, it did have good news. Citing examples from within the UK and beyond, the authors observed that there was plenty of good practice from which to learn. Such schemes could tackle offending behaviour but the Audit Commission's 'big idea' was that reacting to crimes committed was insufficient:

> While public services clearly need to deal effectively with offending behaviour by young people, it would be better to prevent the offending behaviour in the first place. (Audit Commission, 1996)

And the key to effective prevention?

> Although there is no way of predicting accurately which individuals are going to offend, young people in certain categories or circumstances *are at much greater risk* than others. (Audit Commission, 1996, p 58, emphasis added)

The risk-focused prevention paradigm

> The 'risk-focused prevention paradigm' has gained international recognition from governments in recent years as an approach that is both plausible and practical in the light of current knowledge. (Farrington, 2000, cited in YJB, 2001, p 27)

One of the key sources of this 'current knowledge' is the Cambridge Study of Delinquent Development (Farrington, 1989), a study that commenced in 1961 and continues to this day, albeit with diminishing returns for our understanding of contemporary youth offending, the sample of 411 working-class boys from Camberwell in South East London being by now into their early fifties. The boys, aged eight at the time they were first selected, were contacted a further five times up to the age of 21 and a further three times since. The aim of the study, which drew on a combination of official and primary research data, was to identify which of the boys went on to develop a 'criminal career' and investigate those factors that could be seen in retrospect to have correlated with criminogenic behaviour. The researchers concluded that the principal risk factors, those which best predicted future offending, were having criminal/antisocial parents and siblings; poor parental skills and family conflict; low intelligence and attainment at school; psychological disorders such as hyperactivity and impulsivity; low family income; and poor housing.

A review of the 'risk and protective factors associated with youth crime' for the Youth Justice Board, undertaken by among others David Farrington himself, brings together the findings from the Cambridge Study with those from others described as the 'most reliable' and 'most dependable' studies available (YJB, 2001). Applying this knowledge in practice, the paradigm asserts, should ensure that interventions are evidence based and that those more at risk can be identified. Thus, policy and practice are said to be grounded in science. Moreover, it is not only the risks associated with offending that research is said to have uncovered, effective solutions have also been tried and tested.

Evidence about 'what works' in interventions with offenders had been mounting up since the early 1990s (for example, McGuire, 1995; Vennard et al, 1997; Burnett and Roberts, 2004) and this also found its way into *Misspent Youth* (Audit Commission, 1996). To complete the circle, among the key 'features of effective programmes' identified by the Audit Commission was 'matching of the level of risk posed by the individual (based on offending history and perhaps other characteristics) with the level of the intervention' (p 106). In short, risk assessment 'works'.

The appliance of science: *Asset*

Asset puts the risk-focused prevention paradigm into practice. YOT staff are required to complete the form 'before any intervention is made with a young person' and to review and update it at 'the end of an intervention' as well as at other intervals as appropriate and necessary (YJB, 2003, p 32). It is described as a 'structured clinical assessment' tool, which combines the 'professional experience' inherent in clinical approaches to assessment with the 'predictive power' of actuarial methods in a 'comprehensive coverage of risk factors [which] produces a statistical prediction of recidivism and helps practitioners to identify areas for intervention where change might reduce the risk of re-offending' (YJB, 2003, pp 19–21).

The main risk factors assessed using *Asset* are as follows:

- *care history* – for example, whether the offender is subject to a care order, is or has been placed on the child protection register and/or is or has been remanded in local authority accommodation;
- *previous offending and convictions* including time since last arrest;
- *family structure* and *quality of family relationships*;
- *living arrangements*, that is, where the young person lives and with whom;
- *education history and status* – whether there is a history of truancy and/or trouble at school;
- *employment and training status*, if appropriate;
- *type of neighbourhood* in which the young person lives including indicators of problems such as drug dealing, racial tensions, poor transport facilities and so on;
- *lifestyle* – how the young person spends their time, money issues and who they associate/hang out with;
- *substance use* and whether or not there are problems associated with this;

- *physical health and access to healthcare*;
- *emotional and mental health*, taking into account risk of self-harm or suicide;
- *perception of self and others* – for example, difficulties with self-identity, self-esteem, understanding and trust of others and so on;
- *problematic thinking and behaviour* – for example, lack of understanding of consequences, impulsivity, low self-control, destructive of property, manipulative;
- *attitudes towards offending* including victim awareness, sense of responsibility for actions, degree of remorse and so on;
- *motivation to change*.

In addition, young people are invited to complete a 'What do you think' form, which follows a similar structure to that of *Asset*, enabling comparison between the practitioner's and the young person's assessment of the situation and intended as a means of engaging with the client and incorporating their views and feelings in the process.

In theory, then, *Asset* operates like a filtering and sorting device. It indicates the level and type of intervention required, ensuring that account is taken of those risk factors 'known' to correlate with the likelihood of re-offending. It enables YOT staff to distinguish the serious and persistent offender from the less deviant majority and to vary the amount of work done with them accordingly:

> More intensive interventions should be targeted at high-risk young offenders who are likely to continue to offend rather than low-risk offenders who may gain little or no benefit. (YJB, 2003, p 65)

Although *Asset* is not used outside of YOTs, the same 'risk principle' (Andrews and Bonta, 2003) is applied in a large number of New Labour initiatives. Youth Inclusion Programmes, for example, work with 13- to 16-year-old young people identified as being the most 'at risk' within their neighbourhood and aim to reduce re-offending rates by 70% through their inclusion in purposeful activities (Williamson, 2005). Sure Start and the Children's Fund target younger children and their families in deprived areas with the explicit goal (among many others) of nipping youth crime in the bud. Connexions, although a universal service providing advice on education, training and careers to all young people aged 13 and above, nevertheless targets extra resources at those 'at risk' (Tomlinson, 2005) with a view to stemming their involvement in crime. In these different social policy arenas, it is striking how ubiquitous the term 'at risk' has become to the extent that frequently it is not specified quite what this or that child or young person is at risk of. Truancy, school exclusion, antisocial behaviour, social exclusion, re-offending, abuse, neglect, underachievement, low self-esteem – all appear as one big 'joined-up' problem or, in other words, as one big risk.

The story so far

To summarise, the concept of risk has been integral to the recent reorganisation of the youth justice system in three distinct although related ways. First, with an eye to the floating voters needed to secure election in 1997 and beyond (Pitts, 2003; Cohen, 2005), New Labour has invoked the risk or danger posed by young offenders to the well-being of society and promised to get tough in response. Second, New Labour inherited and bought into broader changes in the approach of western governments to crime control in which the identification, management and control of risky populations and situations had assumed growing importance (Feeley and Simon, 1992; Garland, 2001). Characteristic of this new strategy were managerialist concerns with cost-effectiveness and systemic rationality, which, when applied to the existing youth justice system, were found to have been seriously wanting (Audit Commission, 1996). Third, New Labour has drawn on a particular strand of criminological theory, which claims to pinpoint, through neo-scientific, quantitative research, those factors that predispose young people to offend and which can be tackled before they take root so as to prevent crimes from occurring in the future.

The risk assessment tool *Asset* is deployed at the gateway to the new youth justice. It is derived from the risk-factor prevention paradigm and imposes rationality on the system by standardising the assessment process, differentiating between high- and low-risk groups and sorting individuals into the programme or activity that will 'work' for them. New Labour's youth crime prevention strategy is also apparent in a host of initiatives formally outside of the criminal justice system that explicitly target children at risk of entering it.

But does 'what works' work?

One of the problems, or, depending on one's perspective, the advantages, of the longer-term elements of the government's youth crime prevention strategy is that we will not know if it has 'worked' for many years to come. Until the bud has had time to flower, it is more or less impossible to assess whether or not it has been nipped. However, preliminary evaluation of *Asset* has been published as have progress reports of the wider system by the Audit Commission. With New Labour now into a third term of office, critics of the reforms have also had plenty of time to voice their concerns.

The 'official', Youth Justice Board-funded, evaluation of *Asset* is perhaps best described as hopeful. 'On the basis of the evidence currently available', writes one of the researchers in a summary of the findings, '*Asset can be* an asset in many ways' (Baker, 2004, p 85, emphasis added). The most confident claims for success relate to the 'predictive accuracy' of the instrument, that is, its ability to predict which young people will go on to re-offend, which it did in just over two thirds of cases considered (Baker et al, 2002) thereby matching or bettering similar tools used with adult offenders in England and Wales. *Asset* was also found to be reliable in the sense that YOT staff, regardless of their professional background, were arriving at similar ratings of the level of risk posed by young people although the researchers note that consistency in this respect was greater within than between YOTs. In other ways, partly because it is still early days, the evaluation is more circumspect. The potential for *Asset* to provide a measure of change in young people's behaviour and circumstances over time, to promote and facilitate information sharing within YOTs and with outside agencies and to inform resource management and strategic planning decisions has, with odd exceptions, yet to be realised (Baker, 2004).

It is, however, in relation to planning interventions that *Asset* has proved least impressive. In this sense, its ability to 'predict' is misleading because the accuracy of its forecasts can only be known with hindsight. Put another way, we only learn that the risk scores entered onto *Asset* correctly predicted the likelihood of re-offending after the offences have occurred, which in a practical sense is not much use. Back in the present, some YOT workers are reported to view completing the form as an 'isolated piece of work' (Baker, 2004, p 77), not clearly linked to the planning of interventions. Related to this, one of the things that staff appear to most dislike about using the form is its depersonalised, rigid, tick-box quality (Roberts et al, 2001) partly because the insistent focus on negative aspects of their lives can alienate young people and partly because it confronts 'the core beliefs of those [staff] who see a role for individual discretion and creative decision-making in the youth justice system' (Smith, 2003, p 101). In its defence, Baker (2004) argues that *Asset* is designed as an aid to, rather than a replacement for, professional judgement. Implicit here is the view that it is the people who use the form that are the problem, if there is a problem, rather than *Asset* and the thinking behind it. The response to the charge of de-professionalisation, in other words, is that youth justice staff are not professional enough. In its most recent report on the youth justice system, the Audit Commission (2004, p 87) echoes this point, noting that the publication by the Youth Justice Board of effective practice guidelines in respect of assessment and planning interventions 'may help to improve matters'.

The news from the Audit Commission is not all bad. First, more young people are being punished. 'In 2001, nearly one in four young offenders said that nothing happened to them after they were caught by the police' it reports; 'by 2003 it was less than one in ten' (Audit Commission, 2004, p 1). Young people are also being dealt with more quickly, with the average time from arrest to sentence having been halved since 1997 and they are more likely to 'make amends for their wrongdoing', through the introduction of referral and reparation orders. The Commission commends the 'clear national framework' set out by the Youth Justice Board and observes that 'the 155 YOTs are critically placed between criminal justice, health and local government services to co-ordinate and deliver services to young offenders and the courts' (2004, p 2).

The government, its movers, shakers and 'change-makers' (Blair, 2005), have done what they can then, but, alas, the news is by no means all good. 'While some young offenders are benefiting from early pre-court interventions, too many minor offences are taking up valuable time' (Audit Commission, 2004, p 2). In work with higher-level offenders, by contrast, the amount of contact time between offenders and practitioners has barely changed, those on Supervision Orders in 2003, for example, having an average of '1.1 hours' contact per week, about five minutes more than in 1996. The average reconviction rate of young people receiving lower-level punishments has been reduced but the level of recidivism among those more serious and persistent offenders on higher-level orders is unchanged. Moreover, although Final Warnings and reprimands 'show measurable signs of success in reducing reconvictions' (2004, p 11) only 'one in three young people who receive a Final Warning intervention improve the way they think and behave' (2004, p 2). Of continuing concern is that the proportion of young black and mixed race people remanded to custody has increased relative to white young people while the number sentenced to custody remains at around 1 in 12 compared to around 1 in 40 among white young offenders.

Although the overall view of the Audit Commission (2004, p 1) is that 'the new system is a considerable improvement on the old one', the evidence they present lends itself to a more sceptical interpretation and conclusion. To begin this analysis, let us remind ourselves of a famous metaphor, coined more than 20 years ago, to warn against the unintended consequences of avowedly benign intervention in the arena of criminal and youth justice.

Gone fishing

> Imagine that the entrance to the deviancy control system is like a gigantic fishing net. Strange and complex in its appearance and movements, the net is cast by an army of fishermen and fisherwomen working all day and even into the night.... Society is the ocean – vast, troubled and full of uncharted currents, rocks and other hazards. Deviants are the fish. (Cohen, 1985, pp 41-2)

Cohen readily admits that this image is imperfect, noting, for example, that in the real world, deviants are not purchased, cooked and eaten but rather kept alive and processed in any number of ways before being returned, perhaps with a tag (nowadays electronic), to the sea. Nevertheless, in highlighting the relative autonomy of the criminal justice system from the problem it is designed to address and in particular its capacity to grow by drawing in higher numbers of low-level offenders without successfully dealing with and releasing those 'up-tariff', Cohen provides us with an alternative perspective for interpreting the Audit Commission's findings on the impact of the new youth justice.

For this is just what has happened. In the shallow waters of the ocean, among the minnows of the youth offending population, the system has been strengthened such that a significant proportion of young offenders to whom 'nothing used to happen', find themselves subject to a 'preventative' intervention. Ironically, while the general increase in the number of young people to whom 'something is done' in the new system is heralded as good news by the Commission, as noted above, it appears elsewhere to draw the opposite conclusion. In relation to Final Warning schemes, for example, the Commission recommends that 'those with a low risk of re-offending and few needs should not need to complete a programme' while as we have seen they also bemoan the 'valuable *court* time' lost as a result of the fact that the courts, along with YOTs, are having to deal 'with a high volume of low-risk young people' (Audit Commission, 2004, p 22). Meanwhile, up at the deep end, a similar problem has occurred. According to the Commission, 'the proportion of young offenders given 'higher tariff' community sentences has increased' (2004, p 38), 'the likelihood of being sentenced to custody has increased for those aged 10-14' (p 40) (especially among minority ethnic groups and young women) and 'there was a slight increase in the average length of DTOs' (p 40) (Detention and Training Orders – a new sentence combining custodial and community punishment also introduced in the 1998 Crime and Disorder Act). The new youth justice, then, appears to have created bottlenecks at both the entrance to the formal control system and at the point where those truly caught up in it make their (too often temporary) exit. It has become easier to swim in and harder to swim out.

Faced with this dual dilemma, the government and its advisers have looked to 'diversionary' strategies. To avoid the problem of too many low-risk young offenders using up court time, the Audit Commission suggests that they be dealt with as far as possible in the community, via referral to a Youth Offender Panel, a body of (usually three) local volunteers who meet with the young person and others, including if possible victims, in order to 'provide a constructive forum for the young offender to confront the consequences of the crime and agree a programme of meaningful activity to prevent any further offending' (Home Office, 2000, cited in Crawford and Newburn, 2003, p 61). To avoid the problem of there being too many high-risk young people in custody, it is planned to increase the (already growing) number of them who are being dealt with in the community via an Intensive Surveillance and Supervision Package (ISSP) under which young people 'are subject to intensive surveillance in the community for up to 24 hours a day' (Audit Commission, 2004, p 47).

Of course, what is called 'diversion' by some appears to others as a significant blurring of the boundaries of social control along similar lines to those commented on by Cohen some 20 years ago. As proponents of the principles of restorative justice – on which innovations such as the referral order have ostensibly been based – have cautioned, such measures are intended as alternatives to existing retributive and rehabilitative forms of social control, not additions to them (Walgrave, 1995). Yet it seems clear that using Youth Offender Panels to free up court time represents just such an expansion, as against replacement, of the system. Similarly, as the Audit Commission's recent report informs us, there is little evidence that the introduction of ISSPs has reduced custody rates but plenty of reason to believe that their availability alongside pre-existing sanctions 'may be drawing in young offenders who would otherwise have received community sentences' (2004, p 52).

This blurring is even more evident if one considers the spread of youth crime prevention into youth work, health and education-oriented arenas such as Youth Inclusion Programmes, Sure Start and Connexions. The dismal fact that a risk of offending correlates with just about every measure of socioeconomic disadvantage one can think of has been seized upon by politicians and policy makers as an opportunity to tackle crime through tackling social exclusion and to identify 'joined-up solutions' to 'joined-up problems' (SEU, 1998). For others, this approach represents a drift towards the 'criminalisation of social policy' whereby familiar social problems such as family breakdown, housing, unemployment and truancy become 'redefined as "crime problems" which need to be controlled and managed, rather than addressed in themselves' (Crawford, 1998, p 121). The 'risk factor prevention paradigm' is of course central to this project because it highlights the correlation and so blurs the boundaries between social and crime problems and the policies designed to address them. Ironically, therefore, while ostensibly designed to enable practitioners to distinguish between the low and the high risk, the paradigm actually points to what they have in common; it is only a matter of time that separates them. Without benign intervention, the paradigm implies, the 'at risk' are destined to become ever more risky. How do we know this? Because the risky, 'science' has shown, were once 'at risk' themselves.

Distinguishing cause from effect

What is largely missing from the risk factor prevention paradigm is an explanation as to how it is that risk factors become manifest in criminal behaviour:

> Research on individual risk factors has largely failed to specify in any detail the causal mechanisms that link the risk factors to acts of crime and pathways in criminality. (Wikstrom and Sampson, 2003, cited in Armstrong, 2004, p 107)

In the manner identified by Feeley and Simon (1992) in respect of the new penology generally, the problem of causation tends to be sidestepped in risk-factor research, resulting in a kind of 'black box' explanation of youthful transgression whereby causal links are assumed rather than specified. Of course, politicians and policy makers have been happy to infer their own causal explanations on the basis of such findings. Thus, former Home Secretary Jack Straw, for example, asserted in 1998 that 'all the serious research shows that one of the biggest causes of serious juvenile delinquency is inconsistent parenting' (cited in Pitts, 2003, p 45). However, such simplistic reductionism is contradicted by the wide range of factors covered by *Asset*, and indeed by David Farrington and others when reviewing such research for the Youth Justice Board. 'Risk factors can be both symptoms and causes', the Youth Justice Board writes, 'and there is no single factor that can be specified as the 'cause' of antisocial or criminal behaviour' (YJB, 2001, p 7).

One indication of the problem the risk factor prevention paradigm has with causation is that it both under- and over-predicts delinquency. As we have seen, the evaluation of *Asset* suggests that although it fares well next to similar instruments, it only predicts re-offending correctly two times out of three (Baker, 2004). On the other hand, Loeber et al's (2003) review of risk factor research found that a majority of young children identified as at risk of offending did not go on to offend. One therefore begins to understand both the reluctance of some practitioners to base interventions with young people on *Asset* and the recent tendency for young people who have committed relatively minor offences to become the target of unnecessary interventions. On the first point, workers have good reason to believe that *Asset* will regularly (that is, in around one in three cases) generate an inaccurate assessment of risk. On the second, young people who are not in fact at risk will be assessed as being so and targeted accordingly.

The difficulty with difficulty

Actually it is worse than this; in practice, the less risky are frequently targeted because they are less risky and vice versa. In their evaluation of mentoring schemes funded from the Youth Justice Board's Development Fund, for example, Tarling et al (2004, p 24) observe that this form of intervention 'for the most part, was targeted at less serious offenders'. There are various reasons for this, not least of which is that given by some mentors who, when asked why relationships fail, put forward the 'view that some young people were experiencing such traumatic and disruptive events that they were not in a position to commit themselves to a mentoring relationship' (Tarling et al, 2004, p 44). At first sight, then, the targeting policy seems a sensible application of the risk principle: mentoring is a relatively low-level form of intervention, which is best applied to low-risk young people. At the same time, there is a clear danger that in pursuing such a strategy projects will concentrate resources on clients who might well not need a formal intervention and exclude those who do. It seems almost banal to point out that in general it is more difficult to work with more difficult young people. The reason for doing so is that opening the doors of the youth justice system to the at risk in the name of prevention appears to have provided a rationale for doing the opposite, that is, 'easier' work with 'easier' young people. Roberts' (2004) analysis of the impact of offending behaviour programmes provides an echo of this trend from work with adults. Those most likely to successfully complete programmes, he found, were usually in work, had stable family lives and appeared to want to complete their sentences quickly in order to move on. All of which would suggest that they were relatively low risk in the first place.

Conclusion

The concept of risk and the idea that there are measurable risk factors that can be ascertained through rigorous assessment is now embedded in youth justice policy and practice. Yet for all the apparent novelty of recent years – New Labour, a new youth justice system with a new aim and new techniques to tackle offending – it is not so obvious what has fundamentally changed. Seeking to nip offending behaviour in the bud is hardly a fresh idea – the following quotation dates back well over a hundred years:

> One thing, at least, is certain; it would come much cheaper to the country if these budding burglars and pickpockets were caught up and caged away from the community at large, before their natures become too thoroughly pickled in the brine of rascality. (James Greenwood, 1869, cited in Goodman, 2006, p 52)

Nor is the notion that some young people are more at risk than others exactly a breakthrough for all its advocates' talk of a new paradigm. Referring once more to Cohen's visions of social control, for example, we find him citing Intermediate Treatment projects (an older 'new' idea), which distinguished those children who are 'more at risk of getting into trouble with their contemporaries' or which described their provision as being for 'young people at risk of institutionalisation, unemployment, homelessness, family breakdown and lack of work skills' (Cohen, 1985, p 60).

So no, not much has changed. Those young people most at risk of becoming involved in serious and persistent offending behaviour continue to be those who have experienced abusive family or institutional relationships, fared poorly at school, suffered from emotional and psychological problems and grew up in areas of relative and sometimes acute deprivation. Such young people, including those who have developed serious problems with alcohol and or drug addiction, continue to receive inadequate protection and support from the state and continue to be among those in society most at risk of taking their own lives (Goldson, 2002). The 'new youth justice' has failed to stem the growing number of children and young people in custody but has succeeded in increasing the number of relatively low-risk first- and second-time offenders with whom work is done in apparent ignorance of the lessons of the past that such practice threatens to label many unnecessarily and does not address the complex and deep-rooted problems of the few who really are 'at risk' and 'a risk'. Meanwhile, the public, fuelled by the media and in an economic and social context that cannot but exclude and marginalise vulnerable groups, continues to vote for those who promise to get tough. So expect no major changes in youth justice in the near future. Politically, it would be too risky.

References

Andrews, D. A. and Bonta, J. (2003) *The Psychology of Criminal Conduct* (3rd edition), Cincinnati, OH: Anderson Publishing Co.

Armstrong, D. (2004) 'A risky business? Research, policy, governmentality and youth offending', *Youth Justice*, vol 4, no 2, pp 100-16.

Audit Commission (1996) *Misspent Youth ... Young People and Crime*, Abingdon: Audit Commission Publications.

Audit Commission (2004) *Youth Justice 2004*, available at: www.audit-commission.gov.uk/reports

Baker, K. (2004) 'Is Asset really an asset? Assessment of young offenders in practice', in R. Burnett and C. Roberts (eds) *What Works in Probation and Youth Justice*, Cullompton: Willan Publishing, pp 70-88.

Baker, K., Jones, S., Roberts, C. and Merrington, S. (2002) *Validity and Reliability of ASSET: Findings from the First Two Years of its Use*, London: Youth Justice Board.

Blair, T. (2005) Speech to the Labour Party Conference, 27 September, available at: www.labour.org.uk

Burnett, R. and Roberts, C. (2004) *What Works in Probation and Youth Justice*, Cullompton: Willan Publishing.

Cohen, N. (2005) 'Thick end of the wedge', *The Observer*, 22 May.

Cohen, S. (1985) *Visions of Social Control*, Cambridge: Polity Press.

Crawford, A. (1998) *Crime Prevention and Community Safety: Politics, Policies and Practices*, Harlow: Addison Wesley Longman.

Crawford, A. and Newburn, T. (2003) *Youth Offending and Restorative Justice*, Cullompton: Willan Publishing.

Farrington, D. P. (1989) *The Origins of Crime: The Cambridge Study of Delinquent Development*, Home Office Research and Planning Unit, Research Bulletin No. 27, London: Home Office.

Feeley, M. and Simon, J. (1992) 'The new penology: notes on the emerging strategy of corrections and its implementation', *Criminology*, vol 30, no 4, pp 449-71.

Garland, D. (2001) *The Culture of Control*, Oxford: Oxford University Press.

Goldson, B. (2000) *The New Youth Justice*, Lyme Regis: Russell House Publishing.

Goldson, B. (2002) *Vulnerable Inside: Children in Secure and Penal Settings*, London: The Children's Society.

Goodman, A. (2006) 'Whither or wither probation in the twenty first century', *British Journal of Community Justice*, vol 4, no 1, pp 49-66.

Home Office (1997) *No More Excuses: A New Approach to Tackling Youth Crime in England and Wales*, London: The Stationery Office.

Loeber, J., Farrington, D. P. and Petechuk, D. (2003) *Child Delinquency: Early Intervention and Prevention*, Child Delinquency Bulletin Series, Washington, DC: Office of Juvenile Justice and Delinquency Prevention, US Department of Justice.

McGuire, J. (1995) *What Works: Reducing Re-offending: Guidelines from Research and Practice*, Chichester: Wiley.

Pitts, J. (2003) *The New Politics of Youth Crime: Discipline or Solidarity* (2nd edition), Lyme Regis: Russell House Publishing.

Roberts, C. (2004) 'Offending behaviour programmes: emerging evidence and implications for practice', in R. Burnett and C. Roberts (eds) *What Works in Probation and Youth Justice*, Cullompton: Willan Publishing, pp 134-59.

Roberts, C., Baker, K., Jones, S. and Merrington, S. (2001) *Validity and Reliability of ASSET: Interim Report to the Youth Justice Board*, Oxford: Centre for Criminological Research.

SEU (Social Exclusion Unit) (1998) *Bringing Britain Together: A National Strategy for Neighbourhood Renewal*, London: The Stationery Office.

Smith, R. (2003) *Youth Justice: Ideas, Policy, Practice*, Cullompton: Willan Publishing.

Tarling, R., Davison, T. and Clarke, A. (2004) *The National Evaluation of the Youth Justice Board's Mentoring Projects*, available at: www.youth-justice-board.gov.uk

Tomlinson, R. (2005) 'Youth justice at the local level', in T. Bateman and J. Pitts (eds) *The RHP Companion to Youth Justice*, Lyme Regis: Russell House Publishing, pp 32-8.

Vennard, J., Sugg, D. and Hedderman, C. (1997) *Changing Offenders' Attitudes and Behaviour: What Works?*, Home Office Research, Development and Statistics Directorate Research Study 171, London: Home Office.

Walgrave, L. (1995) 'Restorative justice for juveniles: just a technique or a fully fledged alternative', *The Howard Journal of Criminal Justice*, vol 34, no 3, pp 228-49.

Williamson, H. (2005) 'Preventive work in youth justice', in T. Bateman and J. Pitts (eds) *The RHP Companion to Youth Justice*, Lyme Regis: Russell House Publishing, pp 205-10.

YJB (Youth Justice Board) (2001) *Risk and Protective Factors Associated with Youth Crime and Effective Interventions to Prevent It*, London: Youth Justice Board.

YJB (2003) *Assessment, Planning Interventions and Supervision*, London: Youth Justice Board.

Index

Page references for notes are followed by n